e-Governance

Developing hand in hand with e-Business in its use of information and communication technologies (ICTs), e-Government emerged in the 1990s with the promise of a more accessible, efficient and transparent form for public institutions to perform and interact with citizens. The successes – and some critics say, general failures – of e-Government initiatives around the world have led to the development of e-Governance – a broader, more encompassing concept that involves not only public institutions but private ones as well.

Taking a multidisciplinary approach, this book explores e-Governance in theory and practice with an analytical narrative from heterodox perspectives. Covering such essential issues as global governance of the internet, the European Knowledge Economy, the transformative promise of mobile telephony, the rise of e-Universities, internet accessibility for the disabled and e-Governance in transition economies, the book draws on contributions from experienced academics and practitioners with an expertise in an emerging field. In addition, each chapter includes such features as discussion of key issues that draw on case studies in order to facilitate significant discussion questions.

Leslie Budd is a Reader in Social Enterprise at the Open University Business School and Associate of Capital Business Strategies Ltd.

Lisa Harris is a Senior Lecturer at the University of Southampton School of Management, UK.

Routledge e-Business series

Routledge e-Business is a bold new series examining key aspects of the e-Business world, designed to provide students and academics with a more structured learning resource. Introducing issues of marketing, Human Resource Management, ethics, operations management, law, design, computing and the e-Business environment, it offers a broad overview of key e-Business issues from both managerial and technical perspectives.

e-Governance: Managing or Governing?
Edited by Leslie Budd and Lisa Harris

Marketing the e-Business, Second Edition
Lisa Harris and Charles Dennis

e-Economy: Rhetoric or Business Reality?
Edited by Leslie Budd and Lisa Harris

e-Business Fundamentals
Edited by Paul Jackson

e-Retailing
Charles Dennis, Bill Merrilees and Tino French

e-Governance:
Managing or Governing?

Edited by
Leslie Budd and Lisa Harris

Routledge
Taylor & Francis Group

NEW YORK AND LONDON

First published 2009
by Routledge
270 Madison Ave, New York, NY 10016

Simultaneously published in the UK
by Routledge
2 Park Square, Milton Park, Abingdon, Oxon OX14 4RN

Routledge is an imprint of the Taylor & Francis Group, an informa business

Typeset in Caslon by RefineCatch Limited, Bungay, Suffolk
Printed and bound in the United States of America on acid-free paper by
Edwards Brothers, Inc.

Library of Congress Cataloging-in-Publication Data
e-Governance : managing or governing? / edited by Leslie Budd and Lisa Harris.
p. cm.—(Routledge e-business series)
Includes bibliographical references and index.
1. Internet in public administration.   I. Budd, Leslie, 1949–   II. Harris, Lisa,
1968–
JF1525.A8E195 2008
352.3'802854678—dc22
2008030584

ISBN 10: 0–415–96517–9 (hbk)
ISBN 10: 0–415–96518–7 (pbk)
ISBN 10: 0–203–88388–8 (ebk)

ISBN 13: 978–0–415–96517–0 (hbk)
ISBN 13: 978–0–415–96518–7 (pbk)
ISBN 13: 978–0–203–88388–4 (ebk)

Contents

List of Tables and Figures

Tables

Figures

List of Contributors

Leslie Budd is Reader in Social Enterprise at the Open University Business School. He is an economist who has published widely in the area of regional and urban economics in the context of international financial markets and developed an expertise in the governance and management of the public domain. Recent books include: *eEconomy: Rhetoric or Business Reality?* (edited with Lisa Harris), *Key Concepts in Urban Studies* (with Mark Gottdiener), *The Rise of the English Regions?* (edited with M. Baker, P. Benneworth, and I. Hardill) and *Making Policy Happen?* (edited with J. Charlesworth and R. Paton). He is an Academician of the Academy of Social Sciences and former Chair of the Regional Studies Association: a leading international learned society. Leslie is also the Director of the Regional Analysis Innovation Knowledge and Entrepreneurship (RAIKE) Research Exchange at the Open University and an Associate of Capital Business Strategies Ltd.

Lisa Harris is a Senior Lecturer in Marketing at the University of Southampton. Previously at Brunel University Business School where she was Course Director of the Brunel MBA, she developed and ran a cross-faculty undergraduate degree programme in e-commerce at Brunel. Lisa is a Chartered Institute of Marketing Course Tutor and she has run Marketing courses at the University of Weingarten in Germany and Zurich University in Switzerland. Lisa has also recently qualified as an 'e-tutor' for the University of Liverpool online MBA programme. Her research is currently focused upon the usage of new online technologies by small firms, the role of online networks in business development and the development of mobile marketing strategies. Lisa is currently working on a research project called Punch Above Your Weight which is investigating how small firms are promoting themselves and growing their businesses using Web 2.0 technologies. She has co-authored three previous books in the Routledge e-Business Series.

Fintan Clear teaches courses on electronically mediated trading at Brunel University Business School where he pursues research interests in ICT (Information and Communication Technologies) adoption and use by small firms or SMEs (Small and Medium-sized Enterprises). With a background in geography and communications policy, he has worked for a number of organisations including Italcable (Italian telecoms provider), the European Space Agency (ESA), the BBC World Service, and Sainsbury's where he gained extensive development experience in large supply chain information systems. Returning to higher education, he helped set up courses on electronic business and has worked on a number of ICT-related research projects, one of which was a pan-European project called eGap which examined promoters and inhibitors for telework in small firms in France, Italy, Hungary, Finland and the UK. Currently Fintan is involved in a 'WestFocus' research project (a collaborative venture with researchers from Brunel, Royal Holloway and Kingston universities examining ICT adoption issues for SMEs in SE England) in which he was responsible for running the quantitative data gathering exercise (a telephone survey of 378 firms) whilst examining management responses to the data security issues raised by electronic trading. He has published a number of academic papers, reports and a book chapter, all related to use of ICTs.

John Clarke is Professor of Social Policy at the Open University. His basic interest is in the shifting politics and ideologies of welfare, but this starting point has led him in several directions. One is the deconstruction and reconstruction of welfare states in Britain and comparatively. He has been particularly interested in the intersection of political, cultural and organisational changes associated with managerialism in social welfare. This work has been developed through a number of collaboratively produced books: *Managing Social Policy* (edited with Allan Cochrane and Eugene McLaughlin, Sage, 1994); *The Managerial State* (with Janet Newman, Sage, 1997) and *New Managerialism, New Welfare?* (edited with Sharon Gewirtz and Eugene McLaughlin, Sage, 2000).

He has recently been part of a research project on 'Creating Citizen-Consumers: Changing Relationships and Identifications', exploring the impact of consumerism on public services. A book from the project *Creating Citizen-Consumers: Changing Publics and Changing Public Services* was published by Sage in January 2007.

He is also fascinated by how understandings of what the 'social' in social policy are constructed and contested, particularly in relation to dominant political and managerial conceptions of the public and the public interest. He has an interest in the ways in which national, international and transnational processes intersect in the reshaping of social welfare, its social relations and its governance systems. These interests are linked by a commitment to making cultural analysis contribute to the analysis of social policy. This is the focus of a book: *Changing Welfare, Changing States: New Directions in Social Policy*, published by Sage in 2004.

Richard Collins is Professor of Media Studies at the Open University who participated in the WGIG as an accredited civil society representative. He is a former advisor to the Director General of Telecommunications (on broadcasting and convergence) and to the House of Lords (on BBC Charter review). He has published widely and his books include: *The Economics of Television: The UK Case* (1988) [with Nicholas Garnham and Gareth Locksley]; *Satellite Television in Western Europe* (1990); *Culture Communication and National Identity. The Case of Canadian Television* (1990); *New Media, New Policies* [with Cristina Murroni] (1996); *From Satellite to Single Market. New Communication Technology and European Public Service*

Television 1982–1992 (1998) and *Media and Identity in Contemporary Europe. Consequences of Global Convergence* (2002).

Charles Dennis was elected as a Fellow of the Chartered Institute of Marketing (CIM) for work helping to modernise the teaching of the discipline. He is a Chartered Marketer and Senior Lecturer in Marketing and Retail Management at Brunel University, London, UK. In 2005 he was awarded the Vice Chancellor's Award for Teaching Excellence for improving the interactive student learning experience. Charles has been full-time in this post since 1993. Originally a Chartered Chemical Engineer, he spent some years in technical positions, latterly with a 'marketing' emphasis. This was followed by seven years with 'Marketing Methods'; Institute of Marketing as a approved consultant. Charles's PhD concerned consumer behaviour and 'why people shop where they do'. He admits to being obsessed with this research topic (and especially why people e-shop) and has published widely. The textbook *Marketing the E-business* (Harris and Dennis, 2002) and research-based *E-retailing* (Dennis et al, 2004) were published by Routledge; and research monograph *Objects of Desire: Consumer Behaviour in Shopping Centre Choice*, (Dennis, 2005) by Palgrave. His research into shopping styles has received extensive coverage in the popular media.

Colin Gray is Professor of Enterprise Development at the Open University Business School which he joined in 1987. From 1990–2003, Colin led the OU's Small and Medium-sized Enterprise Research Unit with research focused on entrepreneurship, management development and the adoption of technologies in small firms. He has led or participated in a series of externally-funded projects including the EU's Leonardo projects on ICT adoption and management development in small firms, the Learning Support for Small Business (LSSB) ADAPT project, the EU's IST NEWTIME project on broadband in micro-firm networks, the Franco-British Entrepreneurship Club e-Commerce in small firms project and a scoping study for the National Council for Graduate Entrepreneurship in 2004. Since then, his research has been conducted as part of the OU's cross-faculty Innovation, Knowledge and Development (IKD) research centre. He is Chair of Trustees of the Small Enterprise Research Team (an independent research charity based in the School) and a member of the editorial board of the *Journal of Small Business and Entrepreneurship Development*. Colin is a former President of the Institute for Small Business and Entrepreneurship (ISBE), the main UK membership organisation for small business and entrepreneurship, academics, researchers, policy-makers and support agencies. He has also worked widely as a consultant and writer in the broad enterprise field, including projects in Britain, Italy, France, Germany and Egypt.

Simran Grewal is a Lecturer in the Human Resource Management & Organisational Behaviour Group at the School of Management at the University of Bath. She was formerly at the Brunel Business School at Brunel University where she taught for a number of years from 2001. She received a joint award with Lisa Harris for teaching excellence at Brunel University. Her doctoral thesis explored the diffusion of e-mediated learning technology in UK Higher Education and her current research interests include the diffusion of innovations, the role of e-mediated learning technology in higher education and social relations between academic staff and students. She has presented her work at numerous international conferences and is well published in these areas.

Janice Morphet was a senior adviser on local government modernisation and e-government to DCLG 2000–2005. She has also held senior posts in local government as Chief Executive of Rutland and as Director of Technical Services in Woking. Between 1986 and 1990 she was Professorial Head of the Department of Planning and Landscape at the University of Central England. Janice has published on a wide range of issues including planning, e-government and local government. Her recent work includes *Modern Local Government* (2007), *Understanding E Government: A Guide to Principles and Practice* (2003), and she also published a book on Local Authority Chief Executives in 1993. In 2006, Janice joined RMJM Consulting as a Director and also became an associate with a number of consulting firms. She has recently been appointed to the Planning Committee of the London 2012 Olympic Games. She is a Visiting Professor at

UCL, where she is working on a Royal Town Planning Institute (RTPI) sponsored project, Effective Practice in Spatial Planning with Deloitte and is also a member of the UK Research Assessment Exercise (RAE) 2008 panel for planning. Janice has recently been elected to the RTPI General Assembly and joined Summer School in 2006.

Alan Rae is Managing Partner of Ai Consultants – an organisation specialising in Research and Training Programme development – mainly about e-Business in small companies. His company produces a range of small company training products under the www.howtodo business.com and www.1manBrand.co.uk brands. After completing his DPhil in Biochemistry, his first job was for a company that made cranes for steelworks. When he left after four years he was marketing manager. He wrote corporate plans, re-engineered and launched products and negotiated licensing agreements for this 4-site, 1,200-person operation. He then spent the next 15 years running two IT companies specialising in CAD which employed up to 25 people and developed and launched three software products. In 1996 he was taken on to build the Executive Studio in West London. This was a state-of-the-art facility for demonstrating how IT can be used to support company growth. He became Operations Director, organised a management buyout in 2001 and developed workshops, educational content and training programmes in e-Business and IT for Business Link and the DTI's UK online for business programme. He authored 'The MD's guide to the networked economy' and 'Fast Track to e-Commerce success' during that period. Since 2004 he has been creating training programmes, carrying out research and delivering consultancy in marketing, IT and leadership. Recent publications include *1Man Brand* – a complete sales and marketing course for small business and *Market On-Line!* – an e-Book about online promotion. Clients include HP, PCWorld, OneLondon, Virgin Atlantic, SBS, Government of Wales and numerous smaller organisations. Alan is a Chartered Marketer, Technology Means Business accredited adviser and an associate of the Market Research Society.

Antoaneta Serguieva is a lecturer in management science and business computing at Brunel Business School. She has published in the area of intelligent systems, information processing and knowledge representation, and worked on EPSRC research in this field. Antoaneta is a member of the Technical Committee on Computational Finance and Economics of the IEEE Computational Intelligence Society, and participates on the referee panels of four journals from the Decision Sciences section of Elsevier.

Kamen Spassov is a lecturer in e-business at Sofia University, Bulgaria. As Coordinator of the Centre for Information Communication and Management Technologies, under the Bulgaria Council of Ministers and the UNDP, Kamen has been involved in the evaluation and implementation of the e-government strategy. He has experience working on the identity management project within the EC Framework Programme FP6, and delivered presentations to civil servants in several countries.

Jane Vincent joined the Digital World Research Centre as a Research Fellow in 2002 and has worked with them since 1998. Jane spent over 20 years in the UK mobile communications industry working for BT and mmO2 specialising in business transformation, product marketing and strategy development. Her experience spans the evolution of the three generations of mobile communications during which time she has contributed to technological and commercial design and development across all aspects of the value chain.

Jane studied Social Sciences at the University of Leicester and her academic interests now are in the user behaviours associated with mobile communications. Her particular interest is in emotion and mobile phones, the topic of her research PhD with the Sociology Department and on which she has published several papers. She has delivered two studies for the UMTS Forum on the Social Shaping of 3G/UMTS Products and Services and most recently published a report on the use of mobiles by 11–16-year-olds. Jane regularly presents at academic and industry conferences and has been a Final Awards Judge for the GSM Association Awards from 2004 to 2008.

INTRODUCTION

Managing Governance or Governance Management. Is It All in a Digital Day's Work?

LESLIE BUDD AND LISA HARRIS

The prefix 'e' has become synonymous with the word 'electronic' in the late twentieth and early twenty-first centuries. e-Commerce, e-Business, e-Economy, e-Government and so on are the stuff of the brave new world with its own SMS language: B2C, B2B, G2B, B2G. Sexed-up by politicians and commentators, the 'e' word appears to be the magical elixir the imbibing of which opens up the doors to the heavens of the information society and the knowledge economy. Over a decade ago, 'electronic' was a rather sexed-down and mundane term for a number of repetitive transactions that facilitated faster turnover time in business. The world then hadn't embraced the geeks of the developing software worlds as the social studs of our time. Indeed, back then the 'e' world was closely associated with the hedonistic rave culture centred on the drug Ecstasy. Sex and drugs and rock and roll may have been the leitmotif of the 1960s and 1970s, but by the time we arrive in the twenty-first century, we find that these pleasures are much more mediated through digital means so that they appear to take on a virtual reality of their own, and thus seem more manageable.

Similarly, government has been associated in the past with solid if not stolid institutions, arcane processes and procedures whose mainly male participants have faces and dress senses made for radio. The very sense of solidity and permanence of a political class beavering away on behalf of a population that lacked the necessary technocratic or inherent abilities to rule and govern seemed to bestow legitimacy and accountability on the political system. A number of historical disjunctures and disruptions in the post-World War II period – end of the Cold War, quicker onset of globalisation and the apparent hollowing-out of the state, terrorism and apparently rapid changes in demography and migration among others – have been either the backdrop to or the driver for a decline in the importance of democratic politics (Moravcsik, 2004).

Much of this has been harnessed under the term of 'democratic deficit'. In many countries around the world the solution is to provide virtual programmes under the rubric of e-Democracy and e-Participation, for example. At the same time, there has been a perception of the failure of the 'public', with the demand for public and publicly underwritten services outstripping the resources to satisfy this demand. This outcome was chronicled in a literature on the 'fiscal crisis of the state' in the 1970s (O'Connor, 1973). The current climate appears to resonate with the difficulties faced in this earlier period. Moreover, in a seemingly dynamic and consumer-orientated culture, the delivery of public services is seen to be hidebound by a lack of innovation, creativity and flexibility. In this view, public organisations are bureaucratic, impotent and increasingly sterile. Consequently, the idea of digital means to overcome these incapacities has gained currency to deliver optimal outcomes for public policy and service delivery (Klijn and Koopejan, 2000).

The manifestation of this idea in practice is expressed by some as the transition from 'Good Governance' to e-Governance via e-Goverment, e-Business (government electronic business in this setting) and e-Democracy (Okot-Uma, 2000). The components in this transition are important, but they tend to be implemented in isolation and/or on a serial basis. As a result, the creation of a coherent and potentially comprehensive e-Governance space, and eventually system, is inhibited. Figure 1 displays what an e-Governance space ('Infomediation Space') may consist of, but there is a long way to go before this is achievable. The different components and aspects of this space require some common conditions including, *inter alia*, a trust environment and global (in the sense of universal and accessible) communications media and infrastructure. In spite of the ubiquity of the Internet and mobile telephony, their existence and widespread

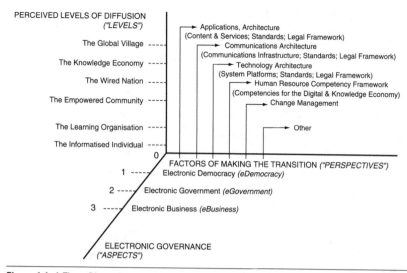

Figure 1.1 A Three-Dimensional Informediation Space for e-Governance relative to the Factors of the Transition to a Digital Epoch and a Knowledge Economy and the Levels of Diffusion in Society. *Source:* Okot-Uma R W' O (2000).

availability and usage is *not* a sufficient condition for enabling the Informediation Space. Moreover, the conditions for moving to a society whose dominant governance institutions are electronic vary by territorial scale and governmental/service function. If one takes a fairly integrated economic space, for example the European Union, one finds the different capacities and capabilities of its territories and sectors constrain convergence towards e-Governance. The different historical trajectories of the institutions within the EU further constrain this convergence. Faced with these difficulties, proponents and promoters of e-Governance have tended to be over-determined by technological solutions. Without comprehensive and detailed scrutiny and implementation of appropriate processes, achieving e-Governance as the governing norm remains a distant prospect.

The development of new government and reinvented government was purported to enable new organisational forms through the embrace and application of new technologies. The boundaries of government were to be liberated by the development of e-Government and the associated organisational innovations that were post-bureaucratic. In this supposedly brave new world the borders between the private and public domains would allegedly break down (Budd, 2007). Experiments with e-Government and e-Business in many countries failed to deliver conclusive outcomes as technological entropy met entrenched bureaucratic interests, for example, the attempt to digitise Medicare in the US and Ford's failed strategy to become the new virtual service company at the end of the 1990s. At the end of the day, the investment set-up and transaction costs were too large for this apparent revolution to succeed. Like Joseph Schumpeter's *'creative destruction'*, the apparent demise of e-Government and e-Business as the main organising principles of economy and society has created the conditions for e-Governance to rise from the ashes; a newly sexed-up *Phoenix* (Schumpeter, 1942). This book represents an opportunity to explore the challenges of a seemingly post-e-Government world by articulating an analytical narrative from heterodox perspectives.

The book attempts to make a major contribution to our understanding of e-Governance and how it has developed out of the relative failure of e-Government as the dominant mode of governing and governance. e-Government is essentially the virtualisation or digitisation of public policy outcomes and the delivery and management of publicly provided or publicly underwritten services. e-Governance is the incorporation of a range of public and private actors and agencies into an institutional framework that delivers the promise of e-Government in a more flexible and innovative way that addresses problems of ICT entropy and organisational rigidity.

According to UNESCO, 'e-Governance is the public sector's use of information and communication technologies with the aim of improving information and service delivery, encouraging citizen participation in the decision-making process and making government more accountable, transparent and effective' (UNESCO, 2005).

A more complete definition is given in Chapter 3 of this book (Budd, 2008). UNESCO sets out the goals of e-Governance as to:

- improve the internal organisational processes of governments,
- provide better information and service delivery,
- increase government transparency in order to reduce corruption,
- reinforce political credibility and accountability, and

- promote democratic practices through public participation and consultation.

Furthermore UNESCO lists the fields of implementation:

- *e-Administration* refers to improving of government processes and of the internal workings of the public sector with new ICT-executed information processes.
- *e-Services* refers to improved delivery of public services to citizens. Some examples of interactive services are requests for public documents, requests for legal documents and certificates, issuing permits and licenses.
- *e-Democracy* implies greater and more active citizen participation and involvement enabled by ICTs in the decision-making process.

These fields of implementation relate to the proposed three-part structure of the book, so as to allow the reader to access and interrogate the contents in a flexible and relevant way. Moreover, it makes international comparisons so as to more fully understand and articulate the role of e-Governance in an emerging environment of global governance, and one in which the boundaries of the public domain are both extending and being penetrated by non-governmental and private agencies and different organisational forms.

I Setting The Governance Scene

We begin by examining the scene of governance and the multiple, puzzling and paradoxical aspects within it. Our starting point is the issue of governance itself, which often tends to be an elastic concept that suffers from a lack of specification. Governance appears to be everywhere and nowhere: in business, in public policy, in academia and its many disciplines; in practice: its 'e' variant appears to be even more of a chimera. In Part I of the book three chapters explore a range of issues under the rubric of *Setting the Governance Scene*. In Leslie Budd's chapter, he uses the following quote to try and get some handle on the slippery concept and practice of governance:

In the literature on public policy and administration the concept of governance now dominates contemporary debates (Newman, 2001). The concept is mostly used to explore the diminishing capacity of the state to direct policy making and implementation, something also portrayed as 'hollowing out of the state' (Rhodes, 1997). The term governance is also used to describe governing arrangements that are more than or greater than merely the institutions of government. Hence users of the term tend to focus on the rupture between the formal political institutions and the growth of governance arrangements – such as networks and partnerships – and the increasing use of deliberative forums for service users (Kelly, 2006; 605).

This definition is a useful starting point in exploring the multi-ness of governance: one of the key strands in John Clarke's insightful chapter. In exploring *Governance Puzzles*, he uses two puzzles: multi-level governance and the performance of governance, to reflect on the possibilities of e-Governance. These possibilities include Digital Era Governance (DEG), which Clarke examines from two perspectives: narrowly technical and socio-technical. Clarke begins by reflecting on how in political science, multi-level governance implies a multiplicity of levels, scales and tiers of government so that differentiated and overlapping authority over governance issues and claims over them is examined. The link to the possibilities of e-Governance is expressed in the sentence: 'We might want to think about the ways in which the "multi-ness" of governance brings new spaces into being, or makes new framings of space visible' (Clarke, 2008). One can conceive of e-Governance as one of these spaces.

Another way of connecting debates about the multi-ness of governance to the prospects for e-Governance is the idea of 'globalising webs' to analyse the transnational characteristic of e-Government initiatives and the narratives that underpin them. Clarke positions governance as multinational and multi-agency: cross-border spaces, transnational processes, etc. interacting with sovereignties at national and sub-national levels whilst different jurisdictions and representations function between a common purpose and engaging in wider processes of governance.

Clarke notes that 'digital technologies seem to represent an enhanced technical capacity for the extension of current governance logics' (Clarke, 2008). He goes on to stress how digital technologies appear to enable the 'multi-ness' of governance by way of their greater connectivity and thus makes the different spaces (transnational, cross-sector, etc.) of governance more easy to manage. These new technologies offer a technical fix to the problems of government and the challenges of governance. However, this underestimates the socio-political and organisational consequences. A socio-technical perspective is one that places these consequences at the heart of configuring e-Governance. In exploring this perspective, Clarke reviews the claims that digital technologies can create a new governance paradigm called Digital Era Governance (DEG) that arose out of the failures of New Public Management (NPM) to transform the management of public services landscape (Dunleavy et al., 2006; Stoker, 2006). Although persuaded by the socio-technical systems perspective, Clarke thinks that the nature of governance puzzles provides a richer vein to mine to explore e-Governance in its multiple manifestations.

The DEG paradigm is one that connects John Clarke's chapter to that of Richard Collins, who explores *e-Governance and the governance of the global Internet*. His starting point is that the literature of e-Governance and DEG has paid little attention to the governance of electronic communications infrastructure, in particular the Internet. As Collins points out, Internet governance shapes e-Governance and it accounts in social science literature and debates about governance: an omission that is doubly baffling. He constructs a dialectic between Netheads and Bellheads to explore this central theme. The former are associated with Internet-type networks and the latter with conventional voice-telephony systems, in particular the Bell telephone company in the United States. For Richard Collins, this opposition resonates with social science perspectives on the evolution from hierarchy to networks. One of the paradoxes, however, is that the Bellhead universe tends to be more distributed and decentralised than the Nethead one.

The Internet tends to be viewed as a single 'thing' because the Domain Name System (DNS) depends on a single authoritative source, known as a root zone file (RZF). To reinforce this statement, Collins points to the central power of Internet Corporation for

Assigned Names and Numbers (ICANN) by using the following quote: 'a single lever by which identity on the Internet can be turned on or off. ICANN has the power to exercise the online equivalent of force' (Crawford, 2004; 703). Collins focuses on the problem of ICANN's governance and criticisms from a range of stakeholders (including Bellheads). There are two strands to this criticism, exemplified by two groups. First, libertarians who point to the informal network governance basis of the Internet in its infancy. Second, representatives of sovereign states who point out that Internet governance should only be determined by properly constituted international institutions. Thus, as Collins indicates, the governance of ICANN is found wanting compared to the vertically ordered and accord-based one of the Bellhead world. This apparent paradox reinforces Clarke's argument about the multi-ness of governance and his criticism of the view that contradictory processes are absent in the digital world.

Collins then goes on to debate whether ICANN represents a failure of network governance. He argues that although there is considerable attention to failure in hierarchical and market forms of governance there is less about network governance failure. The latter is subject to two forms, in his view: failure of representation and failure to bind stakeholders' interests together. For the two main groups of antagonists, ICANN fails on both counts. To address the challenge of network governance in this domain, the UN convened the World Summit on the Information Society (WSIS) to resolve the increasingly contested arena of Internet governance. Contrasting the development of telephony, Collins points to how the new regime of digitally mediated ICT has eroded state sovereignty because of the reduction of monopoly power of national telephony interests. The promise of WSIS has not lasted, confirmed by the United Nations convening of the Internet Governance Forum (IGF) in Spring 2006. It was hoped that IGF would become the basis of shifting ICANN to a more legitimate and accountable form of Internet governance.

Collins concludes by indicating that the challenge of creating institutions which cover the 'global communities of fate' (Held, 2004; 20) is a powerful and ongoing one. He likens ICANN and Internet governance to ad hoc international regimes governing the activities of banks. Like these regimes, ICANN is another example of contemporary globalisation within which global relationships and practices outrun the regulatory capacity of properly constituted institutions. ICANN is an example of network governance in action and one that demonstrates the paradoxical and puzzling nature of governance. Moreover, the salient characteristic of multi-ness of governance appears to be strongest in an 'E' environment.

The themes of paradox and puzzlement are taken up in Leslie Budd's chapter *The limits of post-Lisbon governance in the European Union*. He explores the development of e-Governance in the EU by critically examining the Lisbon Agenda of 2000 which set out the objective of making the EU the most dynamic economy in the world by 2010. Central to achieving this objective is the creation of a European Information Society and a fully developed knowledge economy. The inevitable slippage of the timetable and the challenge that Lisbon represents for the Member States of the EU is the context for this chapter. Budd examines the subsequent Sapir and Kok Reports, gathered together under the rubric of Lisbon II in order to develop a fuller analysis. His chapter connects the regime of economic governance of the EU with the ambitions of Lisbon so as to provide a deeper analysis of governance in general and e-Governance in particular in an expanded and expanding economic union which has developed global reach.

At the heart of his argument is that the regime of economic governance and the objectives of an EU information society and knowledge economy make uneasy bedfellows in the quest for e-Governance. The reasons are that, firstly the former is asymmetrical in that its components lead to unbalanced outcomes, for example, the expansion of the European Union may conflict with the conditions of membership for the single currency area (the Euro). Furthermore, the growth potential of realising the EU knowledge economy through means of developing e-Governance is constrained because of the way in which some of the components of the regime of economic governance operate. He contrasts the two key drivers of economic governance, the Single European Market (SEM) and Lisbon, in order to investigate the possibilities of a European Information Society. By reviewing the building blocks of e-Government Budd critically discusses whether individual projects can be summed up to make the total of e-Governance.

The concept of a 'transactions space' is introduced in order to provide a conceptual framework for Budd's analysis of e-Governance in an EU setting. A transaction space is defined as: 'an abstract n-dimensional space defining the institutional, legal, cultural and languages differences that must be accommodated if a given transaction between two or more agents is to take place' (Wood and Parr, 2005; 4). A transaction space is a concept developed from the interaction of transactions costs ('the costs of doing business' (Arrow, 1969; 4)) and agglomeration economies (the benefits accrued from the co-location of economic activities).

This concept appears to be appropriate to use in order to assess systems of e-Governance as transaction spaces. Furthermore given the cultural, institutional and language differences it appears to be relevant to the EU. The more homogeneous a transaction space, the lower its transaction costs and thus efficiency of its activities and vice versa which poses challenges for the reach of e-Governance at the EU level. For Budd, the above outcome creates a paradox in that a system of e-Governance will of necessity be heterogeneous. But, for the EU e-Governance transaction space to be efficient, it will be have to be more homogeneous thereby generating lower transactions costs.

The challenge for policy makers is to incorporate e-Government initiatives within a European Information Society so that a major outcome would be the creation of an EU e-Governance transaction space. Budd concludes that meeting this challenge may be beyond the EU at present given the combination of the technological over-determination in the Lisbon Agenda and the asymmetrical nature of the regime of economic governance. Thus the limits of the post-Lisbon governance, with e-Governance at its heart, will be reached quickly if the paradox of creating a more homogeneous transaction space from a heterogeneous system is not resolved.

The search for purely technological solutions will not suffice in creating and sustaining e-Governance as the next section of the book demonstrates. It is the interaction with process that helps move towards managing the multi-ness and puzzling nature of governance, especially in its 'e' form.

II Enabling And Managing Technologies

This section of the book draws on three chapters, to demonstrate the breadth and depth of how digital technologies are socially shaping multiple public policy fields and functions, often with puzzling and paradoxical outcomes. The opening chapter in this section *Early adopter' case studies of effective mobile communications between citizens and government* by Jane Vincent and Lisa Harris exemplifies this theme by investigating the role of mobile telephony in enabling more effective interaction between government and governance. This builds on previous work on the social shaping of Universal Mobile Telecommunications Service (UMTS). The ubiquity of mobile telephony appears to make it *the* enabling technology for realising e-Governance. Vincent and Harris draw on a number of case studies to demonstrate this.

The opening arguments in the chapter centre on the rhetoric and reality of m-Government services (with 'm' standing for mobile). Underlying the rhetoric of the technical fix approach is the reality of needing to shape and change social practices if m-government is to become a reality. This chimes with Clarke's review of the socio-technical perspectives in the opening chapter. According to Vincent and Harris, governments have not exploited the possibility of m-government services and its double determination: citizen-facing and operational work. The former covers opportunities to access large amounts of content of online government aimed at citizens. The latter provides better access for fieldworkers and command-and-control centres of public services using mobile communications. They quote Houston's bold statement that the interface for m-government is identical to e-Government. He asserts that e-Government has done the groundwork for m-government in terms of classifications of information, generation of content and its management (Houston, 2006).

Vincent and Harris point out that different technologies have different social practices associated with them. In some senses, this has been the assumption underlying the development of e-Government in the UK which due to its lack of integration and assumption of homogeneous social practices around online transactions is likely to fail. Moreover, as the authors note, there are significantly larger IT projects than current e-Government initiatives. They go on to observe that there are a number of Government to Citizen (G2C) activities but the take-up of m-government will depend on the populace's interest in using mobile telephony to access services and the way in which these services are tailored to citizens' demands.

The chapter moves on to the heart of the matter in developing its critical narrative: social shaping of technology and theories of technological adoption. The former examines the constructive discourse of designers and developers of new technologies creating unintended consequences as their adoption becomes shaped by the social practices of the users that take up these technologies. In reviewing the theoretical basis of technology adoption and related literature, Vincent and Harris point to the advantages bestowed on early adopters. This acts as a demonstration effect to the social practices of users who tend to take up new technologies over time rather than instantaneously. This would appear to be confirmed by the Technology Acceptance Model (TAM) which rests on two main factors 'perceived usefulness' and 'perceived ease of use'.

It is against this conceptual and theoretical background that a number of case studies are used to explore these larger issues and the degree to which m-government may have more promise than e-Government in creating e-Governance. These case studies focus on the key element of the UNESCO approach to e-Governance: e-Administration, e-Services and e-Democracy. By examining different scales – local to international – Vincent and Harris are able to assess the wider and deeper implication of the role and take-up of mobile telephony.

Vincent and Harris's concluding discussion integrates the two elements of the chapter to post a health warning about the embrace of new technologies. The overenthusiasm for new technologies has beset every age. Some old technologies remain the basis of everyday economic and society certainties and one has to be careful of ambitious claims. As they point out, the take-up and use of e-Government and m-government services will depend on their appropriateness. In the arena of mutual shaping of technology and society and how citizens take up virtual technologies in accessing services, the multiple nature of e-Governance manifests itself again; in particular how mobile technologies become distributed to experienced Internet users, further opening up the digital divide rather than closing it.

In Alan Rae's chapter, *Abandoned heroes: The decline of ICT business support*, the use of ICT by small and medium-sized enterprises of electronically-mediated business support is examined; in particular, how this activity, aimed at underpinning SME development and growth, has been reduced in the UK. Rae develops three aspects to his central argument: first, the rise and fall of ICT support over the last decade; second, evaluation of the response to these changes using a sample of SMEs; third, looking at lessons for the UK government in taking a more pragmatic view of SME support. Like many aspects of governance, business support and the increased use of ICT has been a response to external factors. These include, *inter alia*: greater international competition; more efficient operation of supply chains, (which are crucial to many SMEs) and for SMEs to conform to increased regulatory obligations. Without ICT, transactions costs for many SMEs would rise significantly.

The governance of small business support in the UK has been a moving and variable feast. Rae reviews the establishment of Business Link, a one-stop shop for business advice. However, extending business support into the domain of e-Governance processes was seen as being beyond the knowledge of the average BL advisor, who in the great British tradition has been characterised as a 'gifted amateur': a view held by many civil servants. A number of online initiatives were undertaken with degrees of varying success. One of the last, *UK Online for Business*, was wound up in 2004, based on the Government's assumption that online business was now 'mainstream'.

The paradoxical nature of governance is borne out by Rae's observation that there is a gulf between the rhetoric of governmental agencies and the reality of SME ICT support needs on the ground. The turnover of business support and vocational education and skills projects over a number of centuries, is but one manifestation of this gulf as the Vocational Education and Training (VET) and entrepreneurship problem of the UK remains a contemporary problem. A similar comment could be made about e-Government projects that have been deemed as failures by the Government itself. This context is one in which Rae's detailed examination of ICT adoption by SMEs in practice. This examination was undertaken by researchers at two London universities, using a population of 400 firms with a sample of 50 being used to focus on key issues.

The final findings of this study, and those that inform the conclusion of the chapter would make for interesting reading for policy makers, particularly those seeking to address the UK's entrepreneurship and skills problem. That is, for SMEs to be successfully incorporated into an e-Governance framework for business support, then information and training that will become accepted and successful needs to be practical; detailed; structured; bite-sized; informal and non-accredited. This could be equally applied to any governance system but the challenge for supporting SMEs adopting ICT is not to allow government imperatives to limit the domain of this form.

The final chapter in this section, *Collateral damage? The Impact of Government Policy on United Kingdom Higher Education* by Simran Grewal ostensibly represents a case study of an important sector of the economy. Given the transformative nature of higher education (HE) and its role as a positional good (has lifetime effects on employment opportunities, etc.), it is appropriate that it should be analysed in the context of enabling and managing technologies. Grewal explores the adoption and management of e-mediated technologies in UK HE in the context of increasing student numbers and widening participation in the sector. These technologies represent the next stage of modernity for many commentators, and by quoting the work of the British sociologist Anthony Giddens she points to the double-edged sword of modernity. That is, there are downsides to the adoption of new technologies and that an uncritical embrace of the processes associated with these technologies can create unintended consequences and perverse outcomes (Giddens, 1996).

Grewal begins by reviewing the impact of market forces and the introduction of private sector practices. Early attempts to establish an e-University in the UK as a means to introduce a greater element of market forces in HE failed for a variety of reasons. Although primarily technological, the low take-up by students points to a more fundamental socio-economic failure. The UK spends less than its continental European neighbours on HE in terms of proportions of national income and less than half of that of the United States. Given the lack of political will of increasing public expenditure for the sector, the adoption of private sector practices through the adoption of e-mediated technologies has become central to HE policy in the UK. These technologies are seen as offering effective and cost-efficient means of delivering policy objectives.

The policy objectives are covered in a comprehensive review of HE since the 1980s, the drivers of which are increased participation; decreased unit of resource through lower funding; increased accountability; and increased tuition fees. The enabling power of ICT-based technologies would square the circle of apparently conflicting objectives and reshape the social practices of the sector, with the student as consumer at the heart of this different socio-technical universe. This rhetoric has, however, not stood up to the scrutiny of reality as the case study, used to exemplify Grewal's arguments, amply demonstrates.

The case study is based on the take-up of WebCT technology in a mainstream middle-ranking university. Drawing on an ethnographic approach, through a series of interviews, she shows how the social relationship between lecturer and student has been reshaped in the dissemination of expert knowledge. Naively, the senior management of the university in the case study assumed that teaching would become a routine activity, enabled and managed by WebCT, within which a large increase in student numbers could be accommodated at minimal cost. The transaction cost in reshaping the role of lecturer rose significantly as he/she took on a dual role: producer and disseminator of expertise ('expert') and knowledge and manager of the technological delivery system ('lay person') rose. The social reshaping of the lecturer–student relationship now had a dual determination, face-to-face contact and virtual interaction, driving a much higher cultural expectation from the student. As Leslie's Budd discussion in Chapter 3 shows, co-operative relationships based on face-to face communications and co-operative relationships are indicative of efficient transaction spaces and redolent of advanced sectors in the economy. In the context of HE and the case study, lowering of the trust relationship between lecturer and student has resulted from the reshaping of the academic role in universities where this technology has been adopted. A result is additional transaction costs, as well as operational costs as academic staff find that their time is not freed up for more (apparently) productive activities. As Grewal concludes, the paradox is that the net outcome may be one of rising costs rather than savings and a fall in educational standards in HE in the UK at the very time British HE is being marketed as a leading global brand.

III Functional Fields For e-Governance?

So far we have stressed the puzzling and paradoxical nature of e-Governance as well as its multiple nature. In this section of the book the emphasis begins to shift from governing e-Governance to managing e-Governance. Colin Gray's chapter, *e-Governance issues in small and medium-sized enterprises*, follows on from that of Alan Rae. Both chapters stress the continuing importance of developing and sustaining entrepreneurship at all territorial and functional scales. Whereas Rae focuses on the enabling of entrepreneurship by using new technologies, Gray examines how the adoption of these technologies has placed small and medium-sized enterprises (SMEs) at the heart of economic and social governance, and thus assesses their contribution to evolving systems of e-Governance.

The chapter opens with a review of the role of SMEs and the power relations in respect of their networks. In the first part Gray reviews the role of SMEs in innovation and productivity gains and then examines the SME sector in the EU and the UK. Focusing on the key issues he highlights four areas concerning SME networks governance: transaction costs and the vertical disintegration of larger firms; local clusters of complementary SMEs; communities of practices; and family and community ties. Gray then goes on to examine management and governance issues and analyses whether SME networks conform to the EC's five indicators of good governance, namely, openness; participation; accountability; effectiveness; and coherence.

Conforming to good governance is a problem for small firms, not only because of the transactions costs involved but also because of the qualities needed to manage stakeholders to the governance process. One way to mitigate the effects of these costs is for small firms to participate in networks. Gray examines SME typologies and effects by reference to a 2003 study which examined the impact of broadband on networks of micro-firms in the EU. It concluded that the social aspect of networking was as important as business opportunities for these firms. This tends to reinforce the social-technical perspective of e-Governance, expounded elsewhere in this book.

Central to these networks is the importance of supply chains and clusters to the development and sustaining of SMEs. With greater contracting out by larger firms many SMEs have lost their prized independence in acting as autonomous agents. The increased monopsony power created by this change in the industrial environment has powerful implications for the governance of SMEs. In the case of clusters, their development as a major business model has generated positive incentives for the creation of SME networks. However, both these practices have tended to depersonalise social networking among SMEs and has implications for the role of SME networks in e-Governance. Gray goes on to review more traditional models of SME networks: associations and communities of practice.

Moving on to the role of ICT, Gray notes that although the take-up of ICT is not significantly different in the SME sector, its adoption has not been as comprehensive. Drawing on the British Social Attitudes Survey he develops the socio-technical perspective and shows that SME networks appear to correspond to a transaction space of e-Governance in which face-to-face communication and co-operative relations are important. In this setting ICT-mediated communication is drawn upon to access specialist advice but, as the results from the British Social Attitudes Survey show, Internet access is greater than business usage in the SME sector.

In conclusion, he points to the heterogeneous nature of the SME sector. This would suggest that following Budd's discussions, it would not be the site of a very efficient transaction space. However, SMEs cuts across different sectors, business strategies and technological trajectories (including adoption and usage of ICT). As Gray notes, very few SMEs conform to the five factors of good governance and those that do tend to pursue growth strategies and are involved in more high tech sectors. The challenge for the development of e-Governance in this sector is how the governance gap is closed and managed. There are opportunities for ICT in this regard and given the development of traditional SME networks towards that of supply chains and clusters, forms of e-Governance are likely to be generated. However, given the heterogeneous nature of the sector, this will not be a universal process.

One field that perhaps holds out the most promise for e-Governance is local government. Janice Morphet looks at developments in her chapter *e-Governance and local government*. Local government looks ripe for e-Governance given the number of e-Government initiatives in the advanced economies and regional trade agreement areas, for example the EU. Morphet sets out to see ways in which the UNESCO goals of e-Governance; e-Administration; e-Services; and e-Democracy have been used to develop a comprehensive system of e-Government for local authorities. In other words, rather than looking at e-Government projects as building blocks for e-Governance, e-Governance goals are used as building blocks for creating and managing coherent e-Government.

Morphet begins with a review of the 1999 policy to make all public services e-enabled for the citizens of England and Wales by 2005. This target was also applied to central and local government in delivering the UNESCO goals but with rather different emphasis between the different governmental scales. Building capacity through partnerships and joint working and setting clear measuring targets were the two approaches to e-enablement in local government. In doing so, creating e-Government at this level would be seen as part of governance and not an add-on.

A major concern is that of digital exclusion in the delivery and take-up of e-Services within an e-Government agenda. Central to the enablement of e-Service, e-Participation and e-Democracy is the citizen–state contract within which citizens are engaged and the delivery of public services is assured. This contract has a long lineage and has been subject to major theses, including that of Jean Jacques Rousseau and Georg Hegel. In the contemporary world, there is the perception of a shift in the governance relationship between the citizen and the state, as Morphet notes. In moving from subject of state practice to the citizen engaged in a more participatory relationship with the public realm, e-Government may have a key role to play, particularly at decentralised levels. Morphet discusses the relative successes and failures of citizen participation in, and engagement with, governance. This resonates with the case study of a local authority in Jane Vincent and Lisa Harris's chapter.

In the final part of the chapter, Morphet engages in a lengthy discussion of whether local e-Government has been successful, drawing on comparisons with the approaches followed by the EU. In her conclusion, she makes the perceptive point about how the introduction of Government in local government has changed the nature of policy making and the organisational cultures that underpin it. In doing so, Morphet is locating her argument within the new and reinvented government literature in which governance appears to be subservient to managing (Osborne and Gaebler, 1992; Carneiro, 1999) and, perhaps unwittingly in the rescaling of state power arguments that suggest state functions have been turned inside out in the current pressure for public services to be customer focused so that citizens become more like producer interests (Brenner, 1999). This reading of the conclusion may be puzzling and paradoxical, but again shows the multiple nature of governance as local government in the UK shifts towards e-Government in the process of creating e-Governance transaction spaces.

In the penultimate chapter, Fintan Clear and Charles Dennis engage with the e-Inclusion debate by investigating *e-Government, disability and inclusion*. Much has been made of the digital divide between developed and developing economies; what Clear and Dennis contribute is to look more closely at problems of inclusion in a digitally mediated world for the disabled. They begin with a discussion of the concept of disability and its linguistic interpretation taken from a social constructivist perspective.

The following section details legislation dealing with disability discrimination in the UK. The development of the disability rights discourse that has become central to the governance of combating this form of discrimination is the context for this review of UK regulation. The crux of the matter is that disability is heterogeneous and thus it is difficult to frame legislation which combats forms of disability discrimination in most countries that have pursued this form of social policy. Access to the web is not explicitly included nor excluded in this legislation and thus becomes part of the multi-ness of governance.

It is against this background that the substantive parts of the chapter are set out under the heading of 'digital equality' and 'usability'. In the first section of the discussion, the authors refer to the British Household Survey to review the limits of take-up of digital media, particularly the Internet. Again, drawing on the socio-technical perspective, Clear and Dennis point to four discourses around the governance of digital accessibility. At the heart of these discourses is the view that there are technological solutions to the problem of the digitally divided because of disability. However, the social and physiological constraints on the disabled fully accessing their rights of citizenship remain as powerful barriers to their inclusion in the digital world. The section on usability starts off with the critique that the Web is seen primarily as a visual medium, dominated by graphic designers. There is then a long review of the protocols and the implications of legislation and public policy for Internet use for the disabled. What is apparent is that in managing digital exclusion of the disabled we are again in the territory of network governance, from a socio-technical perspective. Moreover, despite the technological and graphic perspectives of Web designers, this issue is not one of management but of network governance in all its complexities.

In the final chapter *e-Governance in transition economies* Antoaneta Serguieva and Kamen Spassov use Bulgaria as a case study on which to investigate this increasingly important issue. As Leslie Budd's chapter discussed, one of the important challenges for the post-Lisbon EU is the creation of a European Information Society in the context of a regime of economic governance of which expanding the Union is a key component. At the heart of Serguieva and Spassov's argument is that e-Governance further embeds democracy in the established EU Member States, whilst for the newer Member States it presents an opportunity to further enable democratisation. The substantive part of their chapter deals with the development of ICT infrastructure and its capacities in Bulgaria by reference to the Digital Opportunity Index. According to this index Bulgaria punches above its international weight when compared to its current economic development and performance.

As a newer Member State of the EU, Bulgaria conforms to the EC's Directives on e-Governance and these provide the legislative

framework in Bulgaria. Serguieva and Spassov discuss the implementation of the Bulgarian government's e-Government Strategy in the
context of interoperability and the implementation of the Action
Plans associated this strategy. The next section reviews the development of e-Government initiatives in respect of different governmental
functions, in the context of Bulgaria's comparative international
performance. The authors then present three case studies of
e-Governance in Bulgaria in some detail. The first looks at the level
of regional government. The second considers the use of the balanced
scorecard as the basis of creating a management information system
for implementing e-Governance at the national level. The third case
looks at the international level in respect of the EU's Government
User Identity for Europe (GUIDE). GUIDE has the object of
creating an EU-wide standard for an interoperable and secure identity
e-Government management architecture. It is interesting to note
the emphasis on technological and management solutions to the
challenges of e-Government and e-Governance in transition economies. In their concluding comments, the authors point to the difficulty of reversing strategies for enabling e-Governance, as shown by
the case studies. In terms of the development trajectory of a transition
economy like Bulgaria, governing appears to be subservient to a
technocratic management project of modernisation. As such a socio-
technical perspective on e-Governance appears secondary. Furthermore, governing appears to be an *ex post* outcome of implementing
e-Governance, but that in itself will throw up some puzzling and paradoxical issues and that the multi-ness of governance also cuts across
time as well as the territorial division of governmental jurisdictions.

On Reflection?

The three parts of this book have attempted to create a critical narrative and a means of navigating the puzzling and paradoxical nature of
e-Governance in all its multiple guises. In an era when everything from
purchasing a parking permit to foreign policy has been sexed up,
perhaps it is time for a more chaste analysis of many the banal and
mundane aspects of the electronic world. The world of early 1990s 'e'
culture centred on the drug Ecstasy has not quite transmitted its

hedonistic pleasure principle to the 'e' world of the late twentieth and early twenty-first centuries, despite many breathless accounts of the new digital world. Some of the old certainties prevail, whether they are associated with technology, product or process. In his analysis of network governance, Richard Collins perceptively points out the paradoxes of the opposition of 'Netheads' versus 'Bellheads' within which one would expect the 'Netheads' to be the efficient trustees of digital governance. In a similar vein, we could oppose 'Onliners' with 'Landliners' and find other paradoxical puzzles to pursue. In other words, new and old technologies are ingredients in the heady brew of different forms of access to an electronic world: the degree of intoxication of the brew not necessarily depending of the amount of 'newness'. Like most parts of the old and contemporary socio-economic universe, boundaries are fuzzy and often elastic and e-Governance is no different.

The boundary between e-Governance and e-Government falls into the fuzzy/elastic category as demonstrated by the cases in this book. Many e-Government projects in a number of countries have 'failed' mainly due to being inappropriate for their intended purposes. Consequently governments have scaled down the resources solely dedicated to e-Government. e-Governance is more difficult to define and more elastic than e-Government. For some the definition of e-Governance is solely: 'about the use of information and communication technology to improve the quality and efficiency of all aspects of the life cycle of legislation' (Gordon, 2000; 1). For others, it is about the electronic delivery of public services and shaping public policy at political levels (Borins, 2002). In both cases, managing and governing combine in the process of e-Governance, and as argued in respect of network governance the proportions of this combination vary for different governmental functions and in different territories. Although the US and Canada appear to be in the forefront of e-Governance developments, service delivery appears to easier to manage than governing changes at the political level (Borins, 2002). This outcome suggests that e-Governance, at least in respect of service delivery is an extension of e-Government. Similarly, the application of knowledge-based legal systems appear to offer most hope for governing e-Governance (Gordon, 2000). It seems to follow that in the same way that e-Government and e-Governance overlap, so managing and governing e-Governance are part of the of the shifting environment within which public policy and service delivery exist. Essentially, the more heterogeneous the transactions space of e-Governance, the less determinate will be its management and vice versa. Thus it ever was, as the following quote from David Landes's excellent book on the Industrial Revolution *The Unbound Prometheus* demonstrates, drawing on the ancient Greek myths. We use this quote to highlight the universal importance of the interaction action between technology and knowledge.

> Prometheus was punished and indeed all mankind for Zeus sent Pandora with her box of evils to compensate the advantages of fire, but Zeus never took back the fire. Daedalus lost his son, but he was the founder of a school of sculptors and craftsmen and passed on much of his cunning on to posterity. In sum, the myths warn us that the wresting and exploitation of knowledge are perilous acts, but that man must follow and will know, and once knowing, will not forget (Landes, 1969; 555).

Prometheus was continuously tortured for stealing fire from the gods and giving it to mankind, from which this ingredient much technology and knowledge was created and developed. Daedulas's son, Icarus, flew too near the Sun and his artificial wings melted. He fell into the sea and drowned. Pandora's curiosity got the better of her and released the evil contents of her box into the world, with hope remaining as the only ingredient in her box. As Landes points out, a serious prognosis cannot be just based on myths and symbols but this narrative approach does point out to some of the continuities and disjunctures in the development of knowledge and technology in the ancient and contemporary worlds.

The contemporary world may sex up new technologies and their adoption and dissemination and sex down old ones and mature processes. But as our metaphorical assignation with the ancient world shows, the creation and development of technology and knowledge is central to the human condition. Within this condition, e-Governance is no different. What is crucial is how the journey of development unfolds. As Mao Tse Tung famously remarked, 'the journey of a thousand miles starts with the first step'. In developing a critical narrative of how e-Governance evolves to be managed or governed, we hope this book has made some significant steps on a road to a little more enlightenment.

Bibliography

Arrow, K. (1969), 'The Organization of Economic Activity: Issues Pertinent to the Choice of Market Versus Nonmarket Allocation'. In *The Analysis of Public Expenditure: The PPB System*. Vol. 1 US Joint Economic Committee, 91st Congress, 1st Session. Washington D.C. US Government Printing Office. pp. 59–73.

Brenner, N. (1999), 'Beyond State-centrism? Space, Territoriality and Geographical Scale in Globalization Studies', *Theory and Society*, 28, 2 pp. 39–78.

Borins, S. (2002), 'On the Frontiers of Electronic Governance: A Report on the United States and Canada', *International Review of Administrative Sciences*, Vol. 69, pp. 199–211.

Budd, L. (2007), 'Post-bureaucracy and Reanimating Public Governance. A Discourse and Practice of Continuity?', *International Journal of Public Sector Management*, Vol. 20 No. 6, pp. 531–47.

Budd, L. (2009), 'The Limits of Post-Lisbon Governance in the European Union'. In L. Budd and L. Harris (eds) *e-Governance: Managing or Governing?* London, Routledge.

Carneiro, R. (1999), 'A Changing Canon of Government: From Custody to Service'. Paper presented to OECD symposium *Government of the Future: Getting from Here to There*, OECD, Paris.

Clarke, J. (2009), 'Governance Puzzles' in L. Budd and L. Harris (eds) op. cit.

Crawford, S. (2004), 'The ICANN Experiment', *Cardozo Journal of International and Company Law*, 12 pp. 701–740. At http://www.scrawford.net/display/Crawford2.pdf on 18.12.2006.

Dunleavy, P., Margetts, H., Bastow, S. and Tinkler, J. (2006), 'New Public Management is Dead – Long Live Digital-era Governance', *Journal of Public Administration Research and Theory*, Vol. 16 No. 3, pp. 467–94.

Giddens, A. (1996), *The Consequences of Modernity*, Cambridge: Polity Press.

Gordon, T. F, *e-Governance and its Value for Public Administration* mimeo, e-Governance Competence Centre, Berlin: FOKUS.

Held, D. (2004), 'Democratic Accountability and Political Effectiveness from a Cosmopolitan Perspective'. Paper presented at the WZB/CARR Conference on Global Governance and the Role of non-State Actors. London School of Economics. 4/5.11.2004.

Houston, D. (2006), 'Mobile Governance', *Juniper Research White Paper*, London.

Kelly, J. (2006), 'Central Regulation of English Local Authorities: An Example of Meta-governance?', *Public Administration*, Vol. 3, pp. 603–21.

Klijn, E-H and Koppenjan, J.F.M. (2000), 'Public Management and Policy Networks; Foundations of a Network Approach to Governance', *Public Management*, 2:2 pp. 135–58.

Landes, D. (1969), *The Unbound Prometheus: Technological Change and Industrial Development in Western Europe from 1750 to the Present*, Cambridge: Cambridge University Press.

Moravcsik, A. (2004), 'Is there a "Democratic Deficit" in World Politics?: A Framework for Analysis', *Government and Opposition*, April.

O'Connor, J. R. (1973), *The Fiscal Crisis of the State*, New York: St. Martins Press.

Osborne, R. and Gaebler, T. (1992), *Reinventing Government: How Entrepreneurial Spirit is Transforming the Public Sector*, Reading MA: Addison-Welsley.

Okot-Uma R. W.'O (2000), 'Electronic Governance: Reflections on Good Governance'. *Commonwealth Institute Working Paper*, London: Commonwealth Institute.

Rhodes, R.A.W. (1997), *Understanding Governance*, Buckingham: Open University Press.

Schumpeter, J. (1942), *The Process of Creative Destruction*, London: Unwin.

Stoker, G. (2006), 'Public Value Management: A New Narrative for Networked Governance?', *American Review of Public Administration*, Vol. 36 No. 2, pp. 41–57.

UNESCO (2005), *e-Governance Capacity Building*, United Nations Educational Scientific and Cultural Organization, Paris. At http://portal.unesco.org/ci/en/ev.php-URL_ID=4404&URL_DO=DO_ TOPIC& URL_SECTION=201.html (accessed 01.06.07).

Wood, G. and Parr, J.B. (2005), 'Transactions Costs, Agglomeration Economies and Industrial Location', *Growth and Change*, Vol. 36(1) pp. 1–15.

PART I

SETTING THE
e-GOVERNANCE
SCENE

1

GOVERNANCE PUZZLES

JOHN CLARKE

Introduction

This chapter focuses primarily on puzzles about changing forms and practices of governance and then addresses the ways in which issues of e-Governance are implicated in these puzzles. Governance has emerged as a key concern of studies of changing relations between state and society or government and people in the last two decades (see, *inter alia*, Cooper, 1998; Kooiman, 1993; Newman, 2001 and 2005; Pierre, 2000; Rhodes, 1997). Despite – or possibly even because of – this growing attention, it remains a somewhat blurred and elusive term, bearing a range of different meanings and interpretations, and carrying the imprint of different theoretical perspectives. Nevertheless, most positions seem to treat governance as a defining feature of the modern/contemporary world – for example, expressed in the claim that we have moved 'from government to governance' (Rhodes, 1997). For others, however, governance refers to a still emergent set of institutional forms, arrangements and practices involved in the coordination of the public realm and its unsettled and uncertain relations with other domains – the private, the domestic and the transnational (Newman, 2005). An alternative view of governance challenges the 'grand narrative' of the shift from government to governance and addresses new governance processes as disorganised and disorganising (Bode, 2007; Clarke, 2006).

In this chapter, I draw on a diverse field of work about governance that ranges from studies of British public service reform to the processes and politics of governing a new social, political and economic space – south-eastern Europe. One end of this range – British public service reform – appears as a 'classic case' of governance studies: the move away from direct government to first 'markets', and then 'networks' as modes of governing the public realm (Rhodes, 1997). While it might be marked by new dimensions of 'multi-level govern-ance' (with levels ranging from the supra-national agencies such as the European Union and the World Trade Organisation to sub-national levels of regional and local governance), it is still framed by a spatial conception of a 'mature democracy', adapting to new governing dynamics. In the process, Britain represents a leading example of new models that may be exported to others (from the New Public Management to Public Private Partnerships).

In contrast, the other end of this range – the governance of an emergent regional space – looks more unsettled. There are problems of defining, much less governing, south-eastern Europe (Syrri and Stubbs, 2005). Political and institutional arrangements have been pro-foundly unsettled, and national spaces and their institutionalisations and interrelationships are still in the process of being worked out. Here, governance and the subjects and objects of governing are in the process of simultaneous and mutual invention or constitution (Lendvai and Stubbs, 2006). However, I will suggest that studies of governance might learn more from such emergent processes than from a focus of 'leading examples'. Indeed, the processes of govern-ance emerging in 'marginal' locations might illuminate what is going on in British governance arrangements. This orientation focuses my attention on 'governance puzzles' – the peculiar and unpredictable dynamics associated with emergent governance arrangements.

The chapter explores two particular 'puzzles': the multi-ness of governance; and the problem of making governance popular. Both of these puzzles are linked to issues about the emergent dynamics of governance and each of them is tied to the rise of e-Governance in distinctive ways.

The Multi-Ness of Governance

In political science, it has become commonplace to refer to the rise of 'multi-level governance', indicating the multiplicity of levels, scales, or tiers of governance bodies or processes that may be nested together (e.g., Bache and Flinders, 2004). Such levels or tiers involve differentiated but overlapping (and possibly even integrated) authority over, and claims on, particular governance issues and governable places. Multi-level governance is associated with what Rhodes (1997) called the 'hollowing out of the state' as nation states are subjected to the authority of superordinate tiers and to processes of devolution or decentralisation to sub-national levels. Processes of both globalisation and Europeanisation have proved fertile terrain for the investigation and elaboration of such concepts (see, *inter alia*, Beyeler, 2003; Ferrera, 2005). There are problems about the concept of level, and about the assumption that it has a corresponding spatial character (see, for example, Allen, 2003). So we are invited to think of levels nested within increasingly larger spaces (from the neighbourhood to the global level). Contemporary approaches in geography suggest that space is not ordered in such tidy and orderly formations (Massey, 2004). We might want to think about the ways in which the 'multi-ness' of governance brings new spaces into being, or makes new framings of space visible. We may see this in governance projects that aim to bring new regions such as 'south-east Europe' into being; that construct neighbourhoods as a site of governing or new governance arrangements for primary health care that claim to address and develop the 'local health economy' (Aldred, 2007; Cochrane, 2006; Lendvai and Stubbs, 2006). In the last case, the 'local' is not a fixed or given category: indeed, the localness of different public services and their governance arrangements may vary substantially, while the 'health economy' has to be constructed and developed, rather than discovered. Similarly, South East Europe has to be imagined, mapped, and brought into being – made into a reality – by the very governance arrangements that name themselves as governing the area, just as 'Europe' has to be defined and reconstructed in the process of its governance through the EU (Walters, 2004). Put simply, the object of governance is constructed in the process of governance – whether this object is a space, a group or an institution. And through governance arrangements, claims are established about who has the authority to govern, the bases of such authority, and the means by which it may be exercised.

This more dynamic understanding of the interrelationship between governance processes and spatial formations reopens the concept of levels (Stubbs, 2002). Where multi-level governance treats the organisation of scale and space as vertical, we can think about governance relationships as multiple, multi-dimensional and overlaid in complicated figures. Some of those relationships are hierarchical and vertical, involving claims about forms of sovereignty and authority, and structured around principles of decentralisation and devolution. But some are horizontal, such as networks within and across national borders. For example, Hansen and Salskov-Iversen use the idea of 'globalising webs' to analyse the transnational articulation of e-Government, arguing that they 'can be seen as one organisational instantiation of how social processes are increasingly unhindered by territorial and jurisdictional barriers and enhance the spread of trans-border practices in economic, political and social domains' (Hansen and Salskov-Iversen, 2005: 230). Other governance relationships may work vertically, but leap over intervening levels (connecting individuals or localities to supra-national agencies) or mix up levels (local partnerships with transnational corporations as one partner). In this way, a spatial perspective alerts us to the ways in which ideas, agents and practices flow in multiple directions.

In this context I am interested in taking the 'multi' of multi-level governance as a pointer to the many 'multi-s' that might be at stake in these new arrangements of governing. For example, governance arrangements that are multi-level are also often multi-national, multi-agency, and multi-ethnic or multi-cultural. I think these different 'multi-s' and their intersections form one central governance puzzle: how to analyse governance arrangements that are both multiple and mobile.

Governance processes are increasingly engaged by the multi-national – in terms of dealing with multiple and overlapping national sovereignties, with cross-border spaces, and with transnational processes taking place both between and within particular national spaces (flows of objects, money and people for example). The increasing significance of such transnational processes, relations and organisations has given many aspects of governance a distinctively multi-national character. This may merely imply that governance arrangements link several national spaces in networks, webs or partnerships. But multi-national governance may require forms of cross-border working or the creation of partnerships that 'transcend' national identification – for example, the economic or social development of 'regions' that cross borders cannot be allocated to a singular national sovereignty claim. Indeed, the region being brought into being may acquire its own powers and capacities beyond singular national sovereignty claims (the European Union, Mercosur and other 'economic' regions embodied in governance entities). As a result, governance arrangements both negotiate and modulate the sovereignty associated with nations as bounded spaces, even as – in some cases – the 'nations' themselves are in the process of being invented, redefined or recreated. This applies equally to the reconfigurations of the countries of the former Yugoslavia as it does to the countries of the increasingly dis-united Kingdom (involving differentiated forms of 'national/regional' devolution).

Governance is, almost by definition, multi-agency: both in the narrow sense of engaging multiple agencies in some common project or concern and in the wider sense of drawing upon different sorts of agents (individuals, groups, organisations) to engage in the business of governing. Governance arrangements, or what Stephen Ball (2006) has called the 'new architecture of governance', require multiple agents because specific projects or objectives are not the sole property of a single entity (government or a government department) but the shared concern of different agents and interests. This understanding of the mutli-agentic character of governance links very different theoretical perspectives: the governance narrative of UK scholars; the dynamic systems view of views of governance as co-steering; and even post-Foucauldian conceptions of governing at a distance (Rhodes, 1997; Kooiman, 2000; Rose, 1999). Governance moves analytic attention beyond the state – opening up questions of its disaggregation (Slaughter, 2004); its decentring (McDonald and Marston, 2006) or its dispersal (Clarke and Newman, 1997). These terms are rather different from some of the epochal claims about the disappearance or even death of the state, insisting that the state persists, albeit in new formations, relationships and assemblages (Sharma and Gupta, 2006).

'Partnership' might be one defining motif of the new governance. Partnership implies the displacement of the (nation) state as the sovereign authority, such that governance involves co-steering between different types of authority, rather than merely being (contingently) devolved authority from the state. Partnership as a mode of governance draws attention to the co-existence of, and possible collaboration between, different sources of authority – the public power of the state and varieties of 'private authority' (corporations, communities, consumers, for example, see Hansen and Salskov-Iversen, forthcoming). In practice, of course, partnerships vary as formations of power and authority. Some enrol multiple sources of authority into new projects; others look more like virtual partnerships or shells for the pursuit of one set of interests (the recurrent criticism levelled at the Private Finance Initiative and its successor form Public Private Partnerships in the UK, where 'corporate welfare' appears to be the main outcome, e.g., Pollock, 2004). Others look like 'compulsory partnerships' where the power of the state is used to enforce partnership between agents and agencies who might not otherwise have sought collaboration (see Glendinning, Powell and Rummery, 2002, on New Labour's approach to partnership making in the UK).

This compulsory/coercive approach to partnership as a mode of governance makes visible what Jessop (and others) have called the relationship between governance and 'meta-governance'. For Jessop 'meta-governance' is one of the ways in which the state may have been displaced, engaging in new roles and relationships – rather than disappearing. Within the complex of new governance mechanisms, the state 'reserves to itself the right to open, close, juggle and re-articulate governance arrangements, not only terms of particular functions, but also from the viewpoint of partisan and overall political advantage' (Jessop 2000: 19).

There are two other dynamics about the multi-agency character of governance that are worth some attention. First, new governance arrangements may have to discover, or even create, the agents that they need to do the business of governing. For example, finding governors, trustees or representatives for particular interests (parents in education governance; tenants in social housing governance) is a task of governance. Such people have to be discovered, groomed and developed to take up their governance roles. They have to possess or acquire the relevant 'expertise' to govern. In a similar way, governance arrangements often need the objects of governance to be 'represented' (embodied in persons who can 'speak for them'). Neighbourhoods, communities, service users, regions, or specified socio-demographic groups have to be 'brought to voice' in governance. In the following section, I will explore some of the complications associated with these processes of representation.

Secondly, however, new governance bodies become agents themselves, acquiring powers, capacities and interests unique to them. However limited, transitory or even virtual such bodies are – they are nevertheless bodies. They have the capacity to enact governance – to make the principles, models and schemas of governance materialise in practice. We cannot, or should not assume, that there are direct transitions from the principles and plans to the practices of governance. What are conventionally described as 'implementation processes' are better understood as processes of translation, in which meanings are subject to inflection, interpretation by active agents in specific locations (Newman, 2006; Lendvai, 2005; Lendvai and Stubbs, 2006, see also Czarniawska and Sevón, 2005). While translation may be true of 'implementation' in general, it has a particular resonance in relation to governance – because governance arrangements are still emergent organisational forms for which previous organisational templates may be a poor guide. Terms such as hybrids, flex organisations, public-private agencies, network governance and even 'partnership' mark out this unstable and unpredictable character of governance arrangements (see, for example, Wedel, 2005). Hansen and Salskov-Iversen draw out these distinctive properties of emergent forms in their discussion of 'globalising webs':

> Globalising webs challenge conventional distinctions between the inside and outside of the nation-state . . . In fact, they connect state institutions across this distinction, across local and national levels of the state and relate them to a host of different actors, including non-state actors and hybrids, indeterminable organisational forms that do not match conventional distinctions between public and private. (2005: 230)

What does this attention to the new forms of agency associated with governance add to the governance puzzle? I think it brings three critical things into visibility. First, it highlights an important question about the forms of knowledge and expertise that are valorised in governance (and the forms that are devalued or de-mobilised). Some of these valued forms of knowledge derive from the field of what Cutler and Waine (1997) call 'generic management' – the belief that all organisations share common characteristics, and thus can be directed using a set of universal principles, knowledge and skills. Secondly, we can see how this may structure who gets to enter into governance roles, with preference being given to those who are the bearers of such 'relevant knowledge and expertise': legal and financial knowledge, business experience and so on (Ball, 2006; Cowan and McDermont, 2006). Others – such as the bearers of lay knowledge, or tacit knowledge of how a service works (from the vantage point of either workers or users) – may find themselves marginalised in the 'business of governance'. Thirdly, and perhaps most strikingly, new governance arrangements create the conditions in which new knowledge, skills and roles may flourish – ones that emphasise cross-boundary working. Transacting, translating, mediating and brokering characterise these new ways of working that are central to the forms of governance as partnerships, networks and collaborations (Lendvai and Stubbs, 2006; Larner and Craig, 2005; Wedel, 2001; 2005). Crossing borders, sectors, cultures, and languages forms a critical element of how governance is being 'made up' in practice.

Returning to the multi-ness of governance, many new forms of governance also have a multi-ethnic or multi-cultural character. In one sense, this reflects the collapse of the imagined geographies that linked 'race and place' in apparently stable or sedimented forms. Such imagined alignments ranged from national to local spaces (where dense conceptions of attachment, belonging and ownership are condensed). This can be viewed as the general character of European modernity (see, for example, Kooiman's conception of governance as related to the complexity, diversity and dynamics of modern societies, 1993). But it can also be seen as the emergence of governmental strategies for governing populations where formations of ethnic/ cultural differentiation have become intensely politicised in transnational, national and local forms (Hesse, 2001; Lewis, 2000; Modood, 2005; Parekh, 2000). New governance arrangements that are structured by this multi-ness aim to accommodate or contain potential social and political antagonisms. Multi-ethnic/cultural governance creates zones of containment that may also be the site of accommodating differences or producing practices of cohabitation or conviviality (Gilroy, 2005). I have deliberately run multi-cultural and multi-ethnic together in this discussion, despite the possible differences and distinctions. The contemporary flux of differences constructed around national identities, ethnic identities and religious/ faith affiliations – and the attempts to make them align with one another – marks a difficult, shifting and troubling field of conflicted and contested identifications. In the process, histories of how 'place and race' are connected to senses of attachment and identification, ownership claims, and ideas of belonging in ways that create a distinctive field of governance problems.

The 'multi-ness' of governance is an integral feature of the rise of governance. It requires us to think about how governance arrangements work on and across categorical distinctions – between nations, levels, sectors, agencies, cultures and more. Governance works across them and reworks them in the processes of governing – borders and boundaries are remade, redrawn or rendered more permeable to some sorts of flows. Hybrid forms emerge that do not simply 'belong' to one side of a boundary or another – they work interstitially in the ambiguous spaces around boundaries. But governance arrangements do not necessarily wholly eradicate such distinctions, rather they both blur and sustain them. Nations are a condition for multi-national governance (even as national sovereignty is reworked in such processes); sectoral distinctions are important for public-private partnerships; multiple ethnicities are both contested and reproduced in 'multi-cultural' governance.

Making Governance Popular?

Conventional accounts of the governance story (as the shift from government to governance) often identify state failure as a driving force in two different ways. One concerns the inadequacies of public agencies (usually coded as 'bureaucracies'). They stand accused of being wasteful or inefficient means of achieving public objectives. A whole era of governance innovations have been directed to resolving such state failures (the New Public Management, contractualisation, marketisation, privatisation, public-private partnerships, the expansion of the not-for-profit sector in service provision and so on). But state failure is also associated with the problems of representative politics, in particular the rise of scepticism, cynicism, and alienation from the institutional processes of politics (registered in declining participation in such indices as party membership and voting, see Stoker, 2006). At the same time, there are concerns about the volatility and vulnerabilities of democratic processes. 'Democracy' is the focus of desires and fears, particularly that democratic politics may be 'captured' and 'exploited' by unrepresentative or unreasonable interests (e.g., the rise of sectarian, extreme left or right wing parties or restorationist ethno-nationalisms, see Kalb, 2005).

One dynamic of governance innovation is thus the concern to reconnect 'ordinary people' in ways that overcome or counterbalance these problems and risks of representative politics. Governance is identified as a site of possible encounters in which people can be re-engaged; the marginal or voiceless may be included; a more representative public may make its views heard; and popular legitimacy may be constructed and affirmed. We can see here the two tendencies that make up the 'crisis of representation' in representative politics (Saward, 2005; 2006). On the one hand, declining participation creates a crisis of legitimacy for political representatives – manifested in declining trust in elected governments and politicians. This is the *institutional* crisis of representation: associated with the institutional forms of parties and governments. On the other hand, in complex societies political representatives are rarely 'representative' of the populations that they seek to represent: they tend to be male, be from majority racial or ethnic groups, be able-bodied rather than disabled and so on. This is the *social* crisis of representation. As the socio-demographics of societies become an object of contestation – as social position and social identity are understood to carry differences of interest – then social representation and representativeness become increasingly difficult terrain for the political process: 'how can they speak for us?'

Governance then appears as both a site where the 'crisis of democracy' may be overcome and a setting for new forms of 'democratic deficit'. Let us consider this paradox of governance a little further. Governance arrangements have often been directed to discovering 'civil society' and bringing people into the processes of governing. At the same time, other governance innovations have been directed to ensuring improved efficiency and effectiveness, for example in the provision of public services. These may not foreground 'participation', preferring models of governance that are 'streamlined' and 'business-like'. Indeed, in some governance contexts, the public may be actively excluded from the business of governance, where business is conducted behind the screen of 'commercial confidentiality'. In such contexts, the agents of governance are likely to be the figures representing organisations, rather than the public or social groups: the partners, the clients and contractors, and (possibly) the regulatory agencies under whose gaze the business is to be conducted. Such representatives are expected to 'do business', although as Aldred (2007) indicates there may be important distinctions between entrepreneurial and managerial discourses of being businesslike. Such governance forms have been criticised for their exclusion of both public and political representatives – being seen as deepening the 'democratic deficit' in contemporary societies. This deficit is also associated with the role played by what John Stewart (1996) called 'the new magistracy' – the appointed, rather than elected, members of governance processes (see also Skelcher, 1998). This reinvention of the 'great and the good' and their enrolment into the architecture of governance also demonstrates the preference for experience in the 'real world' of business and the associated 'can do' culture (Ball, 2006).

But alongside this 'efficiency drive' governance innovations have also sought to re-engage the citizen, the public and communities in governing (see Barnes et al, 2007). A variety of deliberative and participative forms of engaging publics in the process of governing have emerged in the last two decades – in the practices of 'mature democracies' just as much as in 'emerging' or 'developing' nations (Li, forthcoming). For some, such governance arrangements are superior to the imperfections of representative politics. They may be more representative (in socio-demographic terms); they may be more 'open' to multiple interests and voices; they may be more 'authentic' (engaging 'ordinary people' rather than 'professional politicians') and they may avoid the biases and distortions of parties and political machines. For others, such participatory arrangements are characterised by two more troubling dynamics. First, public participation tends to produce, as much as it reflects, 'publics'. Publics are sought out, invited, seduced and constituted in the process of participation. Second, public participation processes are themselves governed – or, perhaps more accurately managed – as part of the work of governing. They have to be staged, peopled, performed – and their consequences taken into other parts of the governing apparatus. This is not to claim that consultation, deliberation and participation are 'stage managed' or merely 'window dressing'. Such processes reflect contexts in which the need to engage the public is powerfully felt. They also have consequences for both the performance and practice of governing. It is the case, however, that such consequences tend to be indeterminate. The fact of consultation may be more important than the effect of consultation.

The recent enthusiasm for 'civil society' often involves a distinction between participation and politics, or between civil society and the state, which treats the former terms as more true, authentic or popularly grounded. In contrast, politics or state institutions tend to be seen as what Elyachar calls 'antipeople and anticommunity' (2002: 496). Civil society, then, appears as a fertile ground for renewing social and political engagement – not least because it is where people, not politics, are located. This popular conception of civil society may also be a populist one, celebrating popular voices against elites and power blocs. In the process, we may be encountering demotic, rather than democratic, modes of governing – in which speaking in the name (and sometimes voice) of 'ordinary people' becomes a political mode in itself (see, for example, Andrews, 2006 on 'postmodern populism' in Italian politics; and Frank, 2001, on 'market populism'). Various communication technologies are bound up with these developments: popular media that claim to be vigorous defenders of the 'public interest' and address their audiences in vernacular and demotic styles; and the rise of 'polling and voting' as technologies of popular media, in both factual and entertainment modes ('You, the jury'. . .). One distinctive element is the growth of on-line opinion sampling and polling, promising more 'immediate' (in both temporal and socially transparent senses) access to popular/public opinion. Such popular 'voicings' might be seen as demotic, rather than democratic, being generally under-determined by systematic conceptions of representation (Clarke et al, 2007).

Here we can see how the crisis of representation returns to haunt other forms of representation. On-line surveys are structured by the underlying distribution of digital access (and the possible social and political predispositions that might be associated with such inequalities). In different ways, generalising claims about 'the public' or 'ordinary people' tend to conceal or occlude distinctions and divisions that may be effective. On the other hand, the pursuit of socio-demographic specificity, often with the purpose of engaging the marginal, excluded or 'hard to reach' demographic segments may risk attributing a unified set of attributes to groups that are internally heterogeneous (women; disabled people; the young; the old; users of services; residents of a locality; minority ethnic groups and so on).

Critics of the civil society and NGO-centred modes of governance have raised a number of problems, two of which are particularly relevant here. One is that NGOs and related organisations evoke the same political ambivalence as states used to: they are both 'representative' of the people and act as a power over them, governing resources, allocating opportunities and establishing conditions of conduct. Of course, different NGOs occupy this field of multiple possibilities in particular ways (just as states vary), but there can be no simple presumption of the more authentic or organic character of the NGO form as a vehicle or site of governance (see, for example, Gardner and Lewis, 1996; Fisher, 1997). Secondly, NGOs, for some of the reasons set out above, are part of what James Ferguson (1990) called the 'anti-politics machine' of development – the processes and mechanisms that displace and disguise the conflicted political character of development policy and practice. Making things 'technical', and subject to regulation through different sorts of expertise, avoids and evades political conflict. Such neutral expertise may include the lay knowledge of 'ordinary people', as well as technical/professional experts, because ordinary people are not 'political' (see Elyachar, 2002).

This second governance puzzle centres on politics – or, more accurately, on the intersection of different aspects and meanings of politics around the forms and practices of governance. Governance stands in an angular relationship to formal or representative political processes – promising to remedy state failure and the crisis of political legitimacy, in part by creating new sites of popular engagement and participation. Governance may expand the reach of political involvement by targeting marginalised or excluded groups, or by engaging 'civil society' groups and organisations. In such processes, governance may also revive the political problems of representation – who is allowed and invited to speak for 'ordinary people' of different kinds. But governance may also involve the drive to 'de-politicise' conflicted or potentially conflictual issues – by turning them into the concern of 'ordinary people' and 'communities' who are constructed as 'outside politics', or by making them the focus of technical knowledge, forms of expertise that are 'above politics'. We might finally note that the design of governance systems, process and organisations might itself be thought of as 'political'. Deciding what sorts of arrangements govern what issues; who is invited to take their place within governance arrangements; what sorts of representation and knowledge are valued; and the horizons of what any governance body may govern are themselves political choices (see, for example, Jessop, 2000, on 'meta-governance' and states). The rise and proliferation of governance arrangements – as well as the specific character of particular governance processes – can be viewed as political processes, rather than just a generic social trend.

'There Must Be Some Way Out Of Here'? e-Governance and Governance Puzzles

These two governance puzzles – the multi-ness of governance and making governance popular – contribute to a view of governance as a field of emergent and unfinished practices. These properties are visible at different levels of analysis in studying governance. They are characteristics of what might be called 'governance systems' – the assemblages of apparatuses, agencies, policies and practices that claim to govern particular spaces, objects or social domains. However, their profoundly unsystematic quality makes 'system' a somewhat risky term to use. They might be better described as formations, constellations or assemblages in order to emphasise their multiple elements and the contingent relationships that hold them together for periods of time. Such terms foregound the combination of instability and innovation that seems typical of governance arrangements.

The same properties can also be observed at the level of individual governance organisations. In part, this reflects the way in which specific governance forms are themselves hybrids or assemblages, bringing different agents into new configurations. But these properties are combined in complicated ways with patterns of institutionalisation, in which particular assemblages crystallise and take on the appearance of solidity and permanence. New organisational forms, valued patterns of knowledge and expertise, and condensations of power and authority become solidified or sedimented. They become 'governance' – its arrangements, its architecture, its processes and its practices.

So, what are the relationships between this difficult dynamic of flux and solidification and the rise of e-Governance? In this final section I explore three views of this intersection. The first treats e-Governance as the inheritor of governance logics (or as the solution to their problems). The second sees e-Governance as a further paradigm shift in the government to governance narrative. The third concentrates on the ways in which e-Governance might reconfigure the management of dispersed and multiple sites of power in the processes of governing.

For governments in particular, digital technologies seem to represent an enhanced technical capacity for the extension of current governance logics. New technologies are seen to 'go with the flow' of current trends in several ways. They provide governmental organisations with significant increases in information management capacities, in terms of the accumulation and use of data in relation to areas that have been, or emerging as, the core business of government (for example, revenue collection; policing – in both domestic and border settings – and aspects of social welfare, particularly fiscal welfare). Secondly, the enhanced 'connectivity' provided by digital systems can enable the 'multi-ness' of dispersed governance, making the transnational, translocal, cross-sector, cross-agency relationships of governance easier to conduct. Thirdly, digital technologies are understood as enabling, and even empowering, the citizen in their interactions with government and other governance agencies. ICTs can make governance popular through providing a dynamic interface between individuals and the state (and its proxies). It provides the immediate means of access to government, a means of addressing enquiries to citizens, and the means of engaging selected or targeted groups: new technologies have a 'democratising' capacity. Finally, digital technologies offer the promise of enabling the 'personalisation' of public services – the greater tailoring of provision to the individual needs, circumstances and wants of the individual. Such personalisation is a core theme in current public service reform (see, for example, Department of Health, 2006 and Leadbetter, 2004) and new technologies represent a critical resource for making the rhetorical move from 'one size fits all' to 'tailor-made' services.

Such conceptions of the 'fit' between contemporary governance logics and new digital technologies both overestimate and underestimate the 'technical' character of these technologies. They also offer a disconcertingly coherent account of governance logics. Overestimating the technical character of ICTs involves a typically desocialising and de-politicising sense of the 'technical': thus ICTs are treated as neutral means for achieving already established governance principles and models. As a 'technical fix', new technologies mean that governments can achieve their objectives – whether these be greater efficiency, greater public engagement, the personalisation or diversification of services, or simply the elaboration of more 'modern' systems of governance. Digital technologies permit and enable all of these.

But this 'technical fix' view of e-Governance also underestimates the technical character of digital technologies in the sense of underestimating the organisational, social and political consequences that such technologies may create. A stronger view of ICTs as 'sociotechnical systems' suggests that new technologies may further some existing governance tendencies, but undermine or displace others (Dunleavy et al, 2006). Such a socio-technical view might also require attention to how digital technologies might reconfigure forms and architectures of power in and around governance. This leads to the second view of e-Governance and governance puzzles. In a recent substantial study, Dunleavy et al (2006) have argued that digital technologies have the capacity to create a new governance paradigm: Digital Era Governance (DEG).

Their view links the rise of e-Government to the waning influence of the New Public Management as the previous dominant governance paradigm. They suggest that the NPM both ran out of steam and produced perverse effects and governance failures, creating a set of conditions in which governance paradigm changes have become possible. While avoiding technological determinism, they suggest that the congruence of digital technologies and governance opportunities and problems forms a distinct opportunity for a new paradigm:

> [G]overnment IT changes are no longer peripheral or routine aspects of contemporary public management and public policy changes, but increasingly important and determinant influences upon what is feasible. IT and information system influences are as salient in current public sector management as they are fundamental in contemporary Weberian rationalisation processes. We see this influence of IT systems as having effects not in any directly technologically determined way but via a wide range of cognitive, behavioural, organisational, political, and cultural changes that are linked to information systems broadly construed . . . DEG processes could achieve productivity and effectiveness improvements while simultaneously simplifying the state apparatus and expanding citizen control of their own affairs. The opportunity to secure such a 'golden mix' of objectives does not occur often in public management. (2006: 217)

Although it is not possible to examine their argument in detail here, Dunleavy and his colleagues claim that DEG involves three clusters of changes. The first, *reintegration*, indicates that digital systems can overcome the fragmentation of government associated with the New Public Management by providing the system basis for drawing functions back into the state. This is likely to be efficient in its own terms, and promises to overcome the inefficiencies and duplications resulting from NPM-driven processes of dispersal and proliferation. The second cluster of changes, *needs-based holism*, involves reforms that 'seek to simplify and change the entire relationship between agencies and their clients . . . It also stresses developing a more "agile" government that can respond speedily and flexibly to changes in the social environment' (2006: 227). The third cluster, *digitisation changes*, involves IT processes and channels moving from secondary or supplementary roles to being the dominant, normal and potentially only mode of doing administration and business (2006: 228). They argue that these technological, or socio-technical developments, go 'with the grain' of current trends in governance, and state-citizen relationships:

> Despite this inevitable indeterminacy, we believe that the current period holds out the promise of a potential transition to a more genuinely integrated and citizen-orientated government, whose organisational operations are visible in detail both to the personnel operating in the fewer, broader public agencies and to citizen and civil society organizations. (2006: 248)

In exploring the conditions of social and political indeterminacy for this possibility, the authors construct a set of scenarios in which it may be achieved, diminished or deflected. Although avoiding the problems of technological determinism is indeed important, for me this analysis suffers from different problems that result from an overly coherent and too narrow view of governance itself. While the NPM was important as a model for fragmenting states, especially in the domain of public services, not all of the governance reforms were driven by its centripetal logic. Some changes involved the centralisation of some forms of power and authority, while others stressed engagement, participation and partnership as we have seen. Still others created 'plural provision' structured by dynamics of competition and choice around services that might prove difficult to reintegrate. The UK has built an elaborate system of planning, finding and evaluating such processes that frames individual organisations in a comparative/competitive logic (Clarke, 2004, Chapter 7). Indeed, the whole field of governance changes looks considerably more heterogeneous than the New Public Management model, even if managerialism provided a distinctive connective discourse (Clarke and Newman, 1997; Newman, 2005). For me, this suggests that digital era governance might be subject to more, and more contradictory, forces and trends than Dunleavy and his co-authors allow for (Clarke, 2006).

There are three tendencies that have the potential to disrupt the optimistic reading of Digital Era Governance. They are tendencies that involve the articulation of forms of power, authority and knowledge in governance processes. Let me begin with the persistently troubled relationships between states and citizens (Clarke, 2005). Dunleavy and his colleagues read this relationship as primarily concerned with the dynamics of empowering and enabling more autonomous citizens. Bleaker views would point to the tendency of states to accumulate knowledge of, and power over, citizens as a dynamic of 'securitisation' of societies (e.g., Huysmans, 2006) or the spread of a culture of control (Garland, 2001). The capacity for the reintegration, or further centralisation, of knowledge and power through digital technologies expands the possibilities for state control over citizens, rather than their autonomisation.

A more sceptical view of autonomised citizens is offered by other perspectives, particularly post-Foucauldian studies of govern-mentalities, which treat autonomisation as a conditional and managed process of 'governing at a distance' (Cruikshank, 1999; Rose, 1999). In this view citizens are being made 'responsible' in specific ways (for their financial welfare, health, work–life balance, security and so on). Such responsibilisation does, of course, create 'autonomy', but it adds other dynamics too. It makes rights more conditional on the performance of responsibilities, creates new frames for judging success and failure, and constructs new governance processes to scrutinise and evaluate the performance of responsibility (see Bauman, 1998, for a particularly bleak view of these changes).

The second governance dynamic concerns the forms of knowledge/power knots that are condensed in governance arrangements and how these might engage with the potentials of DEG. Some of the innovative, hybrid forms of governance arrangement are not simply the effect of NPM fragmentation. The dispersal of the state and its powers was driven by other desires – to subordinate bureau-professional power in public services to better means of discipline (market and/or managerial authority); to remake the relationship between government and corporate capital (in partnerships and contracting relationships); and to engage voluntary, third sector or civil society organisations in a more plural (and cheaper) provision of public services (Clarke and Newman, 1997). What Jessop and others have called a 'politics of scale' points to contested *dimensions*, as well as relations, of governance arrangements (Brenner, 2004; Jessop, 2002). There is no simple rationality for reintegration – rather we encounter a whole series of political, governmental, economic and managerial calculations about the advantages of particular scales, sizes and forms of governing. While Dunleavy and his colleagues make a central feature of the 'contracted out' character of IT development and provision in government, they seem less attentive to the contracted out character of other aspects of the state (and the potential costs of unlocking long-term contracting to enable reintegration). I do not mean to concentrate exclusively on narrow economic calculations around governance (important though they are), but it may be important to think of existing governance arrangements as the site of sunk investments of various kinds (the base for community organisation, the location of distinctive forms of knowledge and power; the place of new skills and careers; the organisational form taken by the 'local' and so on). To these might be added Jessop's 'meta-governance' calculations – of governmental, political and partisan advantage to be gained from governance arrangements. These may well incline towards reinforcing the potentials identified by Dunleavy and colleagues but they are calculations that may be framed by temporalities other than the long-term rationalisation of government.

In the end, I am persuaded by the insistence on treating digital technologies as 'socio-technical systems', rather than technical fixes, but I think that analysing these socio-technical systems needs to be informed by a richer understanding of the social in relation to governance. Reducing governance to two simplifying paradigms misses the heterogeneous character of governance arrangements. In contrast, Governance puzzles – about the multi-ness of governance and the ambivalences involved in making governance popular – provide ways of thinking about how this heterogeneity is the product of the contested and unfinished dynamics of governance.

Bibliography

Aldred, R. (2007) *Governing 'local health economies': The case of NHS Local Improvement Finance Trust (LIFT).* PhD thesis, Goldsmiths College, University of London.

Allen, J. (2003) *Lost Geographies of Power.* Oxford: Blackwell.

Andrews, G. (2006) *Not a Normal Country: Italy after Berlusconi.* London: Pluto Press.

Bache, I. and Flinders, M. (eds) (2004) *Multi-level Governance*. Oxford: Oxford University Press.

Ball, S. (2006) Paper presented at Social Policy Association annual conference, Birmingham, July.

Barnes, M., Newman, J. and Sullivan. H. (2007) *Power, Participation and Political Renewal*. Bristol: The Policy Press.

Bauman, Z. (1998) *Work, Consumerism and the New Poor*. Buckingham: Open University Press.

Beyeler, M. (2003) 'Globalization, Europeanization and Domestic Welfare State Reforms: New Institutionalist Concepts.' *Global Social Policy*, 3(2): 153–72.

Bode, I. (2007) 'New Moral Economies of Welfare: The Case of Domiciliary Elder Care in Germany, France and Britain.' *European Societies*, 9(2): 207–27.

Brenner, N. (2004) *New State Spaces*. Oxford: Oxford University Press.

Clarke, J. (2004) *Changing Welfare, Changing States: New Directions in Social Policy*. London: Sage.

Clarke, J. (2005) 'New Labour's Citizens: Activated, Empowered, Responsibilised, Abandoned?' *Critical Social Policy*, Vol. 25(4), pp. 447–63.

Clarke, J. (2006) 'Disorganizzare Il Publicco?' *La Rivista delle Politiche Sociali*, No. 2 (April–June).

Clarke, J. and Newman, J. (1997) *The Managerial State: Power, Politics and Ideology in the Remaking of Social Welfare*. London: Sage.

Clarke, J., Newman, J., Smith, N., Vidler, E. and Westmarland, L. (2007) *Creating Citizen-Consumers: Changing Publics and Changing Public Services*. London: Sage.

Cochrane, A. (2006) Understanding Urban Policy. Oxford: Blackwell.

Cooper, D. (1998) *Governing Out of Order*. London: Rivers Oram Press.

Cowan, D. and McDermont, M. (2006) *Regulating Social Housing: Governing Decline*. London: The Glasshouse Press.

Cruikshank, B (1999) *The Will to Empower*. Ithaca, NY: Cornell University Press.

Cutler, T. and Waine, B. (1997) *Managing the Welfare State*. Oxford: Berg.

Czarniawska, B. and Sevón, G. (eds) (2005) *Global Ideas: How Ideas, Objects and Practices Travel in the Global Economy*. Copenhagen: Liber and Copenhagen Business School Press.

Dunleavy, P., Margetts, H., Bastow, S. and Tinkler, J. (2006) *Digital Era Governance*. Oxford: Oxford University Press.

Elyachar, J. (2002) 'Empowerment Money: The World Bank, Non-Governmental Organizations, and the Value of Culture in Egypt.' *Public Culture* 14(3): 493–513.

Ferrera, M. (2005) *The Boundaries of Welfare. European Integration and the New Spatial Politics of Solidarity*. Oxford: Oxford University Press.

Ferguson, J. (1990) *The Anti-Politics Machine*. Cambridge: Cambridge University Press.

Ferguson, J. and Gupta, A. (2002) 'Spatializing States: Towards an Ethnography of Neo-liberal Governmentality.' *American Ethnologist*, 29(4): 981–1002.

Fisher, W. F. (1997) 'Doing Good? The Politics and Antipolitics of NGO Practices.' *Annual Review of Anthropology*, Vol. 26: 439–64.

Frank, T. (2001) *One Market Under Good: Extreme Capitalism, Market Populism and the End of Economic Democracy*. New York: Anchor Books.

Garland, D. (2001) *The Culture of Control: Crime and Social Order in Contemporary Society*. Chicago: University of Chicago Press.

Gardner, K. and Lewis, D. (1996) *Anthropology, Development and the Postmodern Challenge*. London: Pluto.

Gilroy, P. (2005) *Postcolonial Melancholia*. New York: Columbia University Press.

Glendinning, C., Powell, M. and Rummery, K. (eds) (2002) *Partnerships, New Labour and the Governance of Welfare*. Bristol: The Policy Press.

Hansen, H.K. and Salskov-Iversen, D. (2005) 'Globalizing Webs: Translation of Public Sector e-Modernization.' In Czarniawska, B. and Sevón, G. (eds) *Global Ideas: How Ideas, Objects and Practices Travel in the Global Economy*. Copenhagen: Liber and Copenhagen Business School Press.

Hansen, H.K. and Salskov-Iversen, D., (eds) (forthcoming) *Critical Perspectives on Private Authority in Global Politics*. Basingstoke: Palgrave Macmillan.

Hesse, B. (ed.) (2001) *Un/Settled Multiculturalisms: Diasporas, Entanglements, Transruptions*. London: Zed Books.

Huysmans, J. (2006) *The Politics of Insecurity: Fear, Migration and Asylum in the EU*. London: Routledge.

Jessop, B. (2000) 'Governance Failure.' In G. Stoker (ed.) *The New Politics of British Local Governance*. Basingstoke: Macmillan.

Kalb, D. (2005) 'From Flows to Violence: Politics and Knowledge in the Debates on Globalization and Empire.' *Anthropological Theory*, Vol. 5(2): 176–204.

Kooiman, J. (ed.) (1993) *Modern Governance: New Government-Society Interactions*. London: Sage.

Larner, W. and Craig, D. (2005) 'After Neoliberalism? Community Activism and Local Partnerships in *Aotearoa* New Zealand.' *Antipode*: 402–24.

Larner, W. and Walters, W., (eds) (2004) *Global Governmentality*. London: Routledge.

Lendvai, N. (2005) 'Remaking European Governance: Transition, Accession and Integration.' In Newman, J. (ed.) (2005) *Remaking Governance: Peoples, Politics and the Public Sphere*. Bristol, The Policy Press.

Lendvai, N. and Stubbs, P. (2006) 'Translation, Intermediaries and Welfare Reforms in South Eastern Europe.' Paper presented at the 4th ESPANET conference, Bremen, September 2006.

Lewis, G. (2000) 'Discursive Histories, the Pursuit of Mutli-culturalism and Social Policy.' In G. Lewis, S. Gewirtz and J. Clarke (eds) *Rethinking Social Policy*. London: Sage.

Li. T. (forthcoming) *The Will to Develop*. Durham, NC: Duke University Press.

McDonald, C. and Marston, G. (eds) (2006) *Analysing Social Policy: A Governmental Approach*. Cheltenham: Edward Elgar.

Massey, D. (2004) *For Space*. London: Sage.

Modood, T. (2005) *Multicultural Politics: Racism, Ethnicity and Muslims in Britain*. Edinburgh: Edinburgh University Press.

Newman, J. (2001) *Modernising Governance* London: Sage.

Newman, J. (ed.) (2005) *Remaking Governance: Peoples, Politics and the Public Sphere*. Bristol: The Policy Press.

Newman, J. (2006) 'Constituting Trans-national Governance: Spaces, Actors and Vocabularies of Power.' Paper presented to 4th ESPANET conference, Bremen, September, 2006.

Parekh, B. (2000) *The Future of Multi-Ethnic Britain (The Report of the Runnymede Trust Commission)*. London: Profile.

Pierre, J. (ed.) (2000) *Debating Governance: Authority, Steering and Democracy*. Oxford: Oxford University Press.

Pollock, A. (2004) *NHS plc*. London: Verso.

Rhodes, R. (1997) *Understanding Governance: Policy Networks, Governance, Reflexivity and Accountability*. Buckingham: Open University Press.

Rose, N. (1999) *Powers of Freedom*. Cambridge: Polity Press.

Saward, M. (2005) 'Governance and the Transformation of Political Representation.' In Newman, J. (ed.) (2005) *Remaking Governance: Peoples, Politics and the Public Sphere*. Bristol: The Policy Press.

Saward, M. 'The Representative Claim.' *Contemporary Political Theory*, 5(3): 297–318.

Sharma, A. and Gupta, A. (2006) 'Rethinking Theories of the State in an Age of Globalization.' In A. Sharma and A. Gupta (eds) *The Anthropology of the State: A Reader*. Oxford: Blackwell Publishing.

Skelcher, C. (1998) *The Appointed State*. Buckingham: The Open University Press.

Slaughter, A. (2004) *A New World Order*. Princeton, NJ: Princeton University Press.

Stewart, J. (1996) 'Reforming The New Magistracy.' In L. Pratchett and D. Wilson (eds) *Local Democracy and Local Government*. Basingstoke: Macmillan.

Stoker, G. (2006) *Why Politics Matters: Making Democracy Work*. Basingstoke: Palgrave Macmillan.

Stubbs, P. (2002) 'Globalisation, Memory and Welfare Regimes in Transition: Towards an anthropology of transnational policy transfers.' *International Journal of Social Welfare*, 11(4): 321–30.

Syrri, D. and Stubbs, P. (2005) 'Viewing Europe from the Outside: Persuasive and Incoherent Stories in the Making of a South East European Cross-border Development Space.' Paper presented to Symposium on 'Nation-building Through Policies of Inclusion/Exclusion: Sources of Transnational Identities?', Oxford, 17–19 June.

Walters, W. (2004) 'The Political Rationality of European Integration.' In W. Larner and W. Walters (eds) *Global Governmentality*. London: Routledge.

Wedel, J. (2001) *Collision and Collusion: The Strange Case of Western Aid to Eastern Europe*. New York: Palgrave.

Wedel, J. and Feldman, G. (2005) 'Why an Anthropology of Public Policy?' *In Anthropology Today*, 21(1): 1–2.

2

e-GOVERNANCE AND THE GOVERNANCE OF THE GLOBAL INTERNET

RICHARD COLLINS

Introduction

Internet governance is the development and application by Governments, the private sector and civil society, in their respective roles, of shared principles, norms, rules, decision-making procedures, and programmes that shape the evolution and use of the Internet (WGIG 2005: 4). All major communications network innovations have given rise to new enterprises, transformed economic, social and political structures, crossed borders, created international disputes, and perhaps most important, eventually led to the development of new coordination or governance frameworks (ITU 2004: 14).

Much recent attention has increasingly been given to e-Governance, defined by UNESCO as the 'exercise of political, economic and administrative authority' via an 'electronic medium' (UNESCO 2005), and embraced by Government bodies around the world. Dunleavy, Margetts, Bastow and Tinkler (2006: 2), for example, propose that 'digital-era governance' (DEG) represents a new norm in governance practice and theory and one which fuzzily (they write 'not in any direct technologically determined way') links 'a wide range of cognitive, behavioural, organisational, political and cultural changes' to 'information systems'. Appointment of the UK Government's e-Envoy in 1999 was but one enactment of such norms: the e-Envoy was to improve 'delivery of public services' and achieve 'long term cost savings by joining-up online government services around the needs of customers. The e-Envoy is responsible for ensuring that all govern-ment services are available electronically' (e-Envoy 2003).

DEG/e-Governance is often characterised as part of a bigger shift in the form of social co-ordination from hierarchical (command and control) and/or market (through prices) to network governance based on trust, co-operation, equality and disinterestedness (see *inter alia* Barabasi 2002, Barry 2007, Thompson 2003); a shift linked to the growing pervasiveness of electronic communication and connectivity (Castells 1996, Taylor 2001) and portending a new type of society – network society (Castells 1996 and 2004).

However, neither the literature of e-Governance/DEG nor con-temporary social science's epochal accounts of change have given much attention to the governance of the electronic communication infrastructure which itself underpins the network society and e-Governance/DEG – that is to the Internet. This gap is surprising given the vital role such accounts attribute to the Internet's significant scholarly literature on Internet governance (see, *inter alia*, Drake 2005, Maclean 2004, Mueller 2002) and the contemporary political salience of Internet governance, (notably at the UN World Summit on the Information Society, WSIS, of 2003–5). Internet governance both shapes e-Governance (because the Internet is the medium of e-Governance) and provides a case study for evaluation of currently salient social scientific accounts of governance. A deservedly well-known study, 'Netheads v Bellheads' (Denton 1999), casts light on these issues by contrasting distinct mentalities and practices in the governance of electronic media.

Netheads v Bellheads

'Netheads v Bellheads' persuasively compared the architectures, mentalities and material interests associated with, on one hand, the classic PSTN (public switched telephone network), circuit switched voice telephony system, characterised by Denton as 'Bellhead' (referring to the Bell telephone systems which long provided service to most North Americans) and, on the other hand, the packet switched, Internet-like, Nethead' system, latterly supplanting circuit switched systems. 'Bellhead' systems are controlled centrally enabling operators to define services, set prices and to determine standards. Whereas packet switched, Internet-like, systems are more open permitting third parties to provide services 'at the edge of the network, without the permission, control or involvement of the network owner' (Denton 1999: 3).

The differences between Bellhead and Nethead networks chime with social scientists' accounts of transition from hierarchical to networked social co-ordination. In distinguishing between network and hierarchy I draw on Thompson's (2003) distinction between hierarchical, market or network governance or co-ordination. In hierarchies governance is by 'command and control', in markets by prices (through which demand and supply are balanced) and in networks through equalitarian collaboration (Thompson 2003: 112). The agents who enact these different systems of governance are, in hierarchies, a specialised body of legitimised governors (politicians, officials and managers), in markets, suppliers and consumers, and in networks, civil society.

Although it is an oversimplification to conceive of the Internet as a single 'thing' (see Collins 2006), with a single locus of control and a single form of governance, many aspects of contemporary Internet co-ordination continue to reflect this collaborative, network, legacy. The Internet is indeed generally permissive at the periphery and with weak central control and developed through networked informal, co-operative, working arrangements. But, in one important respect, the Internet is more centralised than the global PSTN. In both systems messages have to be routed from and to particular addresses – whether between two telephones, each with a unique number, or two Internet users each with a unique IP address. But, PSTN circuit switched addressing systems are not subject to control at a single point whereas the Domain Name System (DNS), which matches Internet names and addresses, depends on a single authoritative root zone file (RZF), control of which happens, for historical reasons, to be in the United States. This difference means, as an official of the International Telecommunication Union (ITU) stated (interview with author 18.4.2005), 'no-one can turn off Switzerland's 'phones' whereas, in theory at least, whoever controls the RZF can 'turn off' the Internet in Switzerland (or elsewhere). Crawford has described the Internet

Corporation for Assigned Names and Numbers (ICANN) the organisation controlling the RZF and administering the DNS, as controlling 'a single lever by which identity on the Internet can be turned on or off. ICANN has the power to exercise the online equivalent of force' (Crawford 2004: 703).

ICANN

ICANN was set up as a not-for-profit corporation following the US Government's celebrated 'Green Paper' (NTIA 1998) in which the US government resolved to 'end its role in the Internet number and name address systems' and establish a new regime characterised by 'private, bottom up co-ordination' (NTIA 1998: np) which vested control of the DNS in ICANN. ICANN, which in the words of one of its most articulate critics, 'rules the root' (Mueller 2002), thus has become the focus of intense international controversy. By virtue of its control of the RZF, ICANN can determine which 'top level domains' (TLDs), if any, are added to the 'root' and, in theory (though in practice such a power may be very difficult to exercise), can remove addresses from the 'root'.

ICANN is subject to criticism for its putative operational failures: notably for its stewardship of gatekeeper power over TLDs which, for some critics, creates rather than mitigates, scarcity (see, *inter alia*, Komaitis and Galloway 2005); for its perceived inefficiency (Mueller 1999 and 2002, Marlin-Bennett 2001, Weinberg 2000); for its control over the root zone file and power to delegate control of country codes (ccTLD) to particular registries (which are usually, but not invariably, authorised by the government of the country concerned); and for its own governance procedures which do not, in critics' eyes, sufficiently empower either national governments or Internet users, as Verhulst argues: 'The central plank of this criticism is that ICANN's organisational structures and activities do not comply with the ethos of participatory and democratic governance' (Verhulst 2001: 1).

ICANN's governance has come under attack both from representatives of Internet users, sometimes with uncertain links to the broad constituency whom they claim to represent, who customarily advocate higher levels of ICANN accountability to, and control by, user representatives and also from some states (and allied 'Bellheads') in international fora (notably the WSIS) who advocate control of the DNS by an international treaty body rather than by ICANN and its Government Advisory Committee (GAC), which currently constitutes the sole formal institutional means through which governments can represent their concerns to ICANN.

The first, user, group of critics is a loose alliance including those who refer back to the informal, network governance, origins of the Internet and the era of John Perry Barlow's Declaration of the Independence of Cyberspace (Barlow 1996) and the Internet Engineering Task Force's (IETF) 'Tao' of 'rough consensus and running code' (see RFC 3160 at http://www.ietf.org/tao.html on 1.4.2006); critics of ICANN's, putatively, anti-competitive use of its monopoly power; and those who hunger for the strong representation of user representatives in ICANN governance envisaged in the NTIA Green Paper. The NTIA proposed a fifteen-member Board, consisting of three representatives of regional registries, two designated by the Internet Architecture Board (IAB), two representing domain name registries and domain name registrars, seven members representing 'at-large' Internet users, and the ICANN CEO *ex officio*. In contrast, the current ICANN Board has reduced user representation.

The second set of critics has argued, straightforwardly, that only duly constituted international institutions could legitimately determine Internet policy. ICANN's 'Government Advisory Committee' is perceived, as its name may suggest, to dilute unacceptably legitimate state sovereignty. For example, China, at the Geneva Working Group on Internet Governance (WGIG) of 18.4.2005, stated that:

> The policy authority for Internet-related public policy issues is the sovereign right of states. They have rights and responsibilities for international Internet-related public policy issues.

ICANN's legitimacy was thus found wanting when compared to that 'Bellhead' hierarchical treaty-based governance through an international body such as the International Telecommunications Union.

In attempting to reconcile the imperatives of efficiency, legitimacy and representativeness, ICANN's governance has undergone many changes. Rony and Rony observed that its Bylaws changed 11 times

between 1998 and 2002 (see http://www.domainhandbook.com/
archives/comp-icannbylaws.html on 18.12.2006). In 2002 the then
President of ICANN, Stuart Lynn, argued that ICANN's governance
and accountability structures were inherently unsatisfactory. He
stated:

> ICANN is still not fully organized, and it is certainly not yet capable of
> shouldering the entire responsibility of global DNS management and
> coordination. ICANN has also not shown that it can be effective,
> nimble, and quick to react to problems. ICANN is overburdened with
> process, and at the same time underfunded and understaffed. For these
> and other more fundamental reasons, ICANN in its current form has
> not become the effective steward of the global Internet's naming and
> address allocation systems as conceived by its founders . . . the original
> concept of a purely private sector body, based on consensus and consent,
> has been shown to be impractical.

Lynn warned against displacing network by hierarchical governance
and explicitly cautioned against 'Bellhead' involvement in DNS
governance:

> I do not believe that there are any better alternatives than a reformed
> ICANN. If the ICANN experiment of private-sector self-management
> cannot work, the default alternative will certainly be some form of
> multinational governmental organization. In my view, this remains an
> unattractive option, for all the same reasons that were so forcefully
> advanced three years ago.

Lynn believed ICANN's governance was flawed because a fuzzily
defined community of Internet users had too much representation and
governments had too little. He proposed that five Board members
be chosen by national governments, to strengthen the authority of
ICANN insiders by reserving five Board places for *ex-officio* nominees
(namely the President of ICANN and a representative from each
three new Policy Councils and a Technical Advisory Committee), and
to replace the direct election of users by and from the 'at-large' constituency by a Nominating Committee's selection of the remaining
five Board members. ICANN's current Bylaws (of 28.2.2006) vest
authority in a fifteen-person Board of whom eight are selected by the

ICANN Nominating Committee and two by each of the Address Supporting Organization, the Country-Code Names Supporting Organization, the Generic Names Supporting Organization with the ICANN President serving *ex officio*. Lynn's proposal for direct government representation was not adopted though his proposal to route representation of users through a Nominating Committee was.

ICANN's formal governance arrangements remain complex, circular and open to criticism. Some members (albeit non-voting) of the Nominating Committee are appointed by the ICANN Board of Directors and others (voting) by the bodies (notably the Address Supporting Organization, the Country-Code Names Supporting Organization and the Generic Names Supporting Organization) entitled to nominate Board members directly. The Bylaws do not make clear how members of these committees come to hold office (though they do specify from where they are to be drawn). The body representing the residuum or the Internet community (to which ICANN is formally accountable, albeit only through 'mechanisms that enhance ICANN's effectiveness'), the At-Large Advisory Committee (ALAC), rather than directly appointing Board members, appoints five voting delegates to the Nominating Committee (and additionally one non-voting liaison member to the ICANN Board) which then selects eight Board members. However, five members of the ALAC are themselves appointed by the Nominating Committee (see ICANN Bylaws of 28.2.2006 Article XI, Section 2.4.b and e)!

Network Governance Failure?

The Bylaws enjoin ICANN boards and committees to ensure diversity and balanced representation among office holders – paying attention to geography, competencies, range of stakeholders, etc. Provisions are also made for reconsideration of Board decisions, for an Ombudsman and for the conduct of business with appropriate openness and transparency. But the legitimacy of the designated bodies is uncertainly grounded in established democratic principles of representation and the power distributed to different stakeholder groups remains contested. However, it is clear that the power and influence of Internet users, *vis à vis* providers, has diminished between the first and latest iteration of ICANN's bylaws – not least because of the intractable difficulties of putting bounds around the constituency to whom ICANN identifies itself as responsible, the 'Internet community' (ICANN Bylaws of 28.2.2006 Article I, Section 2.10).

Thus ICANN has yet to devise durable governance structures. The laudable intention to create an inclusive system, characterised by significant representation for the Internet Community of users and open and participatory procedures, neither sufficiently represented national stakeholders nor found workable and legitimate means of representing the 'Internet community'. Successive iterations of ICANN's 'constitution' may have improved ICANN's administrative functionality and provided a solid basis for representation of key 'producer' interests associated with the DNS, but they have neither built legitimacy with ICANN's two main bodies of critics nor established clear lines of accountability. ICANN governance reflects both positive and negative aspects of network governance, attempts to balance representation of different stakeholder interests in ICANN's governance structures, ICANN's practice of publishing draft proposals and inviting public consultation and deliberation were, and are, positive characteristics of network governance and exemplify its normative attributes of trust and solidarity. However, other aspects of ICANN's governance structure, though similarly characteristic of network governance, such as its uncertain relationship to clearly defined stakeholder groups and its absence of effective mechanisms of representation and accountability when large groups of stakeholders are involved, are less positive.

ICANN's difficulties testify both to the general difficulties posed by global infrastructures, where the relevant 'communities of fate' (Held 2004; 20) are diffuse and dispersed, and to the type of failure to which network governance regimes seem to be prone. Each type of governance defined by Thompson's (2003), hierarchical, market and network, seems to be prone to a distinctive form of governance failure. Governance failure in hierarchical (e.g. ossification, elite capture) and market (e.g. exclusion of the poor, abuse of significant market power, negative externalities) systems of governance is widely recognised (see, *inter alia*, Moran 2003). But network governance failure has received less attention. Network governance failure may take the form of either domination of governance by the interests and viewpoints of those networked, (thus excluding other stakeholders) – a failure of representation, or of a failure to bind sufficiently together many stakeholder interests and viewpoints so making consensus, and thus decisions and actions, difficult to achieve – a failure of effectiveness. ICANN is, in the eyes of its two main groups of critics, subject to both types of failure.

Failure of one type of governance regime tends to lead to the regime in question being replaced by a different type of regime. For example, failure of hierarchy has led to adoption of market governance (liberalisation and privatisation); failure of markets to the adoption of hierarchy (regulation and state control); network failure to liberalisation and/or an adoption of hierarchy. The history of Internet governance, that is governance of the DNS, seems to be a history of network governance failure (the informal early arrangements of 'rough consensus and running code' failing both to scale as the Internet grew and to represent adequately all stakeholders) followed by a different form of network governance in ICANN supplemented by an, as yet immature, mix of market and hierarchical governance.

It may seem incongruous to refer to Internet governance failure for, clearly, the Internet is a striking success story: it functions well, has successfully been scaled up from a geeky connection between a few US research centres to an indispensable global infrastructure, the price of communication has fallen and the accessibility of information increased dramatically. But, just as market failure in voice telephony doesn't mean the phones all stop working, so network governance failure doesn't mean the Internet goes dark. Indeed it is the very effectiveness of the Internet which, in some eyes, constitutes the greatest governance challenge. For governance is not solely a question of what sort of governance (Nethead or Bellhead, hierarchy, market or network) but also the balance between different governance regimes and the relationship of governance institutions to other centres of power and to stakeholder interests. These questions were central issues at the World Summit on the Information Society (WSIS).

Global Governance and the WSIS

The United Nations convened the WSIS in 2003–5 in an attempt, among other goals, to resolve the increasingly intensely contested issue of Internet governance. Both groups of ICANN's critics participated in the WSIS, and its sub-group the Working Group on Internet Governance (WGIG), where ICANN's role in governing the DNS came under continuous critical interrogation. For user representatives, ICANN's governance was too hierarchical and insufficiently represented civil society/user interests, for numerous governments ICANN governance was insufficiently hierarchical and gave too much representation to non-governmental actors such as civil society.

WSIS was the first UN Summit on Communications and provided an effective platform for a 'Bellhead' critique of 'Nethead' governance. ICANN's control of indispensable elements of the Internet, perceived to be tantamount to US Government control, was contrasted to the governance of international posts and telecommunications by the Universal Postal Union (UPU) and the ITU but the issues resonated far beyond the bounded, and somewhat arcane, issue of control and management of the DNS. The WSIS focused on three themes:

- Internet governance,
- The so-called 'political chapeau'/Tunis Commitment – a political declaration on development of a pervasive global information society linking a variety of national initiatives, and
- ICT (Information and Communication Technology) for Development (ICT4D).

Internet governance proved to be the least tractable of these issues and these difficulties led the UN Secretary-General to establish a specialist Working Group on Internet Governance (WGIG), reporting directly to him, in the hope of securing progress which had otherwise proved elusive – these hopes received scant fulfilment (see Collins 2007 and 2007a). Although the tangible outcomes of discussions in the WSIS/WGIG were hardly commensurate with the resources and efforts invested in them, they provided a kind of laboratory, or theatre, in which proponents of rival governance claims, for a network or a hierarchical principle, for *ad hoc* or formalised, treaty based, international regimes, contested the basis of Internet governance.

Discussions at the Summit (and Working Group) were highly charged, for what was at stake was not just the principles and practice of management and governance of a single (albeit important) global communication infrastructure but also the Internet's impact on the PSTN, its governing institutions and the hierarchical principles on which PSTN governance has been based. There were obviously institutional interests at stake, not least that of the ITU itself. Its Secretary-General, Utsumi Yoshio, staked its claim to the DNS stating that the ITU 'is now prepared to take on the coordination and management of critical Internet resources' (Yoshio 2006: 5). But the time-honoured 'Bellhead' regimes of national government/telephone company dominance were also in question.

For a hundred years or so, telephony services characteristically have been provided by national monopolies; either by privately owned and publicly regulated shareholder companies or by state owned corporations. Two such national companies interconnected to provide international communication, handing on traffic to each other and sharing revenues under ITU norms. These arrangements have broken down. As Huston claimed: 'The Internet has accelerated the pace of deregulation of the industry to an extent never thought possible . . . billions of dollars of telephony revenues will be diverted into the Internet market.' (Huston 2002: 3). Instead of costs and revenues being divided between calling partners, as in the old telephony regime which transferred significant sums from the developed 'north' to the less developed 'south', services increasingly are carried on dedicated leased circuits which are customarily provided by global carriers based in the north (and predominantly in the USA) who retain charges.

Not only has the new regime eroded state sovereignty (in respect of the ability to set prices, control market entry and collectively make rules) but telephony can no longer provide a key source of public finance. In many developing countries, high prices for telecommunications services were, in part, paid by foreign callers and for countries which were unable to run efficient revenue collection services telecommunication revenues acted, at best, as a proxy for taxation (and at worst, a source of funds for politically appointed rent seekers). Of course, the new 'Nethead' regime has had profoundly beneficial consequences – new services such as e-mail and web browsing are available, the price of a voice call carried over an IP network has fallen, IP networks make advanced data and other services more widely available and prices to users generally have fallen significantly. But though some benefit others have undoubtedly lost and, crucially, the terms on which some win and others lose characteristically are set by powerful global actors rather than by, for better or worse, domestic political authorities.

What fills the gap left by the decline of 'Bellhead' institutions, such as the ITU and national telecommunication regimes, of hierarchical governance? Essentially, a series of *ad hoc* institutions and practices difficult to describe exhaustively and which could, in any case, only be described at tedious length. ICANN's importance inheres not only in its authority over the DNS and RZF but in its unique status as a high-profile institution of global Internet governance. In consequence, ICANN has acted as a lightning rod through which a multitude of discontents arising from the interconnected changes, from hierarchy to networks, from Bellhead to Nethead networks, from national sovereignty and orderly treaty-based decision making to global institutions and *ad hoc* governance have been discharged.

Civil Society

The WSIS was the first UN Summit where civil society was an official participant and it, and the WGIG in particular, drew in substantial civil society participation significantly augmenting its competencies. Civil society's presence embodied a realisation of the UN's commitment to broadening participation in its activities, and in some sense a formal opening to the network governance which it had been enjoined formally to embrace (see UN 2002 and 2004). The WSIS and WGIG provided opportunities for civil society critics of ICANN, smarting from their reduced place in ICANN governance, to claim a bigger role in Internet governance. But civil society's assertions were matched by significant criticism from numbers of participating Member States who saw civil society's involvement as no less offensive a usurpation of the legitimate powers of governments than they perceived ICANN's administration of the DNS to be. Their objections illuminated some aspects of network governance failure – notably the lack of clear criteria of inclusion within and exclusion from the governance community in question.

Just as the principles underpinning representation on ICANN's Board are uncertain so were the principles of composition of the Working Group on Internet Governance. Some participants of the WGIG clearly represented states, some business and some civil society and some could plausibly be seen as representing more than one constituency. The basis of selection and appointment was opaque (a member of a western national delegation, interviewed by the author on 15.2.2005, stated that the few national representatives on the WGIG were 'appointed rather randomly'). Where procedures were transparent as, commendably, they were for the civil society Internet Governance Caucus, it's clear that few participated in selection of civil society members of the WGIG (Hofmann 2004; 2). And some civil society participants, myself included, were essentially self-appointed (see Collins 2007a).

Outcomes

The formal outcomes of the WSIS/WGIG are the so-called 'Chateau de Bossey' (WGIG 2005) statement of the WGIG and the 'Tunis Agenda' of the WSIS (WSIS 2005). These documents reflect a stalemate between 'Nethead' proponents of the status quo and 'Bell-heads' advocating bringing Internet governance (or at least control of the DNS) under the ITU. The Chateau de Bossey document rather lamely stated that the 'WGIG identified a vacuum within the context of existing structures, since there is no global multi-stakeholder forum to address Internet-related public policy issues. It came to the con-clusion that there would be merit in creating such a space for dialogue among all stakeholders' (WGIG 2005: 10). However, the WGIG could not agree on how the vacuum should be filled and put forward four governance options to the WSIS.

Not surprisingly, the Tunis WSIS was hardly more successful than the WGIG in deciding between the alternatives identified by the

WGIG but identified a way forward by calling for the UN Secretary-General 'in an open and inclusive process, to convene, by the second quarter of 2006, a meeting of the new forum for multi-stakeholder policy dialogue – called the *Internet Governance Forum* (IGF)' (WSIS 2005: Cl 72). Although the IGF was explicitly defined as having no effective power: 'It would be constituted as a neutral, non-duplicative and non-binding process. It would have no involvement in day-to-day or technical operations of the Internet' (WSIS 2005: Cl 77).

The first meeting of the IGF took place in October/November 2006, in his summing up Nitin Desai, the IGF Chair, stated:

> The essential point to realise is that this is a multistakeholder forum. It is an open-door forum. It's not a forum with a fixed membership. It is open to anybody in the stakeholder groups who has an interest and a basic bona fide competence in this area to come and enter and join the meeting. It's in that sense more like an open meeting rather than a fixed membership group. In that sense, it's not possible to speak of anything as being a product of this meeting. So it would be misleading to say that there is any such thing as an agreed conclusion or a product of this meeting in the strict sense of the term, because there is no defined meeting. The meeting is the people who are in the room. (At http://www.intgovforum.org/IGF-SummingUp2–021106am.txt on 18.12.2006.)

Conclusion

Desai's account of the meeting can, charitably, be described as a testimony to the UN's new commitment to networked governance, to open and inclusive forms of deliberation and to creation of a global forum for the discussion, if not the formulation and implementation, of Internet governance policies. But the IGF has done nothing to resolve either the structural problems posed by network governance failure (notably delineation of clear stakeholder constituencies and the establishment of durable and legitimate mechanisms of representation and accountability) or to satisfy the 'Bellhead' critique of ICANN's role and status. The IGF does not take forward the Tunis Agenda's firm assertion that 'Policy authority for Internet-related public policy issues is the sovereign right of States' (WSIS 2005: Cl 35a) but has been welcomed by ICANN as helping to fill the vacuum left by the absence of a global forum for Internet policy – an absence which often led to demands being projected onto ICANN because there was nowhere else to project them.

In 2002, Stuart Lynn had stated that:

> The core ICANN mission includes no mandate to innovate new institutions of global democracy, nor to achieve mathematically equal representation of all affected individuals and organisations, nor to regulate content, nor to solve the problems of the digital divide, nor to embody some idealised (and never-before-realised) model of process or procedure.

Expectations for fulfilment of these objectives had been lodged with ICANN – there was nowhere else to lay them to rest. Now, perhaps, the IGF will fill that vacuum.

It is a truism to observe that there are more and more of what David Held has called global communities of fate (Held 2004: 20) and that these communities lack appropriate instruments and regime of governance. Into the governance vacuum, as global relationships are created *de novo* or supplant what were hitherto national relationships, step various *ad hoc* arrangements. The global Internet and ICANN represent one such *ad hoc* regime, others include the Basel Accords (Basel I and Basel II) governing banks' management of credit and the rules and operating procedures for financial accounting and audit of the International Federation of Accountants (see also, *inter alia*, Held and McGrew 2000). Seen thus, ICANN, and the issues of Internet governance considered at WSIS and in WGIG, are but one more example of a widespread characteristic of contemporary globalisation: that is of global relationships and practices outrunning the capacity of formally constituted political institutions to govern global interdependencies. Moreover, ICANN and the halting development of a durable regime of global Internet governance with which it is inextricably associated, provides an illuminating case study of network governance in action.

Bibliography

Barabasi, A-L. (2002) *Linked: The New Science of Networks*. Cambridge MA: Perseus.

Barry, A. (2001) *Political Machines. Governing a Technological Society*. London: Athlone.

Castells, M. (1996 and 2000) *The Rise of the Network Society*. Cambridge, MA; Oxford, UK: Blackwell.

Castells, M. (2004) *Informationalism, Networks, and the Network Society: A Theoretical Blueprint*. At http://annenberg.usc.edu/images/faculty/facpdfs/Informationalism.pdf on 29.11.2006 (also in M Castells (ed.) *The Network Society: A cross-cultural perspective*. Northampton MA: Edward Elgar.).

Collins, R. (2006) 'Networks, Markets and Hierarchies. Governance and Regulation of the UK Internet'. In *Parliamentary Affairs* 59: 314–30.

Collins, R. (2007) 'Rawls, Fraser, Redistribution, Recognition and The World Summit on the Information Society'. In *International Journal of Communication* 1.

Collins, R. (2007a) 'Trilateralism, Legitimacy and the Working Group on Internet Government'. In *Information Policy*.

Crawford, S. (2004) The ICANN Experiment. *Cardozo Journal of International and Company Law* 12: 701–40. At http://www.scrawford.net/display/Crawford2.pdf on 18.12.2006.

Denton [T M Denton Consultants] (1999) *Netheads versus Bellheads. Research into Emerging Policy Issues in the Development and Deployment of Internet Protocols. Study for the Department of Industry Contract U4525–9–0038*. Ottawa. At http://www.tmdenton.com/pub/bellheads.pdf on 28.1.2006.

Drake, W. (ed.) (2005) *Reforming Internet Governance. Perspectives from the Working Group on Internet Governance (WGIG)*. New York, United Nations Information and Communication Technologies Task Force. At http://www.wgig.org/docs/book/WGIG_book.pdf on 14.3.2006.

Dunleavy, P. and H. Margetts, S. Bastow, J. Tinkler (2006) 'New Public Management is Dead – Long Live Digital-Era Governance'. In *Journal of Public Administration Research and Theory* 16: 467–94.

e-Envoy (2003) *Office of the e-Envoy*. At http://archive.cabinetoffice.gov.uk/e-envoy/index-content.htm on 18.12.2006.

Froomkin, A. M. (2000) 'Wrong Turn in Cyberspace: Using ICANN to Route Around the APA and the Constitution'. *Duke Law Journal* 50: 17–184. At http://personal.law.miami.edu/~froomkin/articles/icann.pdf on 18.12.2006.

GAC [ICANN Governmental Advisory Committee] (1999) *Governmental Advisory Committee Operating Principles*. At http://www.icann.org/committees/gac/operating-principles-25may99.htm on 29.1.2006.

Held, D. (2004) *Democratic Accountability and Political Effectiveness from a Cosmopolitan Perspective*. Paper at the WZB/CARR Conference on Global Governance and the Role of Non-State Actors. London School of Economics. 4/5.11.2004.

Held, D. and A. McGrew (eds) (2000) *Governing Globalization: Power, Authority and Global Governance.* Oxford: Blackwell.

Hofmann, J. (2004) *Notes of Internet Governance Caucus Meeting in Geneva.*

Huston, G. (2002) *Telecommunications Policy and the Internet.* At http://www.isoc.org/oti/articles/1201/huston.html on 29.1.2006.

ITU [International Telecommunications Union] (2004) *Internet Governance.* Geneva: ITU.

Komaitis, K. and J. Galloway (2005) *Does the Need for Internet Governance justify ICANN's Anti-competitive Behaviour?* At http://www.bileta.ac.uk/Document%20Library/1/Does%20the%20Need%20for%20Internet%20Governance%20Justify%20ICANN%E2%80%99s%20Anti-competitive%20Behaviour.pdf on 3.2.2006.

MacLean, D. (2004) *Internet Governance: A Grand Collaboration.* New York. United Nations Department of Economic and Social Affairs. At http://www.unicttaskforce.org/perl/documents.pl?id=1392 on 3.3.2005.

Marlin-Bennett, R. (2001) ICANN and Democracy: Contradictions and Possibilities. In *Info* 3.4 299–311.

Moran, M. (2003) *The British Regulatory State. High Modernism and Hyper-Innovation.* Oxford: OUP.

Mueller, M. (1999) 'ICANN and Internet Governance. Sorting through the Debris of "Self-regulation"'. In *Info* 1.6 497–520.

Mueller, M. (2002) *Ruling the Root.* Cambridge MA: MIT Press.

NTIA (1998) *Improvement of Technical Management of Internet Names and Addresses.* Docket Number: 980212036–8036–01. Washington DC. United States Department of Commerce. At http://www.ntia.doc.gov/ntiahome/domainname/022098fedreg.htm on 19.12.2006.

NTIA (1998a) *Management of Internet Names and Addresses.* Docket Number: 980212036–8146–02. Washington DC. United States Department of Commerce. At http://www.ntia.doc.gov/ntiahome/domainname/6_5_98dns.htm on 19.12.2006.

Raboy, M. (2004) The WSIS as a Political Space in Global Media Governance. In *Continuum* V 18 N 3 September: 347–61.

Taylor, M. (2001) *The Moment of Complexity.* Chicago: University of Chicago Press.

Thompson, G (2003) *Between Hierarchies and Markets. The Logic and Limits of Network Forms of Organization.* Oxford: Oxford University Press.

UN (2002) *Strengthening of the United Nations: An agenda for further change. Report of the Secretary-General General Assembly A/57/387.* New York, United Nations.

UN (2004) *We the Peoples: Civil Society, the United Nations and Global Governance. Report of the Panel of Eminent Persons on United Nations-Civil Society Relations. General Assembly. With note by the Secretary General and Transmittal letter by the Chair. A/58/817.* New York, United Nations.

UNESCO (2005) *Defining e-Governance.* At http://portal.unesco.org/ci/en/ev.php-URL_ID=4404&URL_DO=DO_TOPIC&URL_ SECTION=201.html on 29.11.2006.

Verhulst, S. (2001) *Public Legitimacy. ICANN at the Crossroads.* At http://www.opendemocracy.net/media-internetgovernance/article_35.jsp on 29.1.2006.

Weinberg, J. (2000) 'ICANN and the Problem of Legitimacy'. *Duke Law Journal* 50: 187–260.

WGIG [Working Group on Internet Governance] (2005) *Report of the Working Group on Internet Governance. Château de Bossey.* At http://www.wgig.org/docs/WGIGREPORT.doc.

WSIS [World Summit on the Information Society] (2005) *The Tunis Agenda.* At http://www.itu.int/wsis/docs2/tunis/off/6rev1.html on 8.2.2006.

Yoshio, U. (2006) 'Towards a Bright Future'. In *New Breeze Quarterly of the ITU Association of Japan.* V 18 N1 Winter: 4–6.

3

THE LIMITS OF POST-LISBON GOVERNANCE IN THE EUROPEAN UNION

LESLIE BUDD

Introduction

At the Lisbon Summit in March 2000, the Heads of the Member States of the European Union (EU) agreed to a strategy for growth and employment, based on fulfilling the objective of making the EU 'the most dynamic and competitive knowledge-based economy in the world capable of sustainable economic growth with more and better jobs and greater social cohesion, and respect for the environment' by 2010 (European Council, 2000) At the heart of what has become known as the 'Lisbon Strategy' are five policy areas that have been identified as needing strengthening in order that this objective might be met. In subsequent briefings and publications it has become apparent that the key policy area is:

The knowledge society: Increasing Europe's attractiveness for researchers and scientists, making research and development (R&D) a priority and promoting the use of information and communication technologies (ICTs), within which three main drivers have been identified. Firstly, spreading the use of ICT and mobile technology in order to make the EU a leading information society. Secondly, boosting R&D spending to 3% of EU Gross Domestic Product (GDP) so that the EU becomes the most attractive locale for high-tech activities. Finally, fostering life-long learning through enabling technologies to realise and sustain the knowledge society. (European Council, 2000)

The commitment to developing the knowledge society in order to transform the economies of EU economy is set within the strategic objectives of Lisbon:

1. Increase the trend rate of economic growth in the EU.
2. Raise the employment rate and participation rate of women in the labour market.
3. Develop the Information Society.
4. Establish a European-wide research area.
5. Create an environment in which innovative and start-up business may develop and thrive.
6. Modernise social protection (European Council, 2000).

The heady optimism of the Lisbon Summit of 2000 has given way to a more reflective Lisbon II, as contained in the 2004 Kok Report, with its implicit recognition that the 2010 target is unrealistic and unachievable. In the context of the asymmetrical governance of the EU, the creation of post-Lisbon governance looks like a zero-sum game. That is, the potential benefits of an e-governed knowledge society are insufficient to overcome the costs of asymmetrical economic governance of the EU and variability in the capacities and competences of the Member States. The economic governance of the European Union includes:

- Completion of the Single European Market (SEM), particularly the Services Directive in order to complete the liberalisation of cross-border transactions in business and financial services within the EU.
- The management of the single currency, known as the Euro-Area.
- The expansion of the EU and accession of new states into the economic and political institutions of the European Commission. and
- The policy framework for realising competitiveness agenda of Lisbon and ensure socio-economic cohesion between the richer and poorer regions of the EU.

The regime is asymmetrical because the operations of a number of the components listed tend to lead to unbalanced outcomes. For example, the fiscal rules (in the form of limits on government budget deficits and total government debt as a proportion of national income) constrain the reach and effectiveness of cohesion policy designed to address regional inequality. Similarly, the Lisbon objective of developing an EU information society may run counter to industrial policy that seeks to further and develop existing sector of the economy that are not digitally-based. Perhaps a more important consideration is the nature of governance itself. As John Clarke's chapter that opens this book points out, governance can be a rather vague concept; often 'sexed up' by policy makers and politicians but frequently unsatisfying. The vagueness of the concept is summarised neatly by Josie Kelly as:

> In the literature on public policy and administration the concept of governance now dominates contemporary debates (Newman 2001). The concept is mostly used to explore the diminishing capacity of the state to direct policymaking and implementation, something also portrayed as 'hollowing out of the state' (Rhodes 1997). The term governance is also used to describe governing arrangements that are more than or greater than merely the institutions of government. Hence users of the term tend to focus on the rupture between the formal political institutions and the growth of governance arrangements – such as networks and partnerships – and the increasing use of deliberative forums for service users. (Kelly, 2006; 605).

The problem is compounded by the fact that governance operates at micro and macro levels. At the micro-level governance is frequently associated with corporate governance: the system and rules for managing the legal and business obligations and operations of firms. At the macro-level, governance is seen as a set of obligations and behaviours that encompasses an informal type of government. For example, global governance is defined as a set of inter-governmental relations in an environment of globalisation (Held, 2002). Given the increase in the number of issues that cut across national jurisdictions and beyond the powers of national governments – disease pandemics, genocide, global warming and environmental damage, etc. – there is demand for a range of international organisations and institutions to help form a more comprehensive system of governance on a global scale.

In general, the distinction between government and governance is subtle, but there is a division between the two concepts. Government in democratic societies can be defined as the formal exercise of power and authority through the legitimate and accountable undertaking of functional duties that are underpinned by financial resources on behalf of a constituency. Governance, on the other hand, can be described as the informal attribution of power and authority to a set of institutions, agencies and/or actors who are incorporated into governmental relations by acting as intermediaries on behalf of government or its functional divisions. Governmental bodies and governance institutions both derive their legitimacy from their ability to deliver bargains on behalf of their respective constituencies, for example business associations and trade unions in the case of governance. The difference is that in the former case, the attribution of power is formal and the latter is informal (Offe, 1985). If governance is a container for a range of concepts, ideas and practice around the process of governing, will the development of governance by digital means contribute to a better understanding and application of the concept and practice of governance? Governance is thus a broader concept and appears to be appropriate as an organising concept and principle for investigating the prospect for electronic and/or digital forms of governing at different territorial and functional scales.

Building Blocks of e-Governance

The establishment of e-Government is often promoted on the grounds of economic efficiency. Central to this argument is that Using Information and Communication Technologies (ICTs) will lower transactions costs[1] by reducing the amount of bureaucratic procedures in public administrations (commonly known as 'red tape') (European Commission, 2007a). In the EU, public procurement accounts for about 15–20% of the aggregate EU Gross Domestic Product (GDP), the standard measure of national income. This amounts to about €1.5 trillion to €2.0 trillion, at 2007 prices. The European Commission claims that use of this type of e-Government service will generate 5% in annual cost savings over the long term. Furthermore, the role of e-Government in improving public sector efficiency and innovation was highlighted in the 2004 'Competitiveness Report' (EC, 2004). This evidence does tend to show that e-Goverment is a narrower concept than e-Goverance. e-Government includes e-Health, e-Learning and e-Taxation, for example. Proponents of e-Government appear to stress its operational effectiveness rather than its strategic potential. e-Governance, on the other hand, is broader and covers a host of relationships and networks based on the use of ICT within and across government and governance institutions that function outside the realm of formal government. The latter institutions include non-profit organisations and private organisations that are incorporated into the public domain, for example managing and operating some public services. The prefix, 'e' represents the electronic platform or infrastructure that enables these two concepts (Sheridan and Riley, 2006).

The United Nations Educational Scientific and Cultural Organization (UNESCO) defines e-Governance as 'the public sector's use of ICT with the aim of improving information and service delivery, encouraging citizen participation in the decision-making process and making government more accountable, transparent and effective' (UNESCO, 2005). Their more complete definition suggests that:

Governance refers to the exercise of political, economic and administrative authority in the management of a country's affairs, including citizens' articulation of their interests and exercise of their legal rights and obligations. e-Governance may be understood as the performance of this governance via the electronic medium in order to facilitate an efficient, speedy and transparent process of disseminating information to the public, and other agencies, and for performing government administration activities. e-Governance is generally considered as a wider concept than e-Government, since it can bring about a change in the way that citizens relate to governments and to each other. e-governance can bring forth new concepts of citizenship, both in terms of citizen needs and responsibilities. Its objective is to engage, enable and empower the citizen.

UNESCO sets out the specific goals of e-Governance as enabling better organisation of governments' internal processes; endow more efficient delivery of services and information; create more transparency, legitimacy and accountability so increased public consultation and participation results. UNESCO sets out three fields of implementation for achieving these goals:

1. *e-Administration* – effectively e-Government that uses ICT to create more efficacious management of governmental policies and practices.
2. *e-Services* – the evolution and sustaining of interactive accessed public services.
3. *e-Democracy* – active and direct of engagement of all citizens in the political process and the management of governmental outcomes.

From these approaches what are the possibilities of e-Governance in realising an information or knowledge society in the EU? Moreover, can the development of a comprehensive e-Governance system lead to the main objective of the Lisbon Agenda, of making the EU the most dynamic knowledge economy in the world by 2010, being achieved? This chapter explores the limits of a Lisbon e-Governed EU and the potential of the EU to break out of its unbalanced forms of economic governance through virtual means.

The Promise and Potential Failure of the Lisbon Agenda

The strategic priorities of the Lisbon Agenda were stated above, but have been subject to a number of criticisms and challenges. In response, the EC sought to develop better means of following these priorities. The subsequent Sapir and Kok Reports, commissioned by the EC, stress the utility of the Lisbon growth strategy in enabling cohesion through the EU economy reaching its potential. The former was published as a result of the President of the EC inviting a group of independent experts, known as the 'High-Level Group' to analyse the strategic economic goals set out in the Lisbon Agenda with sustainable economic growth and greater social cohesion in July 2002. The Group was asked to review the entire regime of EU economic policies and to propose a strategy for delivering faster growth together with stability and cohesion in an enlarged EU. It subsequently became known as the 'Sapir Report' after the name of the Chair of the Group.

Central to the Sapir Report is a six-point agenda that is set out to help achieve the goals of Lisbon:

1. To make the Single Market more dynamic through better co-ordination of regulatory and competition polices to stimulate new market entry; invest in infrastructure to increase greater connectivity within the wider European economy.
2. To boost investment in knowledge through stimulating research, R&D by use of tax credits and create a single EU science-and-research institution.
3. To improve the macroeconomic policy framework for EMU through encouraging Members States to operate fiscal policy according to cyclical norms (surpluses during upturns and deficits during downturns) and to implement a more flexible and effective Growth and Stability Pact (GSP).
4. To redesign policies for convergence and restructuring through concentrating on low-income nations and not regions with priority given to institution building and investment in human and physical capital with EU funds complementing national welfare polices to restructure individual's participation on the labour market.
5. To achieve effectiveness in decision taking and regulation through more flexible and coherent allocation of policy com-petences between EU and Member State levels; devolution of some economic management and regulatory function to independent Europe-wide bodies; as well as a leaner Commis-sion and more Qualified Majority Voting (QMV) in economic policy matters.
6. To refocus the EU budget through creating three new funds: growth; convergence; and restructuring so as to radically reorganise that part of the EU budget pertaining to economic performance, albeit within the 1.24% of EU GDP ceiling established by Agenda 2000 and the subsequent 3rd Cohesion Plan (Sapir et al, 2002; ii).

The strategic priorities of the Lisbon Agenda and the six-point agenda of the Sapir Report take place against the background of the regime of economic governance of the EU. The major elements are:

- completing the Single European Market (SEM) in the context of the EU fulfilling its obligations to the World Trade Organisation (WTO);
- management of Euro-Area macroeconomic policy, founded in part on the Maastricht Treaty rules (Buiter 1992, 2006) and the constraints of the Growth and Stability Pact (GSP) which restrict the use of fiscal activism to ameliorate the effects of industrial and regional shocks; and
- the enlargement to 27 Member States and possibly more in the future.

The Sapir Report focuses on the components of two key policy drivers within the regime of economic governance, as shown in Table 3.1. It is against this background that the development of a European Information Society needs to be investigated, and in particular, how this

Table 3.1 Policy Elements of Two Key Drivers of Economic Governance

	Single Market	Lisbon
Ultimate aim	Integration and growth	Growth, social cohesion, employment
Intermediate objectives	Cuts on cost of cross-border transactions for products and services	Advances in education and innovation, Increase in R&D spending Liberalisation for service industries Increase in labour force participation and employment rates
Means	Elimination of border controls Harmonisation and approximation of laws	Definition of common targets Performance reporting and benchmarking Joint monitoring
Instruments	EU directives Enforcement by case law	Mostly national (spending, taxation, regulation)

Source: (Sapir, 2001)

development will contribute to achieving the objectives of the Lisbon Agenda. The Lisbon Agenda and its commitment to develop the information society and create a knowledge economy has been 'sexed up' by politicians, for example former UK Prime Minister Tony Blair. This sexing-up has tended to lead to an uncritical acceptance of new technology driving new industries, as the solution to the EU's perceived economic weaknesses and the lack of dynamism of European societies. The evidence for this assertion rests on comparative evidence on the productivity performance of the EU and US economies. Behind the headlines, associated with this evidence, is a more variable picture so that digital sexing-up may not necessarily be appropriate to marrying the EU's development to the information society (Budd, 2004). Moreover, there is a danger that policy makers become divorced from reality because of a poor understanding and specification of the information society.

The current seductive appeal of the information society is frequently associated with the work of the sociologist, Manuel Castells. His trilogy of books: *The Information Age: Economic, Society and Culture* has been influential among academics, policy makers and practitioners engaged with the interface between technology and society. Castells claims that informationalism is a new technological paradigm that is creating the network society that is transforming the way we all live. The rather breathless account of this transformation suggests that Castells is too much in love with the possibilities of ICT. He tends to give little credit to the provenance of information society, particularly the role of the work economists like Fritz Machlup and his work on the knowledge industry; and the management writer Peter Drucker's observations on the shift to a knowledge-based economy (Machlup, 1962, Drucker, 1969). One common reference suggests that:

> An information society is a society in which the creation, distribution, diffusion, use, and manipulation of information is a significant, political and cultural activity. The knowledge economy is its economic counterpart whereby wealth is created through economic exploitation of understanding. (http://en.wikipedia.org/wiki/Information_society accessed 01/06/07)

The fact that all societies are essentially information societies (notwithstanding the overexcited use of this term) distracts us from a real understanding of the role of ICT and the potential of new developments, for example, e-Governance. By endlessly stressing the 'new' and the 'modern', politicians and policy makers reduce many virtual or digital initiatives to impotence.

The idea that the information society will be some kind of societal stimulant in the twenty-first century is one that ignores the rather mundane and chaste nature of the reality behind it, as a historian of science notes:

> There is no doubt that the rise in employment in service industries in the rich countries is one of the major economic changes in the last thirty years. A number of analysts have, perversely, identified this growth of service employment with the rise of an 'information society' with connotations of weightlessness or indeed the 'dematerialised' economy. This was a fashionable, and misleading, way of saying little more than that the service industries now account for very large proportions of GDP and employment. This is partly the result of mis-specification because services include a vast range of activities, many of them far from weightless or indeed new. (Edgerton, 2006; 70)

Our ability to experience shock and awe in the face of the 'old', and old technologies in particular, should not be underestimated (Landes, 2003). After all, the principles of the internal combustion engine; the aeroplane; and the railways have been with us for over a century. Thus the claims for the liberating effects of an EU information society, based on ICT and its applications, should be treated with healthy scepticism, something that the promoters of the Lisbon Agenda appear to forget.

Realising a European Information Society?

A European information society owes its lineage to modernist thinkers of the nineteenth century, but has most recently triumphed in the Lisbon Agenda. In reflecting on an EU Information Society, the Kok Report points to the transformative nature of the 'knowledge society' in boosting productivity, economic growth and employment.

The report flags up the possibilities of new business models that can be more easily adapted to the needs of networks and tailored to individual demands. The 'economic' perspective on the knowledge society is in line with the major objectives of Lisbon, as well as those of the Sapir Report. But, beyond stating the utility of ICT, the Kok Report does not expand on how the knowledge society is to be achieved. There is little or no mention of the role of the public sector in the Kok Report, beyond a discussion of regulatory reform. In contrast the Sapir Report engages in a detailed debate on budgetary reform at the EU level, but in both cases the role of e-Government and e-Governance in enabling an EU information society is missing.

The main policy vehicle for an EU Information Society is i2010. This is the Commission of the European Union's strategic framework to promote the digital economy and ICT research in order to help achieve the Lisbon objectives of making the EU the most dynamic, sustainable and socially inclusive economy in the world. A number of policy instruments have been created to support i2010, including joint research projects with stakeholders, as well as new regulatory procedures. According the Commission's Annual Report on the development of Information Society in Europe, growth has been steady (EC, 2007b). The recent growth trends are shown in Table 3.2. The i2010 project builds on the previous *2005 eEurope Action Plan* which was launched at the Seville European Council, in order to fulfil the demands of the Lisbon Council of 2002 and Barcelona of 2004.

Table 3.2 Growth in ICT Services and GDP in the EU

	Share of ICT Sector (2006)	Growth Rates		
		2004–5	*2005–6*	*2006–7*
Software & IT services	31%	5.8%	5.7%	5.9%
Electronic Communications services	45%	3.5%	2.3%	1.4%
Growth in Gross Domestic Product*	–	2.2%	1.7%	2.4%

* The twenty-five Member States of the EU known as EU25

Source: EITO, 2007 (not including Malta and Cyprus), National Institute Review (2007)

Central to these demands are the modernising of public services and developing opportunities for a dynamic e-Business sector. Satisfying these demands is conditional on greater access to broadband at competitive prices and secure ICT infrastructure.

The EC's 2005 communication '*i2010 – A European Information Society for Growth and Employment*' points to the need to have policy convergence to accompany and enable the EC's claim for digital convergence. The EC sets out three priorities:

1. Competing in a 'Single European Information Space'.
2. Promoting growth and employment in higher-value added occupations, by reinforcing innovation and investment in research into ICT.
3. Creating an inclusive information society in Europe in order to integrate better public services and quality of life with growth and employment objectives, all within a commitment to sustainable development.

For the purposes of this chapter, we focus on the third priority. The Communication stresses the benefits to all EU citizens from the greater usage of ICT. By making public services more accessible, by means of this type of technology, the quality of life will be improved and efficiency gains will be created for public procurement. That is, the buying of goods and services from the private and non-profit sectors by the public in order to deliver cost-effective public services. In the EC's view, giving greater access to ICT-based public services will also help overcome the challenges of e-inclusion, defined as overcoming the digital divide between nations and regions and among citizens. It has proposed a European Initiative on e-inclusion in 2008, focused primarily on the e-procurement and e-health aspects of e-Government by means of the vehicle of Actions Plans for these two areas of e-Governance.

The *Annual Information Society Report 2007* builds on these initiatives, but again does not escape the constraints imposed by the regime of economic governance that underlies the Lisbon Agenda. The seemingly serial stalking nature of the Lisbon cycle does place constraints on the development of a comprehensive form of e-Governance in the EU. The sado-masochistic preferences of policy makers for the market adjustment agenda of Lisbon to whip EU e-inclusion into shape undermines the very basis of developing a fuller system of e-Governance. In other words, without appropriate public sector action and institutions, satisfying the demands for e-inclusion will be a frustrating and ultimately unsatisfactory experience. The question of policy deviancy in developing e-Governance is examined in the next section.

e-Government to e-Governance in the EU?

The previous section argued that the dominance of the Lisbon Agenda in promoting an EU Information Society has overlooked the means by which its objectives will be achieved. Underneath the Actions Plans and the i2010, one finds a number of e-Government initiatives but no real explicit move towards developing a comprehensive system of e-Governance. Clearly, the boundaries between e-Government and e-Governance are fuzzy and we do need to remind ourselves about the subtle but important differences between the two concepts and how they function in reality. That is, e-Government involves managing and delivering public and publicly-underwritten services using electronic media. e-Governance is the set of institutional arrangements for formulating and managing public policy in pursuit of governing electronically-mediated services. According to Sheridan and Riley, 'Information sharing, knowledge sharing, and jurisdictional cooperation (horizontality), are the means to achieve e-Governance' (2006; 4). The challenge for the EU is the degree to which horizontality can be achieved across 27 Member States: Member States, moreover, with differing economic capacities and development paths. Information and knowledge sharing may be difficult in an environment in which the digital divide is experienced between countries and within countries.

The telecommunications market in the EU has been liberalised since the late 1990s, with five Directives covering its completion by 2003:

1. *Framework Directive*: Outlines the general principles, objectives and procedures.

2. *Authorisation Directive*: Replaces individual licences by general authorisations to provide communications services.
3. *Access and Interconnection Directive*: Sets out rules for a multi-carrier marketplace, ensuring access to networks and services, interoperability, etc.
4. *Universal Service Directive*: Guarantees basic rights for consumers and minimum levels of availability and affordability.
5. *e-privacy or Data Protection Directive*: Covers protection of privacy and personal data communicated over public networks.

These Directives initially only covered the EU15 (the Member States from Western Europe). Although newer Member States have also to comply with these Directives, their full implementation does bring difficulties because of the lack of a relatively sophisticated market and the need for new infrastructure. In 2007, there were 90 outstanding cases against Member States in breach of one or more of these Directives, many of them in the newer states whose infrastructure is less developed and who are recipients of the EU's Cohesion Funds. The crucial issue for the development of e-Governance in the EU, particularly in economically less developed Member States, is creating capacity in e-Government structures and processes that provide the building blocks of the former.

The Commission's proposals for the review of the telecommunications regulatory framework were adopted in 2007. They focus on the four areas of: increasing competition; better regulation; strengthening the internal market; and protecting consumers. Two things need noting: the telecommunications sector has many characteristics of a natural monopoly. That is, the minimum efficient scale of operations necessitates the market being dominated by very few large producers. Furthermore, as the EU expands, the benefits of scale economies created by the internal market are offset by the costs associated with diseconomies of scale of operating beyond an optimal scale. In this situation, achieving better regulation and protecting consumers may prove difficult. Moreover, generating standard service levels for e-Government processes and operations in a union of nations with differing capacities and capabilities inhibits the creation of the appropriate set of institutions of e-Governance.

The Lisbon perspective tends to dominate the development of e-Government capacity as shown in Figure 3.1. That is, the development of a European Information Society appears to be determined by the realisation of the knowledge economy within the EU economic space: the emphasis of which is on the transformative power of research and development in itself. The bias towards technology rather than process seems to be a barrier in moving from e-Government to e-Governance. The approach to the five main elements of Figure 3.1 can be summarised as:

1. *Knowledge Management and Organizational Innovation*: The EU views organisational innovation as one of the key drivers of e-Government. By creating online access for routine services, more complex services can be created and managed by government officials efficaciously. Through knowledge enhanced ICT-based services it is claimed that democratic processes, public policies and public services will be improved. The main vehicle for making these changes is Knowledge-enhanced e-Government (KEEG).

2. *InterOperability and Pan-European Services*: The advantage of providing e-Government services stems from gaining economies of scale and scope as a result of standardisation of ICT systems. Public administrations in the EU, however, have developed digitally-based services at different governmental scales so that the take-up of these services will be constrained. By creating Pan-European interoperability, then the scale and rate of take-up of e-Government services should increase significantly.

3. *Secure e-Government and Identity Management*: In order to overcome cross-border constraints on EU citizens accessing public services, electronic forms of pan-European identity are proposed. It is planned that the EU population will be able to exercise its rights and responsibilities as citizens and reinforce the objectives of inter-operability and pan-EU services. But, there are a number of technological and organisational challenges such as security and privacy and the fear of the rise of 'surveillance society'. Creating 'frictionless' access

is central to achieving these aims, as well as those of Pan-EU services.

4. *User Interaction and Mobile Services*: This function is directly related to interoperability, but includes a wider frame of reference and resources. It consists of combating the digital divide to overcome inequalities in access due to, *inter alia*, age, income, employment and personal formation and social exclusion as well as disability that limits access to on-line infrastructure and resources. The ubiquity of mobile telephony appears to promote the idea of mobile e-Government as the dominant form. Not all public services are accessible through this type of communication so that the EC is proposing that all wireless forms should be included for consideration as delivery vehicles. This sort of e-Government includes internal transactions as well as external ones leading to claims of significant cost savings with public administrations and associated non-profit and private agencies. The issue of mobile access to government services is developed further by Vincent and Harris in Chapter 4.

5. *e-Democracy*: The EC's definition of e-Government is 'the use of Information & Communication Technologies (ICTs) to make public administrations more efficient and effective, promoting growth by cutting red tape. This is something which anyone who has spent hours waiting in line in a government building can appreciate' (European Commission, 2007b). It is claimed that the effective introduction of e-Government and sustaining it can make a significant contribution to overcoming the 'democratic deficit'. This term covers the apparent dissatisfaction with democratic politics in the EU and elsewhere. However, introduction of innovative ICT to enable public administrations to manage multiple, complex and conflicting 'expressions of will' in a democratic society more readily may be longer on promise than delivery. To date, this kind of response has not been a major driver of e-Government. But, unless e-Government is underwritten by trust and accountability, then no technological imperative will overcome the democratic deficit. By promoting different forms of engagement between

the citizen and government through different channels, under the rubric of e-Participation, some of the current weaknesses in e-Democracy may be overcome.

Prospects for an e-Governance Transaction Space in the EU

The actioning of these five drivers present a major challenge to the creation of what can be termed an e-Governance transaction space in the European Union because of the heterogeneous nature of various e-Government initiatives and the differing e-Capacities of participating Member States. A transaction space is defined as, 'an abstract n-dimensional space defining the institutional, legal, cultural and language differences that must be accommodated if a given transaction between two or more agents is to take place' (Wood and

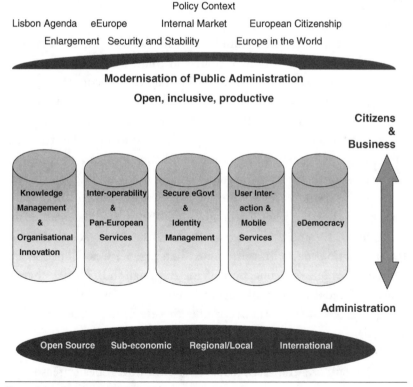

Figure 3.1 e-Government R&D Focus.

Source: European Commission (2007b). Reprinted with permission.

Parr, 2005; 4). The idea of a transaction space is one that is developed from the relationship between transactions costs and agglomeration economies. Transactions costs are incurred in any exchange of good or service as each party engages in a formal or informal contract, enforced by some procedures so that each party complies with the conditions of the exchange. In international trade, transaction costs are incurred in the form of transport and insurance costs to ensure that traded goods and services arrive at designated markets (Wood and Parr, 2005). Agglomeration economies are those that are external to the firm in the form of co-location of business activities. They take the form of pooled labour markets and shared market intelligence in the same activity in a particular locale. These kind are known as localisation economies. For unlike activities in the same place, the provision of transport infrastructure, research and development facilities form the basis of what is known as 'urbanisation economies'. There is a third category of agglomeration economies, known as 'activity-complex economies': 'they refer to economies that emerge from the joint location of unlike activities which have substantial trading links with one another' (Parr and Budd, 2000; 603).

Activity-complex economies can be likened to economic growth poles in which economic activities are developed and sustained by proximity to each other, for example financial centres; innovation networks and so on. The benefit of proximity is expressed in the form of gaining agglomeration economies and thus lowering the transactions costs for the firms involved. The more that a transaction space is homogeneous, the lower will be the transactions costs of constituent forms and thus the transaction space will be more efficient. On the other hand, the more heterogeneous a transaction space the higher the transactions costs. In this context heterogeneity, is defined as the degree to which the collection of institutional and cultural characteristics faced by economic agents' transactions is different across the geographical space that separates these agents (Wood and Parr, 2005; 5).

The evidence that transactions costs are positively related to the heterogeneity of a transaction space rests on three lines of reasoning. Firstly, the span of control shortens as the transaction space becomes more homogeneous and vice versa. In the former case, the number of economic agents that are needed to co-operate and the regulatory institutions to be complied with in undertaking a transaction is smaller (Williamson, 1975). The more that economies of communications are realised, the less the probability of loss of control by the transacting agents. Secondly, the rules, regulations and control procedures covering transactions will be more effective in a more homogeneous transaction space and vice versa. That is, standardisation of contracts will be more effectively enforced and limit exploiting opportunism in dealings between firms (Sokoloff, 1995). Thirdly, conflict between transacting or contracting agents is reduced as a result of the co-location of firms in a particular place. Market information is more easily distributed and shared and co-operative relationships develop from greater face-to-face communication, leading to transaction spaces that are more homogeneous and thus lower transactions costs (Wood and Parr, 2005).

More effective trust relationships tend to be created in more homogeneous spaces because of proximity and face-to-face contact. It has been argued that these types of arrangements are essential to the survival of specialist businesses and those operating in complex supply chains (Stuart and Sorenson, 2003). There is also an increasing amount of evidence that supports the hypothesis of the importance of strong links between trust, reputation and face-to-face contact (Glaeser et al, 2000). In an age that is apparently dominated by ICT and a population seduced by the ubiquity of this technology and one which lusts after the next 'new' digital device, this conclusion may seem surprising. However, both the biotechnology and finance sectors of the advanced economies have lower transaction costs where agglomeration economies are largest (Parr and Budd, 2000; Stuart and Sorenson, 2003). The relationship between firm co-location and co-operation, face-to-face contacts and communications and trust and reputation suggest that the more homogeneous a transaction space, the more efficient will be business transactions (Wood and Parr, 2005).

Given this discussion, it is apparent that if a framework in which institutional, cultural and language differences can be created, then combining a set of e-Government initiatives will not be enough to create a system of e-Governance. That framework is the transaction

space which is sufficiently homogeneous to limit increasing transactions costs. The paradox is that any system of governance is
necessarily heterogeneous, given our definitional elements of networks, partnership and fora in which service users deliberate in. But,
in order to function efficiently (lower transaction costs) a transaction
space of e-Governance must be more homogeneous. Furthermore, the
relationship between agglomeration economies and more efficient
transaction spaces is a severe challenge for any form of virtual
organisation and its operational management. Given the unstable
nature of networks and partnerships over the longer term, the ability
to create the conditions for an EU Information Society in which
e-Governance is enabled is doubtful. The youthful promise of social
networking sites like Face Book, YouTube and Second Life among
others, notwithstanding, matching the benefits of face-to-face contact
and communications is a difficult and frequently unsatisfactory
pursuit.

At present the major Lisbon objective of an Information Society in
which the EU Knowledge Economy progresses is a description and
not a basis for action and creating the necessary agency to fulfil this
objective. Therein lies the rub, the technologically and R&D over-
determined nature of the Lisbon Agenda inhibits the development of
the necessary institutional processes and procedures in which digital
and virtual technology can generate more homogeneous transaction
spaces. The starting point of initiating any form of governance is to
cohere the appropriate networks and partnerships around a central set
of objectives, potential outcomes and the institutional basis to produce
these elements, as well as matching them to governmental functions.
Aggregating the parts of e-Government programmes driven by R&D
will not add up to the total sum of e-Governance. That is, by having
R&D and technologically-driven e-Government projects that are
not set within an efficient transaction space will not create a system of
e-Governance.

One can start to see why the Lisbon Agenda seems to be creating
the possibility of a zero-sum game. On the one hand ICT and its
application will not in themselves create an EU Information Society
and thus the conditions for EU e-Governance. On the other hand, the
regime of asymmetrical economic governance, based on the primacy

of market adjustment inhibits the development of a world-beating knowledge economy, whose benefits are distributed among the populace. Is there any way out of this conundrum?

One possible solution is the extension of the Open Method of Co-ordination (OMC) in the development of governance structures and processes. OMC can be seen as an attempt to integrate the operations of EU-level and Member State policy processes in a more flexible manner and consists of:

* subjecting national policies to EU-wide guidelines;
* establishing measures of best practice against which the performance of member states can be compared; and
* calling on member states to adopt action plans in order to operationalise EU guidelines. (Budd, 2007; 358)

The OMC operates by establishing a series of 'soft law' agreements to make the operation of formal EU governmental rules ('hard laws'). For example, the implementation of legislation to deregulate and liberalise telecommunications markets, in the context of achieving the Action Plans for e-inclusion and e-health. The challenge for a Lisbon-inspired EU Information Society and e-Governance is that elements of e-Government projects can be successfully established at national and sub-national levels. For example, e-Democracy through e-Participation may be appropriate to some local initiatives or simple governmental programmes, but once these are ramped up to EU-wide levels then manifold problems may occur. As argued above, a transaction space of e-Governance will be less efficient if it is more heterogeneous. One of the Lisbon Agenda's main drivers is the creation of an EU Information Society. This entity requires a degree of heterogeneity for it to be implemented and leads to the potentially paradoxical outcome of it undermining the logic of the Lisbon Agenda itself.

Conclusion: Prospects beyond a Zero-Sum Result?

Many of the objectives of the Lisbon Agenda of 2000 are laudable. Few can argue with making the EU the most dynamic, socially inclusive and sustainable economy in the world. Nor for that matter, with harnessing the potential and possibilities of ICT to create an Information Society in order to overcome the digital divide. Like most politically inspired programmes, the 2010 deadline for the achievement of its objectives is overambitious. This was recognised in the subsequent Sapir and Kok Reports, expressed in the moniker: Lisbon II. One could be accused of being cynical if one were to identify this process with the serial thriller and sex movies: Die Hard, II and III or the prospect of Deep Throat I–IV. Sexing up movies as brands to sell more cinema tickets and merchandise may be one thing, but the legitimacy and accountability of supra-national development programmes in Europe is another matter altogether. This is particularly the case when using the Lisbon Agenda to drive through the development of complex public policy changes such as the introduction of e-Government programmes in order to create a transaction space and eventually a system of e-Governance.

The underlying rationale of the Lisbon Agenda is that competitive markets will ensure economic dynamism and ensure social cohesion. Aided and abetted by the EU's regime of economic governance, the conditions for creating an EU Information Society and a knowledge economy will accordingly be fulfilled by the application of ICT and R&D. Desire may be a stronger emotion than rationality in the human condition, but by overlooking the role of process in all its complexity, EU and Member State policy makers may be generating a zero-sum game. (A zero-sum game is one in which all the winnings are matched by the losses, for example poker.) The regime of economic governance is asymmetrical and lacks the institutional basis needed to fulfil the objectives of the Lisbon Agenda, as noted in the Sapir and Kok Reports. It restricts the development of an EU Information Society and the distribution of its benefits to the wider population because of the operation of the assumptions that technology, in and of itself, and market adjustment are sufficient conditions for creating and sustaining a dynamic knowledge economy. Given these parameters, creating an e-Governance transaction space will be very challenging.

This chapter has contended that the more heterogeneous a transaction space the larger will be the transactions costs, and thus the efficiency of the transaction space. The importance of agglomeration in the form of co-location that creates greater co-operation and trust has been noted by observers of advanced industries (Glaeser et al 2000; 113). In order to make an e-Governance transaction space more homogeneous, virtual and digital forms of agglomeration must be developed so that an abstract space that encompasses institutional, cultural and language difficulties can be simulated and created. However, the very existence of significant differences in language, culture and institutions across the EU suggest that creating digital versions of social inclusion, participation or democracy will not of themselves address this challenge. Summing together individual e-Government projects will not generate the total of e-Governance, whatever the utility of these projects. e-Governance in the EU is pregnant with possibilities and conceiving of it as a transaction space is a starting point. But, the gains and losses will cancel each out if the post-Lisbon environment is over-determined by technological and R&D imperatives, buttressed by an asymmetrical regime of economic governance which distorts the development path of the European Union.

Bibliography

Budd, L. (2004) 'Death of the New? Re-materialising the Economy'. In Budd, L. and Harris, L. (eds) *The e-Economy: Rhetoric or Reality?* London: Routledge.

Budd, L. (2007) 'A Cohesion Pact for the Regions: A Role for Industrial Policy?', *Policy Studies*, Vol. 28, No. 4, pp. 347–64.

Buiter, W. (1992) *Should we Worry about the Fiscal Numerology of Maastricht?* Yale University. Economic Growth Center, Discussion Paper No. 654.

Buiter, W. (2006) 'The Sense and Nonsense of Maastricht Revisited; What have we Learnt about Stabilization in EMU?' *Journal of Contemporary European Studies*, Vol. 44, No. 4, pp. 687–710.

Castells, M. (2000) *The Rise of Network Society, The Information Age: Economic, Society and Culture*. Vol. 1. Malden: Blackwell.

Drucker, P. (1969) *The Age of Discontinuity*. London: Heinemann.

Edgerton, D. (2006) *The Shock of the Old: Technology and Global History Since 1900*. London: Profile Books.

European Commission (2004) *2004 Competitiveness Report*. Brussels: European Commission.

European Commission (2005) Communication from the Commission to the Council, the European Parliament, the European Economic and Social Committee and the Committee of the Regions – i2010 – *A European Information Society for Growth and Employment* [SEC (2005) 717]. Brussels: European Commission at http://ec.europa.eu/

information_society/eeurope/i2010/key_documents/index_en.htm
#i2010_ Communication (accessed 15/02/07).

European Commission (2007a) *Putting People First*. Brussels: European Commission at http://ec.europa.eu/information_society/soccul/egov/index_en.htm (accessed 1/06/07).

European Commission (2007b) *Annual Information Society Report 2007*. Brussels: European Commission at http://ec.europa.eu/information_society/eeurope/i2010/docs/annual_report/2007/i2010_ ar_2007_en.pdf (accessed 01/01/08).

European Council (2000) *Lisbon Council: Presidency Conclusions*. Brussels: European Council.

European Information Technology Observatory (2007) *ICT Markets*. Frankfurt: EITO.

Glaeser, E.L., Laibson, D.I., Scheinkman, J.A., and Soutter, C.L. (2000) 'Measuring Trust', *Quarterly Journal of Economics*, Vol. 115, No. 3, pp. 811–46.

Held, D. 'Cosmopolitanism: Ideas, Realities and Deficits'. In D. Heald and A. McGrew (eds) *Governing Globalization: Power, Authority and Governance*. Cambridge: Polity Press.

Kelly, J. (2006) 'Central Regulation of English Local Authorities: An Example of Meta-governance?', *Public Administration*, Vol. 84, No. 3, pp. 603–21.

Landes, D.S (2003) *The Unbound Prometheus: Technological Change and Industrial Development in Western Europe from 1750 to the Present*. Cambridge: Cambridge University Press.

Machlup, F. (1962) *The Production of and Distribution of Knowledge in the United States*. Princeton: Princeton University Press.

Newman, J. (2001) *Modernising Governance: New Labour, Policy and Society*. London: Sage.

Offe, C. (1985) *Disorganised Capitalism*. Cambridge: Polity Press.

Parr, J.B. and Budd, L. (2000) 'Financial Services and the Urban System', *Urban Studies*, Vol. 37, No. 3, 593–610.

Rhodes, R.A.W. (1997) *Understanding Governance*. Buckingham: Open University Press.

Sapir, A., Bertola, G., Hellwig, M., Pisani-Ferry, J., Rosati, D., Vinal, J. and Wallace, H. (2002) *An Agenda for a Growing Europe: The Sapir Report*. Oxford: Oxford University Press.

Sheridan, W. and Riley, T.B. (2006) *Comparing E-government vs E-governance* at www.rileyis.com (accessed 01/06/07).

Solokoff, K.L. (1995) 'Comment on Enright'. In N.R. Lamoreaux and D.M.G.Raff (eds) *Coordination and Information: Historical Perspectives on the Organization of the Enterprise*. Chicago: University of Chicago Press.

Stuart, T.E. and Sorenson, D. (2003) 'The Geography of Opportunity: Spatial Heterogeneity in Founding Rates and the Performance of Biotechnology Firms', *Research Policy*, Vol. 32, No. 2. pp. 229–53.

UNESCO (2005) *E-Governance Capacity Building*. Paris: United Nations Educational Scientific and Cultural Organization at http://portal.

unesco.org/ci/en/ev.php-URL_ID=4404&URL_DO=DO_TOPIC&
URL_SECTION=201.html (accessed 01/06/07).

Williamson, O.E. (1975) *Markets and Hierarchies: Analysis and Antitrust
Implication*. New York: Free Press.

Wood, G.A. and Parr, J.B. (2005) 'Transactions Costs, Agglomeration
Economies, and Industrial Location', *Growth and Change*, Vol. 36, No. 1.
pp. 1–15

PART II

ENABLING AND MANAGING TECHNOLOGIES

4

'EARLY ADOPTER' CASE STUDIES OF EFFECTIVE MOBILE COMMUNICATIONS BETWEEN CITIZENS AND GOVERNMENT

JANE VINCENT AND LISA HARRIS

Introduction

This chapter investigates what is needed to make the mobile phone an effective tool for the interaction between government and governed, building upon our earlier work reported in Social Shaping of UMTS – Preparing the 3G Customer (Vincent and Harper 2003). To date, a number of m-Government projects have been successfully established, but their usage still tends to be confined within small niche markets (Institute of Public Finance, 2006). Recent studies have also shown that a significant proportion of the UK population have no interest in the Internet and no intention of accessing it (Dutton et al, 2005). However, it is reported that there are more web-enabled mobile phones than there are PCs in the UK (Mobile Data Association 2006). It would appear, therefore, that mobile phones may well offer the most viable electronic channel through which to encourage large-scale take-up of online public services. Our chapter begins by reviewing recent research in this area in an attempt to distinguish the 'reality' from the 'rhetoric'. We then discuss relevant theories of technological adoption and diffusion and draw upon case studies of best practice from around the world to highlight the emerging ways in which mainstream usage of this type of government/citizen interaction can be encouraged. We also point out some pitfalls to avoid and highlight areas where further research is required.

The Rhetoric and Reality of m-Government Services

The availability of hand-held wire-free communication tools that work in almost any urban location globally has created a major transformation in business and personal life. Mobile phones or cellphones had been used as private radio services for many years, but the licensing of public mobile communications services met latent demand that is still not sated in many nations. At the same time as improvements in international air travel were opening up business opportunities in previously inaccessible regions, the development of mobile phones was gathering apace. The powerful combination of these and other developing technologies such as the World Wide Web has augmented new business opportunities by giving communications access to employees in more remote locations, as well as enabling people to use the time when they were on a journey or not in the office to keep in contact.

Mobile phone products in the UK were first made available over public networks in the mid-1980s and were initially targeted at business customers. It was over five years before a consumer tariff was designed to attract a broader base and during the 1990s, the acceptance or rejection of new technologies relied on the response of this mass-market consumer base (Vincent, Haddon and Hamill 2005). Accordingly, texting (short message service or SMS) was adopted at such a rate that the mobile communications companies supplying the service and the technologies supporting it were hard put to keep up with demand. On the other hand, WAP – (wireless application protocol) or mobile internet – was initially rejected by customers, although with the arrival of email and more advanced wireless broadband technologies this is now gaining more widespread use many years on.

The origins of SMS are found in its engineering function as part of the maintenance layer of the GSM infrastructure, and it was the development of the unified GSM standard in Europe that provided the technological infrastructure to support the general availability of this form of data exchange (Taylor and Vincent 2005). Notwithstanding the more than 10 year development cycle for the GSM technology that supports present-day mobile communications, WAP is an example of a technology that has taken an unplanned additional number of years to be adopted by its users. Thus it is a process of continual refinement and absorption of both the technological advances and the users' response to it that eventually finds an acceptable solution, one that in the case of texting is still developing as pictures, video and sound are included in this new communications argot. In the UK text messages are now being sent at a rate of over 100 million per day (Mobile Data Association 2006) and are supported by services that did not exist five years ago:

> Over the last six years text.it (www.text.it) has witnessed text messaging grow from a popular craze to becoming an essential communication tool, inclusive to all age groups. The MDA has forecast that figures will continue to rise this year to deliver an annual total of 45 billion text messages for 2007, with an average of 3.75 billion messages being sent per month and 123 million messages per day [in the UK] (www.themda.org, 2007).

Using mobile phones for talk and text has thus become integrated into our everyday lives, but unless there is a substantial change in social practices, we believe that the much heralded 'm-government' will take many more years to become a reality. Those who communicate electronically with government are not yet lifelong users of mobile phones and tend to see them and their personal computer as serving very functional and separate roles (Vincent 2006). Although mobile phones are omnipresent in UK society, and they seem to pervade almost every avenue of private, public, business and personal communication, they are not yet fully endorsed and used by everyone. Our research has shown that most people use their mobile phone for social contact to communicate with people they already know, and that official communications are still often made from a fixed phone. Indeed mobile phones appear to be different from any other computational device in that people have a unique attachment to them. They are associated strongly with social and close family contact that is maintained through the device. This finding poses a challenge for the development of m-government services, as people tend not to regard their interactions with local or national government as being in this elite category of personal communication. Mobile technologies do, however, offer huge potential to represent mainstream government/ citizen interaction if these issues can be addressed.

People already use text and photos to record unexpected events such as road traffic or public incidents and the appearance of celebrities. As new generation mobile phones provide easier access to the World Wide Web there is increasing opportunity to leverage these capabilities for m-government solutions. According to the recent government report 'Transformational Government Strategy' (March 2006): 'Technologies have emerged into widespread use – for example the mobile phone and other mobile technologies – which government services have yet properly to exploit.' (2006, point 19)

This oversight is borne out by industry forecasts such as those by Jupiter Research (Houston 2006) highlighting an increase in revenue opportunities for suppliers of interoperable mobile and wireless networks for delivering online government services. It should be noted that in common with government policy documents, industry research discusses e-Government in terms of both the citizen user and the operational (government) user. Houston refers to this as 'citizen-facing m-government' and 'operational work': the former being 'user friendly approaches to accessing the enormous amounts of content now available for citizen-facing online government' (p 4) and the latter offering mobile communications access to fieldworkers and especially to command and control centres, both non-emergency and emergency.

The methodology for developing the taxonomy of information and information access is a moot point. Houston states:

> e-Government has done the groundwork for m-government in terms of the fundamental taxonomies of information, modes of effective online presentation, and content production and management. The challenges of citizen-facing m-government relate chiefly to the limitation of display, user input and overall device functionality. (Houston, 2006: 3)

This is a bold statement not least in that it makes the assumption that the interface for m-government is identical to that of e-Government, however, as we shall discuss later, the social practices of a mobile phone user are not the same as for other communication technologies so this assumption may well be erroneous.

The UK government, which is committed to putting all government services online, has so far spent around £8bn on obliging its departments and the wider public sector to comply with its targets. There is very little evidence yet that all customers want or need online transactions, let alone any degree of payback from the investment. (Vincent 2004a and Curthoys 2004) and recent research by Jackson and Irani (2007) claim that the current lack of a joined-up approach to UK e-Government will result in its failure. e-Government spending to date will be dwarfed in the next few years by projects such as the NHS National Programme for IT and the integration of Customs and Excise and Inland Revenue information systems. Historically, the success rate for implementation of large-scale computer projects is low (Harris 2001). The 'dotcom' crash is another recent example of the consequences of 'blind faith' in new technology without consideration of the social implications, and it would appear that the UK government is now exercising some cautious optimism with the statement that 'some of the newer technologies today will be mainstream by 2011 and the time will be right to roll out their widespread exploitation' (Cabinet Office 2006, p 19). It is not clear from this whether planning should begin now in readiness for 2011, or whether we should wait until that date to see what has happened and then exploit it.

Thus it would appear that technology in some form is already in place or ready for purchase to support all kinds of online G2C activity in a variety of locations. However, for m-government to be taken up successfully there does need to be corresponding enthusiasm among the citizens who will use the services they support. To access services online and via mobile phones or some other wireless device is assumed in UK policy, but how this will be implemented is not clear, nor is it apparent how services can be tailored to the particular ways that citizens are prepared to access them. Recent research on mobile phones finds that people are willing to adopt new technologies only if they are presented in a familiar guise to pre-existing services, such as the ways that the exemplar of email over a PC is used as the basis for wireless local area networks or email over cellphone technology (Mallard 2005). Thus although the technology may be completely new, the actual product or service that it supports remains familiar such as with the experience of voice calls, text messaging, email and photographs. These findings have important implications for the development of m-government services, examples of which will be discussed later in this chapter. To the user this presents a dichotomy; wanting the familiar but recognising that there may be advantages to them in changing the ways that things are done. In this context, the change is less about adopting new technologies and products, and more about using a personal device that is associated exclusively with social and family uses for less personal public services. If such attitudes prevail then mainstream usage of m-government is unlikely to be facilitated. We will now go on to examine the theoretical under-pinning to the relationship between these social and technical aspects of new technology adoption in more detail.

The Social Shaping of Technology

Acknowledgement of the role that society and people have in the making and adoption of technology is a relatively new, for until the 1990s it was generally held that the technology would determine the social uses of products and services. Mackenzie and Wacjman (1999) asserted that technology had been viewed as 'a separate sphere, developing independently of society; following its own autonomous logic and then having effects on society' (Mackenzie and Wacjman, 1999; XVIII).

In their discourse on the topic Grint and Woolgar (1997) argue that rather than this previous essentialist approach in which new technology results from the purely scientific development of past technological inventions, the current approach is more constructivist, or 'anti-essentialist'. 'Technological artefacts do not possess capacities by virtue of extrapolation from previous technical states of affairs but rather that the nature, form and capacity of a technology is the upshot of various antecedent circumstances involved in its development' (Grint and Woolgar 1997; 97).

It is not only the designers and developers of new technologies that imbue its capabilities with their own social experiences but also the social practices of people who adopt and adapt the new technologies. Appropriating a new technology may result in it being used in different ways than were intended by its developers such as in the insatiable demand for SMS text messaging on mobile phones discussed above. The use of camera phones also exemplifies this point; intended to be an augmented texting service in which images would be taken by the phone user and sent via a multi-media text message (MMS) the users quickly found better uses for the camera, especially after finding that sending messages was complicated, costly and often did not work at all. Quick snaps taken on the spur of the moment were instead shown and shared with friends and downloaded onto personal computers or to other mobile phones using Bluetooth or Infrared. What had been intended as a network messaging service turned out to be a new service created by the users. Learning from this, the mobile phone manufacturers improved the quality of the cameras and have built on the desire to show and share to offer a vast array of content-based services that are downloadable to mobiles.

It is only in more recent times, with more assured quality of service, that the sending of images has become more commonplace such as in the aftermath of disaster or to record a special event (Vincent 2006). The role of citizen journalism is now accepted practice as people are entreated to send images of events that may be of public interest. The first images of many events, particularly disasters, are now usually taken on mobile phones by bystanders. As for technologies that are rejected completely, it is a moot point as to whether this is social shaping or merely the purveyors of the technology removing access such as with the first generation of mobile phone games and ring tones that are no longer available free except in return for a download fee.

The social practices of the mass users remain constant but the technologies that support it do not. Whilst this is due in part to the development and augmentation of design, artefacts and technical capabilities, it would appear that the seemingly faster pace of technological change is a consequence of the ways that technology, business and the economics of everyday life interweave with society.

These ways that people appropriate technologies was examined by Haddon and Silverstone (1993) in their domestication theory and is cited by Anderson (2003) in his exploration of information communication technologies in European homes and in particular what happens to them once they have been purchased, especially by those for whom the technology can appear threatening. What has been observed is that 'Over time familiarisation, experience, training and (perhaps most importantly) experimentation lead to a domestication cycle', whereby eventually the technology is absorbed in everyday life. Referring to the mobile phone, Anderson states:

> This is most easily seen in the recent domestication of the mobile telephone which has become a tool of business, of safety and security, an item of fashion, of convenience and, most dramatically, of young people's fervid social communication. The same device, the same service, the same ICT but radically different places in the lives of these different people. (Anderson, 2003)

Once again, there are clear lessons here from the user perspective for the development of effective m-government services which will be explored with some empirical examples later in the chapter.

Theories of Technological Adoption

At this point it is worth reiterating that just because modern communications technology is now widely available, it does not necessarily follow that people will be prepared to change their established practices and use their mobile phones to interact with government. Moving the discussion on to a more micro level, 'diffusion of innovations' theory provides some insight into how mainstream usage might be expedited. According to Rogers (1962) an individual's decision to adopt a new technology is a process consisting of a series of actions taking place over a period of time, rather than an instantaneous act. This absorption rate of the technology is enhanced if users perceive it to offer greater value than they enjoyed previously. Jacobsen (2000) suggested that when peers share positive evaluations of a new technology, like-minded individuals become motivated to adopt it. Hamilton and Thompson (1992) presented a useful summary of personality characteristics displayed by these so-called 'early adopters' in their research into the adoption of an electronic network for educators. They studied the development of an electronic communications network that allowed a link to be created between students and faculty members. The aims of the network were to decrease the isolation often experienced by students, increase the availability of faculty expertise and raise faculty awareness of any problems in the field. The early adopters in this project were found to possess similar levels of education, social status and social participation. They had a cosmopolitan view, accessed data from mass media channels, were part of broad interpersonal communications networks, exhibited a high level of innovation, held a positive view towards risk and change and held impartial attitudes towards failure. The role of the early adopters was critical in encouraging wider use of the network, as their enthusiastic endorsement influenced the rate of subsequent adoption of the technology by others.

There is clearly a lesson here for the adoption of m-Government services. Rogers' approach has been applied to research on the adoption of mobile phones (Ling 2002 and Mallard 2005). However, the latter argues for caution in the application of the diffusion approach in the introduction of new technologies. He suggests that people who are commonly selected as the 'lead users' or 'early adopters' of new innovations may not be the best judges of its success or otherwise:

> Indeed, it is dangerous to reify the innovative potential of people since a particular category of the population can be lead users in a domain and conservative in another one – compare for instance the capacity to innovate in matter of clothes and in matters of new technology. In this sense, the notion of lead user is weakly predictive. (Mallard, 2005; 3)

We will discuss this important point in more detail later in the chapter.

Another model that explores the adoption of new technology, this time from a behavioural perspective, is the Technology Acceptance Model (TAM) referring to the process that users go through to accept and use computing technology. Davis (1989) suggests that when a user is presented with new computing technology, two main factors determine whether and when the individual will use that technology:

1. 'Perceived Usefulness' is the degree to which an individual believes that using a particular system would enhance his or her job performance.

2. 'Perceived Ease of Use' is the degree to which an individual believes that using a particular system would be free from effort.

Influential studies carried out by Shih and Venkatesh (2004), extend the original TAM model to describe perceived usefulness and usage intentions based on social influence. They observed that the greater the perceived job relevance (the degree to which the individual perceives the technology to be applicable to his or her job) of a new system, the more important output quality becomes. They recommended that in order for the technology to be accepted by an individual or a social unit, the effectiveness of the system should be demonstrated to potential users and, preferably by those people that the potential users considered important. This point comes across quite strongly from our case studies to which we will now turn.

Case Studies

Although mobile phones are omnipresent globally their use is by no means ubiquitous, nor are they accessible to all. In addition it would appear that the mobile phone is not generally perceived as a formal means of communicating with government, particularly at national level. Household and business-based internet connectivity remains probably the most commonly used and preferred digital communications media for accessing government departments in addition to the fixed phone. Indeed, notwithstanding the fact that many people will use their mobile phone to make a call to their local authority, as we have noted earlier the use of mobile communications within e-Government is by no means yet commonplace. The presence and role that mobile phones play in citizens' everyday lives is, however, being leveraged by some local governments to offer access via text messaging in particular, albeit on a piecemeal basis at present. At a national level there are a few examples of using text messaging but mostly the mobile phone is used in *ad hoc* novel ways within the process of government. In the case studies that follow we examine some of the ways that digitally mediated communications are being adopted within local and national government and how the mobile phone figures in some, where in others it is unlikely to have a role for some years to come.

Case Study 1 – e-Voting in Estonia, India and the Russian Federation

Much is talked about electronic voting, not least how any voting system is required to be extremely secure. Already a Netherlands-based organisation claims to have hacked into one system planned for adoption in some EU countries. In this case study three types of electronic voting are explored; two of which, in Estonia and India, make no use of mobile phones as part of the voting process and the third, in the Russian Federation, that leverages mobile phone use to participate in monitoring the results of the election. In the Estonian example the voting process could be adapted for mobile phone users, and although India might make use of mobile communications network infrastructure indirectly, at present it has little in common with mobile phone practices and has no dependence on individual, household or business ownership of communications technologies such as personal computers and mobile phones.

Looking first at Estonia, they provided the opportunity for e-Voting for their elections in 2005 and 2007. The system is linked closely with their mandatory national identity card and requires the use of a reader attached to a computer and the use of two passwords. The reader has to be purchased for the sum of approximately 6–12 Euros. Estonia's population of 1.3 million has 1 million ID cardholders with electronic chips in use that enable them to be used online. Despite optimistic predictions the number of people who actually 'e-Voted' was lower than expected – less than 10,000 rather than the anticipated 20,000–30,000. Quite a number of the e-voters used their work computer, particularly those in the banking and telecommunications industry, suggesting that they were already more computer literate in this regard, or they simply found that the voting online process was familiar with their everyday work practices. However, although e-Votes represented only 3% of turnout the number of e-Voters in 2007 doubled from the first election in 2005 when e-Voting was first made available. There is no mention in the literature of transferring the e-voting capability to mobile phones and it would appear that even as the internet capabilities of mobile communications mature the use of a reader already purchased and attached to a computer might have fixed the voting to the home PC.

Although this is a small volume of voters in a nation with less than a million voters, electronic voting is by no means constrained by the scale of operation required to support high volume of voters, as has been demonstrated in India which has a wholly electronic voting system. In Estonia the technologies made available for voting can be done from a home PC, whereas in India the system has been set up in polling centres and aims to offer diversity in voting capturing the illiterate as well as literate voter. India has an electorate of more than 668 million in 543 parliamentary constituencies, many of whom are remotely located and poor voters. The electronic voting system introduced in recent years now has over one million machines made by two Indian companies. Unlike the Estonian example above where voting can be done on any enabled PC, in India it can only be done at a polling station. In Estonia the electronic voting appeals to the computer literate and the domestic user whereas in India it is targeted more at ensuring all voters, many of whom have previously voted with their thumbprint, are enfranchised in this vast democratic state. The ballot paper itself is presented on a device with each candidate having a button alongside their name which must be pressed to cast the vote. The voting is done in private with the polling station staff activating and deactivating the balloting unit to prevent any more votes being cast than is allowed per voter. With the maximum number of voters per polling station being 1,500 the fact that each electronic voting machine can record five votes a minute or an estimated 2,700 in a polling day it should be more than capable of coping with the volumes. After progressively introducing the system the Indian Government used only electronic voting machines for the first time in the Lok Sabha election in 2004.

In the Russian Federation electronic voting is being trialled in Veliky Novgorod. The importance of maintaining the secrecy of the vote is paramount and accordingly the voting system has been set up within the polling station. In his speech to the Council of Europe session of experts of electronic voting Yaschenko (2006) commented on the difficulties of a voting system that used remotely located devices, registering concern at the potential breach of 'secret suffrage' of the Estonian remote voting system: 'There is no solution to guarantee that when a voter votes with the use of a mobile phone, Internet or digital television there is no person or group of people nearby who would know for sure who he/she gave the vote to' (Yaschenko 2006).

The trial that took place on October 8 2006 enabled the Central Election Commission of Russia to learn more about the voters' responses to the electronic voting system offered at five polling stations. They found that some people were less willing to stop using a paper-based voting system, preferring not to vote at all when voting booths were full, whereas others want to have the choice to vote electronically. The issue of trusting an automated electoral system has in part already been addressed by the successful introduction of the SAS – the State Automated System (SAS) known as 'Vybory' that is used mostly for the planning and electronic registration of voters and only a small amount for the summarising of results. These results are available as they arrive online to the 22 million Internet users in Russia, and as part of the trial similar information about the results can be sent to mobile phones via SMS or MMS messages. As there are more than 80 million mobile phone users this significantly increases the number of people who could actively participate in monitoring the results of an election as they come through. It is clear that in Russia electronic voting is not going to replace the paper-based system that is trusted by the voters and the CEC alikes but the integration of new technologies into the process of monitoring results is a major move towards the adoption of mobile phones as part of the whole election process and a recognition of the most favoured means of communication of its citizens.

Case Study 2: Push and Pull Text Messaging Services: UK

This case study examines some of the *ad hoc* systems that have been set up in the UK within different local authorities that make use of people's everyday use of mobile phones. These involve the use of 'push and pull' services. Push services provide a range of information services that people can subscribe to (currently free of charge) whereby they are automatically sent information that they request.

The pull services are provided to receive information from citizens who wish to report deficiencies in local amenities such as broken street lights or potholes. In Hillingdon these include news alerts via email or SMS and access to council services 24 hours a day. In common with other local authorities Hillingdon has targeted services that affect daily life such as street services and information services. 'Request recycling bags, report a broken street light or request street cleaning by text message from your mobile phone'. www.hillingdon.gov.uk/index.jsp?articleid=7694.

Services where citizens can text into their local authority are limited, but there are a number of text alerts whereby news from the council about jobs, events and even food safety warnings are on offer. Some of these services, such as job vacancy alerts, are only available by text – they are not offered via email. Lewisham offers a service whereby you can photograph a problem and send it by mobile phone to them for action:

> The London Borough of Lewisham uses Cam2Web technology. A citizen (or council worker, or politician) can report an environmental problem by taking a digital picture on their mobile phone and sending it to the council. The incident is inserted directly into the council's database, and then resolved by the appropriate team. An email or SMS message is then sent to the citizen to confirm the action taken. (TGT 2006)

The costs of the text messages to the council are borne by the user and a note to this effect is included on the website address. This service called 'Love Lewisham', not only reports progress in attending to the problems, it does so against the published image online which introduces an element of public shaming of the offending location and its perpetrators. It also appeals to a sense of outrage on the part of the citizen who is empowered to take action, much as one would do in an emergency call for assistance. The use of the emotional epithet 'love' in the call for reports of problems also appeals to citizens and how they might be being affected by the actions of others. This service was championed by an individual councillor, no longer in office but still an active user. New councillors and local wardens have been issued with mobile phones by their council specifically to photograph the problem areas to demonstrate their 'hands on' approach to their role as elected representatives. A typical photograph will be of graffiti or fly-tipping, which once posted is monitored and the corrective action taken is noted on the website so that the entire process is transparent to local residents.

Case Study 3: Mobile Internet Access to Government Authorities:
Norway, Malaysia, UK

In accordance with Government policy all UK local authorities have website access to their services although the extent to which this is accessible to its citizens and the amount of information available varies considerably from region to region. However, as we already know there are more Internet-enabled mobile phones in the UK (and globally) than there are Internet-enabled PCs, and more people are trying out these services as access becomes more reliable. Filling out a self-assessment form for social services such as is possible in Kent via its www.kent.gov.uk/SocialCare/adults-and-older-people/self-assessment/portal, may not be an obvious use of web access via a mobile phone, but it could become part of the access process. Checking out what is on the web and using it to find data such as opening hours of local council offices and leisure amenities would be better examples, however, this type of data would most likely be accessed by people familiar with using the Internet on their mobile phone (such as for work or to get train times), and it may not occur to someone who rarely, if ever, uses the Internet capability on their mobile.

Interaction with government may be merely a procedural matter, such as in the case of tax returns when no new data needs to be submitted but confirmation of status is required. In Norway it was recognised that a large proportion of the population regularly returned their tax forms unchanged and so these people are offered the option to do so via SMS (O2 2004: 61). Reporting on the success of electronic tax returns, the Norwegian tax office advised that in 2005 over 1.8 million Norwegians chose to deliver their tax returns electronically, of which 257,000 used SMS (www.skatteetaten.no). In Malaysia the road transport department uses SMS to alert citizens to the status of their road tax and licence enabling them to renew them and avoid fines (O2 2004: 14). The take-up of these services is, of course, reliant on both an awareness of the service and on the willingness of citizens to be contacted in this way. In the instance of electronic voting set up for local authority elections in the UK, it was suggested that whilst the service may have attracted some new voters it mainly appealed to existing voters who chose to use the service because it was more convenient for them. (O2 2004: 78) – a situation in common with the Estonian case study above. This is an important consideration when introducing m-government services which, as suggested above, may initially benefit mostly those citizens who are already aware of such services rather than improve interaction with 'hard to reach' groups of the population. The danger with this of course is that, despite best intentions, the so-called 'digital divide' is increased rather than reduced.

Case Study 4: 'Pull' Information and Content from Posters and Billboards to Mobiles

This service is obtained in response to a request from the mobile phone owner responding to static advertising in a particular location using Bluetooth capability. One provider of this type of service is 'Qwikker' who supply the capability to deliver music clips at rock concerts and local information from London Underground posters. In 2006 the Department for Transport (DfT) used Qwikker to produce a mobile game as part of their campaign to stop young people drinking and driving. Pub goers were alerted to the game on flat screen television in the pub that advised them to switch on their Bluetooth. They could then download for free a game in which players had to drink-drive a car home from a pub in the process of which accidents, injury and involvement with the police was used to draw attention to the dangers of drinking and driving. The Bluetooth technology is freely available to all and can be used by anyone to pass on information, but only with the active permission of those involved. Careless use of Bluetooth might lead to transfer of unwanted material, but as with the DfT example above using a familiar method of data transfer to appeal to a specific audience such as the youth market might augur well for governmental organisations.

Discussion and Conclusion

So far we have highlighted the dichotomy that exists between the technological advances that continue apace in all aspects of twenty-first century life and the continuing familiar social practices that underpin it. We have also noted that while a number of innovative m-government examples now exist, mainstream usage is still a long way off. In this final section we will extract the lessons and recommendations that have emerged from the research undertaken in order to help address this issue.

While our case studies demonstrate that using mobile communications for accessing e-Government services is still very much in its infancy, the examples given do show, however, that people are beginning to make use of text and WAP services that complement the familiar social practices of their mobile phone use today, such as the taking and sending of images from public places. It was reported by the Mobile Data Association in August 2006 that: 'Close to 20% of [UK] mobile phone users are now regularly using the WAP capability on their phones to download ringtones, games, wallpapers or to simply browse the internet whilst on the move' (MDA 2006a). This is a positive step for m-government opportunities but note that the services currently accessed are more for personal and fun use.

The case studies demonstrate the breadth of service applications being developed that make use of mobile phones as the communications medium, as well as highlighting that even when mobile phones can be used they may not be the desired or optimum solution for users. In these examples the mobile phone is used because it is already a familiar device, something that people take for granted as being an everyday item in their lives. More than that, it has become a means of greater involvement with a particular event or community or a simple means of achieving the mundane such as a nil tax return, a necessity that is often neglected due to inertia, or the difficulty of understanding another organisation's system and a process that appears to add little value to your life. Electronic voting is a revolutionary way of enfranchising eligible voters who may not previously have been able to vote due to remoteness, lack of registration or simply the hassle factors involved in making it happen.

New technology moves us forward but it isn't necessarily replacing old ways of doing things – as we learn from the example of the Russian Federation and their voting process which, in common with India, remains cautious when it comes to the potential loss of free and secret suffrage. There is often considerable rhetoric that makes claims to usage of new technologies when in reality their take-up is slow or non-existent, such as, for example, the 3% turnout of e-voters in Estonia. In some ways the apparent reluctance by UK Government to fully endorse and programme the introduction of m-Government services could be construed as tacit acknowledgement of this uncertainty. However, it is more likely a response to the decision to push online Internet-based services as the way forward, despite the fact that there are fewer households with Internet-enabled computers than there are with Internet-enabled mobile phones. Now that digital media are diverse and being adopted in niche ways this policy may be short-sighted.

In any event some local authorities are finding their own ways to meet the needs of their local citizens. Thus in addition to the blanket policy to introduce all government services online – for the operational benefit of the authority as well as to the citizen – there are niche services emerging that respond to the ways people like to communicate. Thus LoveLewisham, Hillingdon's SMS alerts and electronic voting all offer local citizens a service that, when taken together and effectively promoted, could be regarded as leading by example as a starting point for establishing mainstream citizen-led digitally mediated communications.

It is clear that new technology in itself rarely instigates significant change, and it certainly offers no panacea for success. As Budd and Harris (2004) demonstrate, the underlying continuities emerging from the use of new technology can be more enlightening than the optimistic expectation of change. Every age believes it is new and different:

> The claims made by the disciples of the Information Age, Knowledge Economy and the new e-economies, at the end of the second millennium, are no different from those of Adam Smith and Karl Marx in the 18th and 19th centuries or the proponents of modernity at the turn of the [20th] century.' (Budd and Harris 2004; 22)

The rhetoric of new ways of organising business through technology may influence decision making, but the promise of the new is rarely matched by performance delivery in the short term. The lesson here is that government should seek ways of engaging the interest and active participation of citizens and demonstrating the effectiveness of the services (as in the 'Love Lewisham' example) rather than expect m-Government services to be utilised simply because the necessary technology has been made available. When assessing levels of usage it should also be remembered that changing people's established social practices may take a significant amount of time.

Some of the case studies offer a more optimistic outlook with an indication of the type of mobile phone based services that citizens are already beginning to take up. However, to register with the services online Internet access is usually required although local authorities may benefit from viral marketing of the service by satisfied users. Earlier we made the point that governments need to be *inclusive* in terms of the service deliver-channels that they offer. Compelling people to use online government services by the withdrawal of any other means of access is already causing some concern, such as access to employment rights leaflets that are only available online. 'Citizens Advice estimated that if someone wanted to print these out in their library they may now cost the consumer around £6' (Sinclair 2006).

Our research also highlights the danger of relying too much on Roger's generally accepted diffusion of innovations model. Gladwell (2000) criticises this with his claim that early adopters are apparently influential only because they are very visible by virtue of the fact of being 'in there' early. Instead, he notes that the quality of referrals by influential 'connectors' operating through effective social networks and providing peer endorsement is what makes the difference between mass market acceptance and rejection. Surowiecki (2005) supports this argument with his historical example of the development of standardised screws in the 1860s. Previously these items were individually handmade and gave considerable power to the machinists that made them. William Sellers managed to get his own design accepted as a national standard by targeting influential users such as the US Navy and Pennsylvania Railroad. This generated credibility and momentum for his product until a critical mass of users was achieved.

So how can the principle of focusing on influential connectors be applied to the adoption of m-government services? Rosen (2000) has developed a screening profile for identifying these 'connector' individuals, known as an ACTIVE profile. The characteristics are:

Ahead in adoption
Connected (socially and electronically)
Travellers
Information Hungry
Vocal
Exposed to media.

Companies such as Procter and Gamble are recruiting such individuals into research partnerships and panels (see their Tremor group of influential teenagers, www.tremor.com) to generate goodwill and word of mouth for new products. As the individual connector is disproportionately powerful within his/her community, the network effect quickly kicks in to 'spread the word'. Similar marketing strategies could be adopted to promote m-government services into mainstream usage.

Another key point to emphasise is that the e-Government (and m-Government) channels offered must be appropriate for the user. Critically, this need may vary at different stages of the process. It means that not only will services have to be accessible via a number of digital and non-digital interfaces (with obvious economic consequences for the provider) but that for any one government service specific stages of it may be best suited to different channels. For example, when paying the London congestion charge by text one first has to register online through a PC. Another example of integration of channels within one service provision could be to allow a simple yes/no response to be sent by text to a tax return or car parking permit scheme that involves no change in circumstances. The example of online registration to Kent Social Services described above has won many awards, but the process is currently complicated by access restrictions whereby an initial approach off-line cannot then be adjusted to allow subsequent assessment online. While providing this flexibility would have obvious appeal to users, there are also clearly huge workflow implications internally which would need careful consideration if a multiple channel system is to work effectively. This is an area which the next phase of our research will investigate in more detail.

In this chapter we have explored the mutual shaping of technology and society and the ways that people prefer to use familiar ways of doing things as a means of adopting the new technologies. We have shown that old technologies are not simply replaced by the new, and the m-Government services that have had most success to date have been those, such as 'Love Lewisham', which resonate with people's emotional attachment to their mobile as a means of personal communication. We have also highlighted the dangers of new m-Government services inflating the digital divide by merely adding choice and convenience to experienced Internet users without bringing new user groups into the fold.

Bibliography

Anderson, B. (2003) 'The Domestication of Information and Communication Technologies'. In K. Christensen and D. Levinson (eds). *Encyclopedia of Community: From the Village to the Virtual World*. London: Sage: pp. 774–77.

Budd, L. and Harris, L. (2004) 'The Virtuality of Reality'. In Budd L. and Harris L. (eds) *e-Economy: Rhetoric or Business Reality?* London: Routledge.

Cabinet Office (2006) 'Transformational Government Enabled By Technology', Norwich: TSO (The Stationery Office).

Cabinet Office (2006) 'Transformational Government Implementation Plan', Norwich: TSO (The Stationery Office).

Cross, M. (2005) 'Our Failures are Behind Us, Promise Ministers', *Technology Guardian* 13th October, p. 6.

Curthoys, N. (2004) 'e-Government: From Utopian Rhetoric to Practical Realism'. In Budd L. and Harris L. (eds) *e-Economy: Rhetoric or Business Reality?* London: Routledge.

David, P.A. (1991) 'Computer and Dynamo: The Modern Productivity Paradox in a Not-Too-Distant Mirror'. In *Technology and Productivity – The Challenge for Economic Policy*, Paris: OECD.

Davis, F.D. (1989) 'Perceived Usefulness, Perceived Ease of Use and User Acceptance of Information Technology', *MIS Quarterly*, 13(3) pp. 319–40.

Dutton, W., di Gennaro, C. and Hargrave, A. M. (2005) 'The Internet in Britain'. *The Oxford Internet Survey* (OxIS) May.

EDRI-gram: European e-Voting machines cracked by Dutch group (11.10.2006) http://www.edri.org/edrigram/number4.19/e-voting.

Election Commission of India http://www.eci.gov.in/ElectoralSystem/the_function.asp#howthevoting April 19 2007.

Estonian National Electoral Committee Election Results 2007 http://www.vvk.ee/r07/paeveng.stm.

Estonians will be first to allow Internet votes in national election http://www.iht.com/articles/2007/02/22/business/evote.php February 22 2007.

Forester, T. (1985) *The Information Technology Revolution*, Oxford: Blackwell.

Franke, R.H. (1987) 'Technological Revolution and Productivity Decline: The Case of US Banks', *Technological Forecasting and Social Change*, Vol. 31 pp. 143–54.

Freeman, C. (1988) 'The Factory of the Future: The Productivity Paradox, Japanese Just-in-Time and Information Technology', *Programme on Information and Communication Technologies Research Paper*.

Gladwell, M. (2000) *The Tipping Point*, New York: Little Brown.

Grint, K. and Woolgar S. (1997) *The Machine at Work: Technology, Work and Organization*, Oxford: Polity Press.

Haddon, L. and Silverstone, R. (1993) Teleworking in the 1990s: A View From the Home, SPRU/CICT Report Series, No. 10, University of Sussex, August.

Hamilton, J. and Thompson, A. (1992) 'The Adoption and Diffusion of an Electronic Network for Education', Proceedings of Convention of the Association for Educational Communications and Technology Division, ERIC Document Reproduction Service No: ED 347 99.

Houston, D. (2006) 'Mobile Governance', *Juniper Research White Paper*, London.

India Elections http://news.bbc.co.uk/1/hi/world/south_asia/3493474.stm.

Jacobsen, D.M. (2000) 'Examining Technology Adoption Patterns by Faculty in Higher Education', Proceedings of Ace 2000, Learning Technologies, Teaching and the Future of Schools, Melbourne, Australia.

Jackson, P. and Irani, Z. (2007) The Virtual Research Institute into e-Government, available at www.iseing.org.

Kent County Council (2006) http://www.kent.gov.uk/SocialCare/adults-and-older-people/self-assessment/ accessed August 2006.

Ling, R. (2002) 'The Diffusion of Mobile Telephony Among Norwegian Teens: A Report from After the Revolution', *Annales des télécommunications* 47 pp. 210–25.

Love Lewisham (2006) http://www.lovelewisham.org accessed April 2008.

MacKenzie, D. and Wajcman, J. (1999) (eds) *The Social Shaping of Technology*, Buckingham: Open University, 2nd edn.

Mallard, A. (2005) 'Following the Emergence of Unpredictable Use? New Stakes and Tasks for a Social Scientific Understanding of ICT Uses'.

In *The Good, Bad, Irrelevant: The User and the Future of Information and Communication Technologies*, Conference Proceedings 3–5 Sept, pp. 116–24.

Mobile Data Association (2006) Press Release 15 August www.themda.org.

O2 (2004) 'Options: Mobile Technology in Public Service' Christian Asare (compiler) mmO2 Slough.

Porter, M.E. and Millar, V.E. (1985) 'How Information gives you Competitive Advantage', *Harvard Business Review*, 63(4) pp. 149–60.

Rogers, E.M. (1962) *Diffusion of Innovations*, New York: Free Press.

Rosen, E. (2000) *The Anatomy of Buzz*, New York: Doubleday.

Sellen, A. and Harper R. (2001) *The Myth of the Paperless Office*, Cambridge, MA: MIT.

Shih and Venkatesh (2004) Beyond Adoption: Development and Application of a Use-Diffusion Model, *Journal of Marketing*, 68(1) pp. 59–74.

Simon, H.A. (1987) 'The Steam Engine and the Computer: What Makes Technology Revolutionary' *EDUCOM Bulletin*, 22(1) pp. 2–5.

Sinclair, D. (2006) e-Government, public services and older people http://www.egovmonitor.com/node/6662 17 July.

Surowiecki, J. (2005) *The Wisdom of Crowds*, London: Abacus.

Taylor, A. and Vincent J. (2005) 'An SMS History'. In Hamill L. and Lasen A. (eds). *Mobiles, Past Present and Future*, London: Springer.

Vincent, J. (2004a) 'Social Shaping of e-Government – What can we Learn from Mobile Mediated Communications?' In Budd L. and Harris L. (eds). *e-Economy: Rhetoric or Business Reality?* London: Routledge.

Vincent, J. Haddon, L. and Hamill, L. (2005) 'The Influence Of Mobile Phone Users On The Design Of 3G Products And Services'. In *The Journal of Communications Network* Vol. 4. Part 4 Oct–Dec.

Vincent, J. (2006) 'I Just Can't Live Without My Mobile' *Vodafone receiver* #15 www.vodafone.receiver.com.

Vincent, J. and Harper, R. (2003) 'Social Shaping of UMTS – Preparing the 3G Customer' Report 26 *UMTS Forum* at www.umts-forum.org.

Yaschenko, V.V. (2006). Thesis of the speech by the Head of the Federal Centre for Informatization under the Central Election Commission of Russia V.V. Yaschenko at the session of experts on electronic voting of the member states of the Council of Europe on November 23–24, 2006 in the city of Strasbourg (France) http://www.coe.int/t/e/integrated_projects/democracy/EVoting/Speech%20Yaschenko% 20Nov% 2006.doc.

5

ABANDONED HEROES:

The Decline of ICT Business Support

ALAN RAE

Introduction

This chapter looks at the issues of how SMEs use IT, and how the support available to them as they seek to develop and grow their businesses has been progressively reduced. It draws upon the findings of a continuing research project which examines how small firms in the UK use IT and seeks to make some policy recommendations for addressing this problem. Specifically, the chapter falls into three separate sections:

- A review of the rise and fall of government funded ICT support over the last 10 years.
- An account of what these issues look like to some representative SMEs that we interviewed.
- Some thoughts from the analysis of these interviews as to what progress could be made if a more pragmatic approach were to be taken by government towards small business support.

The Rise and Fall of ICT Support for Small Business in the UK – The Quest for Productivity

Small business support has had a chequered history in the UK over the last 10 years. The main channel for support during this period has been Business Link, originally set up in around 1994 by Michael Heseltine during his period as President of the Board of Trade.

It is probably worth rehearsing the argument for why small businesses should be supported at all. After all – they have decided to take their chances with the market and should be prepared to stand or fall by their own efforts. The short answer is that small businesses account for 46.8 per cent of employment and 36.4 per cent of total turnover in the UK (Small Business Service, 2006).

They are for the most part run by 'gifted amateurs' – not in the sense of being amateur in what they do, but in that they generally lack much formal business training and tend, quite rightly, to be suspicious of too much qualification, accreditation and regulation and indeed of those who promulgate it without having to take the consequences. However, growth of these organisations to provide the yeast that UK plc so badly needs requires that they are able to deal successfully with the standards of more formal working as their companies grow.

In today's world the only way that small firms can cope with the demands of their corporate partners and the regulatory authorities for structured information is to use ICT in an increasingly sophisticated and effective way. One of the unexpected findings of the research project that the author carried out recently in conjunction with academic colleagues at Brunel and Royal Holloway Universities is the extent to which regulation is a key driver of ICT uptake in the logistics and food manufacturing sectors – mainly due to the exigencies of the drive time and ingredient traceability regulations respectively (Rae et al, 2007).

It seems only right that if government seeks to impose additional costs on small businesses they should be prepared to fund the learning that is required to comply with this imposition in the first place. British governments perennially agonise about how business in general, and small business in particular, fails to measure up to the exemplars of the day. Today the obsession is the perceived productivity gap between UK small business and their transatlantic cousins. This is further documented in the SEEDA regional economic strategy evidence base. It identifies that even the best performing UK regions in terms of GVA and productivity per head lag seriously (>50 per cent) behind equivalent regions in Europe and the US.

Traditionally most research work into productivity has been carried out on the performance of manufacturing companies – mainly because it has proven difficult to come to an overall structure for service companies. Where organisations are transactionally based – such as gas, electricity or phone – the value of what is delivered is relatively easy to quantify. Services are based on outcomes – such as 'have I got better?', 'has this advice allowed me to save money?', 'how much revenue has this marketing campaign actually generated?' – are intrinsically more difficult to measure. Current thinking looks at the growth of value in the organisation based on Gross Value Added per employee or Return on Capital Employed. For listed companies, Tobins 'Q' is a useful measure that compares the book value of the assets with market value as represented on the stock market.

In fact, productivity gains have been achieved largely by taking cost out of communication and transaction through use of the Internet. There has been considerable debate as to why US companies have been so much more successful at boosting productivity through IT, but deeper analysis shows that it comes almost entirely from three sectors – Publishing, Retail and Wholesale. The reasons are spelled out in a paper entitled 'Where are the profits in e-Commerce?' presented at the World ICT congress in 2000. Professor Paul Strassner identified that profits from e-Commerce come from reduction of information costs in retail and wholesale activities.

Table 5.1 illustrates where the savings can be made in a typical distribution chain. This issue, however, runs deeper than simply throwing ICT at the problem. Bloom et al (2005) compared productivity in US, UK, French and German manufacturing companies and found that the key variables were best management practices, but inversely related to company age. The key data are set out in Table 5.2.

Table 5.1 Distribution Chain Savings (Strassner 2000)

	Relative Size	Information Costs	% From Which Productivity Can Come
Manufacturing	100	34	34
Wholesale	27	23.5	87.04
Retail	31	24	77.42
Total	158	81.5	51.58

Table 5.2 Productivity by Company Size and Country of Operation

	Total	UK	US	Germany	France
Firms	731	152	289	154	136
Median Size	690	418	1,251	974	311
% MBAs	1	0.97	1.89	0.07	0.2
% Graduates	21	13.5	30.6	14.2	15.4
ROCE	9.94	10.89	5.84	12.9	15.38
Tobin's Q	2.51	2.01	2.87	1.77	1.31

The study jointly carried out between the LSE and McKinsey's found that productivity is gained by documentation, targets and performance management and obtaining and rewarding the best people to run processes that take cost out of the business model wherever possible. This means through use of ICT in general, and Internet-mediated processes in particular, but it also requires a substantial amount of focused people management to make it work effectively.

The whole issue of staff motivation and customer orientation is key, particularly for a service business. Olins (2003) says that the difference between selling products and services is that getting consistency is much harder in a service business: 'Chocolate doesn't get tired, it doesn't get sick, it doesn't answer back'. He goes on to observe that in services, 50 per cent of time, energy and marketing budget has to go on motivating the troops to stay on message.

The problem for a small business is that while the founder is doing the work, this looks after itself. Once the business starts to scale, however, it gets lost because the founders forget that other people do not have their motivation and commitment to the business. Developing such a company culture requires looking at the business holistically and integrating the numbers with the people with the vision with the customer interface. Much of this is intangible value which most small companies are at a loss as to how to measure and track.

The thought leaders in measuring the role of intangibles in business development are the Swedish insurance company Skandia. They publish some of these indicators in their balance sheet. Broadly speaking they follow the principles of the balanced scorecard. They combine hard-edged financial measures with some equally specific measures of their outputs. It is essential to decide what are the key outputs for the business in question and combine them with some more generic ones.

Benchmarking data are available in the public domain. The SBS commissioned Cranfield to measure a representative sample of small and medium organisations across all major business sectors (Neely, 2002). A suggested spread of measures suitable for SMEs was developed by the author in a project called e-Tranee which aimed at e-enablement of Eastern European transport companies. We came to believe that it would be beneficial to use some of these indicators to monitor the effect on business performance brought about by the application of ICTs including internet operations. More details are available here at: www.bcsmanagementservices.com/assets/applets/ Closing_the_Gap_3.pdf.

These can be related to a full balanced scorecard or a simpler schema shown in Figure 5.1 which essentially asks the questions:

1. Are we relating well to the customers?
2. Are our internal operational procedures ok?
3. Do we get the stuff to the customers ok?

If we could get small companies to ask these questions in a structured and logical way and use it to decide what the next sensible IT investment should be, then some real progress would be made.

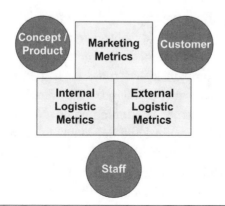

Figure 5.1 Indicators of Business Performance.

Realising this productivity means using IT – to manage relationships with the customer, to track progress, to promote the business and take cost out of its processes and to handle the increased burden of compliance, quality and traceability dictated by the twin pressures of globalisation and government regulation. This is why ICT support is so crucial. No ICT skills means no vibrant small business sector, which means stagnation and unemployment for UK plc.

The history of business support in the UK over the last 15 years is the story of Business Link. To be fair, in the early days of the Business Link, some real attempts were made to encourage companies to carry out joined-up thinking. For example, in Business Link London West a balanced scorecard analysis was for a time the gateway into funded subsidised consultancy. This included a sensible number of IT and process-related questions. Some noble successes were achieved but the gains were squandered by a policy which was suspicious of technology, did not operate in a joined-up way itself and had no feel for the integration of strategy and tactics which successful entrepreneurs both display themselves and require from whatever training they believe is needed by their organisations.

At the time the UK Government set up Business Link, German industry was still riding high and Heseltine and his team wondered why the UK was not able to support the Mittelstand, that phalanx of companies employing between 500 and 2,000 individuals that formed the backbone of the German Economy. It was probably not appreciated at the time the extent to which this represented markets that had been arrested from consolidation by regulation. It was thought that if only we could persuade and train UK owner-managers to go for growth we could solve several related problems from unemployment to innovation. So a structure was put in place so that would focus on companies that could be helped to grow. Business Link duly recruited teams of advisers who were initially intended to be people with experience of running comparable businesses so that the advice would be practical and delivered with sufficient gravitas to be taken seriously. In practice a salary of £29k was only enough to attract retired bank managers or individuals (like the author) who were in the process of re-inventing themselves. The mix included individuals with skills in marketing, HR and finance plus some specialists in design, innovation and ICT. In those days the emphasis was on direct solution provision and the advisors were targeted on doing a certain amount of direct delivery; and in fact they had income generation targets based on this. While some of the quality of this advice was at best mediocre there was a core group who did some good work with their clients.

Because ICT was traditionally perceived, rightly, as a topic beyond the ordinary advisor's capabilities, the DTI launched the Information Society Initiative in 1995. This provided £100k pump-priming money for each Business Link area of which there were at that time over 100 in England. In addition several major vendors provided free equipment – each ISI centre was provided with a teleconferencing system and one vendor offered a small network of three machines. Microsoft allowed each centre to have free software under their MSDN (developers programme) and Sage followed suit. Most Business Links recruited a full-time manager who was intended to be the ICT adviser, do some proactive work on his or her own account and sweep up queries that his more technically challenged colleagues were unable to deal with.

The Information Society Initiative (ISI) attracted a considerable amount of support in kind from the UK ICT industry and under the guidance of the DTI, organisations such as BT, Oracle, Intel and IBM contributed money and personnel to a number of other supporting initiatives such as the National e-Commerce Awards, Technology Means Business, an accreditation for advisors to ensure that IT advice was given in a business context, and senior individuals such as David Baxter from BT, Jenny Searle from Oracle and Liz Grant from IBM were seconded to head the initiative.

The ISI was renamed UK Online for Business in 1999 and deployed a team of 200–300 advisors, produced a large amount of educational material and was quite heavily funded for the next few years as part of the government's ambition to make the UK the best place to do electronic business. In the early days of the Blair Government, various white papers were produced by the DTI which focused on the need to e-enable small businesses and a clear e-Adoption ladder was defined with various diagnostics being produced, as shown in Figure 5.2.

E-adoption ladder

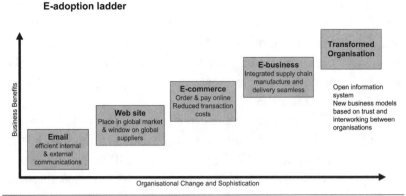

Figure 5.2 The DTI e-Adoption Ladder (DTI 1999).

The ladder has since been criticised for being too simplistic and not reflective of reality where different types of business enter at different points on the ladder, and for some the lower levels are quite sufficient. A survey of the situation in the East Midlands around 2005 defined eight levels defined in a more operational way – asking questions such as 'did the companies accept or make payments online, did they trade online or offer online tracking?' For more details see www. ebusinessclub.biz/projects/eAdoption_Survey.html. The advisors were supported by an active network management programme which made provision for annual conferences, best practice surveys for centre management, a list server and central database of information which allowed advisors to effectively ask the audience for help on problems that they couldn't deal with from their own immediate experience. This enabled the collective knowledge bank of 200–300 advisers to be focused on customer issues.

However, there is an inherent gulf between the view of the world that the SME has, and the 'official' view of the world taken by Policy Makers and the Education and IT industries. In essence the official view is that there are users of technology on the one hand and IT professionals on the other. This of course ignores the great majority of SMEs that have networks, broadband connections and systems that are managed by 'gifted amateurs', namely people with a different day-job. The decisions as to what was appropriate content were generally made by a combination of senior people in the DTI and senior individuals in the vendor organisations. In the UK the vendors tend to be sales and marketing operations that do not have any great expertise of how the products are used directly. The channel structure for distribution means that the actual knowledge is held with the value added resellers.

Senior staff of large organisations often miss something else which is fundamental to the way in which small businesses operate – and that is the integration of strategy with implementation. Most large organisations operate on the view that senior people 'do strategy' and that the wise leader does not get bogged down in the detail of how the vision is actually implemented. In a small organisation the owner manager does not have that luxury as he will often be one of the workers himself. This means that the attitude to detail will be dramatically different. Small business owners will often want technical answers to technical problems in fairly short order, but not in quite the same way that an IT professional will. This caused some anomalies, because most of the training materials that were produced were long on vision and short on the 'how to'. The accreditation standards that were produced tended to be commissioned to fit into the NVQ framework which had been devised to suit the needs of further education dealing with school leavers, rather than for mature individuals with a lifetime of achievement behind them. Consequently they were 'over-engineered for purpose' and met with resistance from the individuals that they were designed to help.

In 2001, the Government implemented a change in the way small business support was delivered. The Business Link organisations – which had been up to that point organised in different ways in different areas – for example as a subsidiary of the Training and Enterprise Councils (TECs), run by the local Chamber of Commerce, or subcontracted to third-party organisations – were put on a common footing. Considerable amalgamation took place; in London for instance eight Business Links were merged into one organisation and these were henceforth to be treated as franchises to be bid for. In most cases the incumbent organisation was successful. The emphasis at this time was changed so that instead of 'competing' with the private sector for delivery of consultancy, a 'coaching and mentoring' model would be adopted. In parallel with this, considerable funds were made available for expansions of the UK Online for Business offer. One, called the Local Partnership Fund, was earmarked for developing the service offer. The other was to expand the number of individuals available to give advice.

The additional manpower was viewed as a mixed blessing as the funding was only to run for two years. As most of the organisations were struggling with the TUPE (transfer under protected employment) issues caused by closing one set of organisations down and starting up another set, many Business Links considered it imprudent to recruit staff they would later have to shed, and instead spent the money on subcontracted advice. The Local Partnership fund fared better. In some areas, the advisors were able to get together, specify what they needed and organise to develop the training programmes, fact sheets and diagnostics that they needed to give effective advice. From 2001 to 2004, the Government was still keen to be seen to be encouraging e-enablement and much good work went into producing case studies to encourage SMEs, both paper-based and video.

A less successful initiative at this time was the e-Commerce clubs which were set up in partnership with the National Chamber of Commerce movement. These allowed for UK Online for Business advisers and representatives of the major sponsoring vendors to run events to help SMEs engage with the e-Business agenda. Unfortunately the prevailing ethos of 'let's not get too technical' meant that the representatives put forward were unable to answer the questions raised by the few genuine owners who attended.

In parallel with these developments in the Business Link/Uk Online for Business area, the TECs were abolished and replaced with what was effectively direct rule from the DfES in the form of the Learning and Skills Councils. These were far more prescriptive than the organisations they replaced and struggled from the fact that the brightest and best of the TEC employees voted with their feet and moved on. Five years on they have been reorganised three times and have effectively channelled most of the discretionary adult vocational funding into remedial reading and writing for 16–19-year-olds. They seem to display no awareness of the importance of IT and almost exclusively focus on NVQ level 2 qualifications based on the current requirements for training providers under 'Train to Gain' – the current small business training offer (2008).

The net effect of all these changes was an increasing bureaucratisation as to how funded projects were managed, and a progressive reduction in the ability for innovative approaches suited to the particular psychological needs of small organisations to be funded. By 2004 it was considered necessary to take photostats of beneficiaries' passports in order to deliver basic IT training. Compliance and monitoring actually had become more important than the suitability of the content. In 2004 the UK Online for Business initiative was wound up on the assumption that ICT in business advice was now 'mainstream' and that any generalist business adviser should be able to rise to the occasion. In parallel with this the other specialist advisors in innovation and design were phased out. This resulted in all of the SME-orientated literature being withdrawn including a substantial number of useful case studies. The Business Link itself has progressively streamlined the service it offers and has moved almost entirely to a diagnostic and brokerage service. Brokerage had been ostensibly to a National Consultants Register. This is currently in the process of being wound up. Management of funding has been transferred from the DTI to the Regional Development Agencies, while the number of initiatives and programmes has been drastically cut, thus losing an invaluable repository of information about what small organisations were actually doing. The evolution of these initiatives is summarised in Figure 5.3.

Before progressing to the review of the current situation for small company support, it is worth reviewing the performance of two key players in this space: Sector Skills Council and the Technology Means Business Accreditation. Sector Skills Councils (SSCs) were set up to be the vehicle for ascertaining and implementing the training needs of particular industries. Some industrial sectors were still not covered, but e-skills has done a sound job in collating and structuring an approach to IT skills with initiatives such as the e-Skills Passport and SFIA (Skills Framework for the Information Age) which is a complete framework tied back to the NVQ system for assessing training for users and IT professionals. It is currently developing a diagnostic tool to aid small businesses in selecting appropriate technologies.

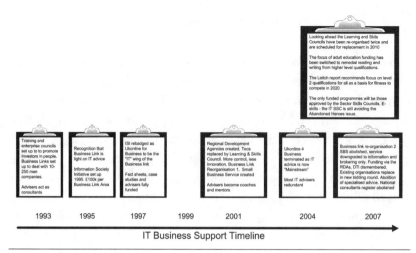

Figure 5.3 Business Link Timeline.

However, it has not recognised the need for some 'IT Paramedic' Training to suit the needs of small businesses who have to maintain sometimes moderately complex systems without any officially qualified IT staff. It is possible that a new approach, the National Vocational Qualification for IT Users (ITQ) which demonstrates staff competence in the use of IT in the workplace will address some of these issues.

Technology Means Business was a bold attempt to deal with the perennial problem that IT companies tend to promote products and services and analyse the technological solutions that are required purely in IT terms without reference to the business objectives. The original programme was funded by the DTI and major vendors such as BT, Intel and HP. The original implementation was contracted to an organisation which based it on an intensive NVQ-type 'tick-boxing' approach. This meant that it was extremely cumbersome and time-consuming to complete. Originally it was to be mandatory for individuals giving ICT advice within the Business Link. BT and PC World were also originally part of the scheme and were committed to putting their advisers through the programme. However, the complexity of it caused them to abandon the scheme so that eventually only the Business Link advisors and a few independents bought into the accreditation – which at £1,000 a head was not cheap. The scheme has been amended twice. The re-accreditation process was simplified and eventually became a good system consisting of a knowledge test and an updatable portfolio of evidence that checked the individual's ability to deliver advice in a business context (for more details see www.tmb.org.uk). HP did use the system for a while for their larger SME-orientated partnerships, but no other major player committed to it. With the transfer of responsibility for SME business support to the RDAs its future looks uncertain, mainly because its initial complication caused the mainstream ICT industry to lose interest.

The next section of the chapter will examine some practical implications of the changing nature of government business support as discussed above with reference to the experiences of a number of case study firms.

SME ICT Adoption in Practice

Many SMEs find themselves in a difficult situation where IT is concerned. They are often too small to be able to afford to employ a dedicated ICT expert and lack the money to buy consultancy advice (or the experience to have confidence in its reliability). Despite all the efforts describe in the introduction, they often have limited experience in selecting, implementing and evaluating suggested ICT solutions. So the provision of effective ICT support to SMEs is still considered an area of market failure. As the introduction shows, supporting the SME sector has been a key policy aim of successive UK governments but the amount of resource available in today's climate is much less than in the past.

The research team from Royal Holloway and Brunel carried out research in two main phases. The first focused on how small companies use IT to run and promote their business. The second phase culminated in the development of a workshop and other training materials which collectively became known as 'Punch above your Weight'. We carried out a number of in-depth interviews with early adopters who were specifically using Web 2.0 techniques to leverage their online marketing in a way that was integrated into the fabric of their business in a holistic way. Many of this group were consciously adopting some of the behaviour patterns that were identified by conversations with some of the more advanced members of the first phase of the project.

In the first phase we talked to over 400 SMEs in the food, logistics, media and Internet services industries. These industries are particularly important to the economy of the region. The aim was to identify good practice amongst SMEs and highlight any areas of concern. The firms were initially contacted by phone, and over 50 of these also provided follow up face-to-face in-depth interviews.

The findings have been published in a report called 'Abandoned Heroes' Rae et al (2007) which is available via www.howtodo business.com or www.westfocus.org.uk/ICT/Home_3.aspx.

In summary:

- We found enormous creativity and self-reliance in the small business sector. Use of broadband, email and the Internet is pervasive and most find that their use of ICT has been beneficial. Eighty-five per cent of those surveyed said they had got good value for money from their ICT investments.
- They use ICT to keep up with their competitors, to increase their sales and marketing activity and to reduce costs through operational efficiency and improved quality. ICT enables them to collaborate more closely with their customers, suppliers and other supply chain partners. Many see the use of ICT as an opportunity to operate nationally and internationally and not just regionally. Interestingly, most of this investment is funded from retained profits.
- They believe in training their staff in order to upgrade their ICT skills, but are concerned about the costs of so doing. They are not so worried that if they train them they will move on, being confident of their ability to inspire loyalty in those who work with them.
- There is a degree of complacency exhibited about ICT security. Surprisingly, this was worse in the media and internet services sectors, with the food and logistics sectors seemingly more used to operating with the discipline needed for high levels of security. This seems to be connected to the need for systematic working in these sectors driven by the pressure of compliance. In

particular, operating in the food industry imposes demands for food traceability and in the logistics industry sectors there are requirements for recording drivers' working times. So one unexpected finding of the study was the degree to which the need for compliance is a major driver of ICT practice in these groups.

- We found that progress in the deployment of ICT typically depends on a single individual with vision who takes full responsibility for ICT initiatives, as well as continuing with their regular business activities. They often have to rely on their own self-taught expertise and feel ill-equipped to carry out the implementation tasks required of them.

- They make little use of the formal methods of ICT project management or evaluation and feel at the mercy of the external consultants and suppliers on whom they have to rely. They tend to choose these on the basis of personal recommendations, past experience and cost. Nonetheless, they typically bring in ICT projects on time and on budget, despite having to overcome the most challenging aspect of implementation – overcoming resistance to change.

- Our findings were generally supported by a study carried out by the IOD (2006) who found that most of their members were already committed to wi-fi, were using laptops in place of desk-top computers and, most interestingly, were moving to hybrid support solutions where external providers carried out some of the work in conjunction with an individual working within the organisation itself.

These individuals are the 'Abandoned Heroes' of this report's title which was inspired because they make very little use of Government funded support, expressing the view that what is available simply doesn't relate to their real issues. They find it difficult to get good ICT advice, and they feel let down by the commercial sector, being concerned by the costs and vested interests associated with suppliers and consultants. However, they also feel neglected by government-supported sources of advice and guidance. Less than a quarter of the companies surveyed had had any contact with Business Link. There was scarcely any interaction with any other government organisation, with only one company (out of over 400 surveyed) having had any interaction with e-Skills.

Our interviewees expressed the need for access to detailed quality technical advice, available in a way and at a price that met their needs. SMEs have very different needs from large corporates, as they typically lack ICT professionals. We found that while the companies and individuals involved were very ready to rise to ICT challenges, they often found that the process was demanding and actually quite difficult for them personally: 'Just the thought of backing all that data up makes me want to go and hide under the desk' said one interviewee.

SMEs are notoriously averse to committing to extended formal training. They feel they need to be able to see a quick return and they are keenly aware of the opportunity costs of time spent out of the office. The truth for SMEs is that 'free' is not really free, it is the time spent with the eye off the ball that deters the owner manager. They don't seem to trust the ICT industry. There is a real structural issue as there is insufficient margin for larger Value Added Resellers (VARs) to focus much attention on SMEs. Progress can occur if a trust relationship is built with an affordable ICT supplier, and indeed some success has been achieved by the industry in remote support of SME systems from both local VARs and organisations such as PC World. The SMEs recognised that they were often overdependent on outside contractors – over half used external consultants to implement ICT. However around 30 per cent used 'other' methods – from the evidence of the in-depth interviews we interpret this as meaning that they are solving the problems themselves – hence the title of Abandoned Heroes.

About 20 per cent of the companies surveyed were using out-of-date or unreliable equipment. They recognised that something needed to be done but were holding back. The main barriers to implementation were:

- uncertainty about the cost,
- lack of trust in the ICT firms who pitch for the business because they do not have the in-house skills to check if the information they are given is correct, and

- inability to afford the disruption that will occur if things do not go smoothly.

Money seemed to be less of a barrier than fear of getting into something they cannot get out of. They reported that keeping to time and budget is the most challenging aspect of implementation, followed by overcoming resistance to change. This means they wait until they find a supplier they can trust based on personal recommendation, past experience and cost – or they do it themselves.

However, review of the in-depth interviews suggested that there was more than one way of doing it yourself. Companies in more traditional businesses often struggle to provide an entry level version of the official way of building and supporting a network. However some of the early adopters we studied, particularly in the media, IT and business services segments of the market, have started to take another route entirely and are operating successfully using tools such as social networking sites, collaborative document sharing environments such as Basecamp and other externally hosted services accessed via an online browser to connect with their data and collaborating organisations. In its pure form this means a company can function effectively with a laptop and a wi-fi broadband connection. They have the choice of following the conventional route of progressively increasing both their IT skills and their IT intensity, or they can simply increase their own IT skills and keep the amount of IT equipment they use to the minimum. We have christened these Route A for the conventional route and Route B for those who take the more innovative approach.

When we interviewed individuals who had chosen to follow Route B and keep the IT intensity low, it appeared that they had all achieved a reasonable standard of IT proficiency suitable for their needs as a 'Web 2.0 warrior'. However, they had largely acquired the necessary expertise either on their own by trial and error, or they had learned it from their peers. There was little evidence of any attempt to learn through the 'official' channels which were generally perceived as out-of-date and time-consuming. And little interest in the kind of formal training and accreditation routes beloved of the education industry, professional bodies, sector skills councils and the authors of the Leitch report (2006).

Our report concluded that if we are ever to re-develop an effective IT small business support regime in the UK, policy makers will need to engage more effectively with the motivations and requirements of the small business community.

The Way Forward

If the 'Abandoned Heroes' of our research are to be helped, they need various support structures to help them:

- identify what they need to do next,
- reduce the uncertainty and risk attached to what often feels like a leap in the dark, and
- acquire, inexpensively and expeditiously, the knowledge that they need to confidently support the implementation that they need to carry out.

They need images of what is possible, plus the reassurance that it is possible for them to achieve the same thing with the knowledge and support necessary for such transformations to be carried through safely. They need knowledge to be supplied on demand in 'bite-sized chunks'. If they need to follow Route A and be able to support and troubleshoot a network once it is set up, then a suitable course needs to be put together on a 'need to know' basis using sections of industry standard training such as A+ and Net+ and delivered in ways appropriate to time-poor audiences.

The images could be dealt with by case studies which show what other companies have achieved. These might build on the excellent precursors from the UKOnline4Business project, but should also contain somewhat more technical detail so as to act as a 'recipe' as well as an inspiration. These might be tied to the key areas in a business where people know they need to make progress to get traction. Our research showed that a shortlist of suitable topics that individuals need help with might look like this:

- wireless and VPN,
- customer databases and CRM,

- effective use of Internet tools to build a comprehensive and effective web presence,
- how to use collaborative tools such as Basecamp to strengthen their position in the market through collaboration with other knowledge professionals,
- backup, storage and disaster recovery, and
- industry-specific software and issues.

However, above all we need an effective, grounded theory of small business growth within a holistic model which allows tracking of the successful development of the business. This typology was one of the outputs from our research. Overwhelmingly, small businesses only employ the founder, and these individuals are often loners who can be reluctant to work with others. Alternatively, two people working together can be a very productive association, as shown by the many husband and wife companies. We found that many of the barriers that companies struggle with at the lower end are due to a lifestyle business obtaining some success before starting to hit the limits of the founder to grow the business unaided. In some cases they did not want to engage with the formality and the discipline of working as part of a team that emerges as the business grows.

The first 'sweet spot' is the traditional 5–12 person 'hunter gatherer' band. It is easy enough for one person to lead a team of this size. However, much employee legislation starts to impact when there are more than five employees, meaning that the growing company has to start to cope with regulatory and compliance issues. In addition, the need to secure a baseline sales pipeline is likely to require interacting with larger organisations that may demand more formal ways of doing business, such as a formal Pre-qualification Questionnaire and tendering process, meeting rigorous Service Level Agreements (SLAs) and Key Performance Indicators (KPIs).

These considerations drive a transition which we refer to as the 'Dawn of Formality'. It is the point where systems are put in place, investment in an IT infrastructure needs to occur, and delivery as well as sales is starting to become an issue. Our study highlighted that organisations cannot deal effectively with this transition unless they have someone at senior level who is able to deal with the process effectively, but many small business owners simply do not want to go there. They either continue to ply their trade as 'technicians' or they find ways to collaborate with other professionals to provide a complete solution informally and avoid the need to formalise themselves. We discuss the techniques used by this group of gifted amateurs to promote themselves effectively in another paper (Harris, Rae and Grewal 2008).

Once the company has grown to 20 employees, with a core management team in place, the next task is to grow to 'own its niche' and to develop 'proof of concept' for its business model. For many growth businesses this activity will be aimed at getting the business ready for sale or for additional financial injection. This means creating an entity which is either going to be a 'cash cow' or is going to be scalable so that its proven niche model can become global. We have defined this as the 'scalability' transition. To achieve this, the organisation will need to ensure that its delivery, IT and HR systems are both robust and scalable. In addition it will need to develop its innovation capacity so that it can identify and deliver new products and services as required.

Jones and Hwang (2002) found that focusing on the following key behaviours led to consistent timely, reliable, responsive and friendly service and delivered greater profit based on budgeting, objectives and controls, efficient use of labour and lower marketing costs:

- delegation;
- multi-skilling;
- recognition, pay, rewards, incentives;
- appraisal;
- more careful recruitment of new staff;
- high degree of team working and
- strong partnership with stakeholders.

Creating these systems and behaviours are the key tasks of an organisation moving towards scalability. The rewards will be lower staff turnover and higher average customer spend. Our work showed that businesses cluster at certain preferred sizes due to interpersonal dynamics. The key issue is that in order to break through any of the identified barriers, a business has to change the way it behaves.

To be fair, the original incarnation of the Business Link idea did aim to get people to think in an integrated way. While the skills and enterprise agendas were united prior to the dissolution of the TECs in 2001, the pressure to get small companies to sign up for 'Investors in People' did push the agenda towards joined-up management. The adoption of the Business Excellence Model as a template (which is still retained as part of the rhetoric) at least does take a holistic approach with the right-hand side of the map aligned quite closely to the balanced scorecard. The trouble is that it has never been effectively mapped to the underpinning IT systems that are required to deliver on the vision. With the move to the brokerage model, the name of the game has become a quick diagnosis followed by identification of enough private sector providers to allow a competitive bidding operation to take place. Since these tend to be selected for their specialist abilities, the role of the adviser as the overall consultative guardian of the integrity of the joined-up vision has been lost.

Companies embark on a journey. There are some critical milestones that have to be faced and passed. Not all companies want to grow. In fact the vast majority of them will never employ more than four people. These stages are:

- defining the offer,
- finding customers,
- getting established,
- achieving the dawn of formality,
- achieving the cornerstone management team,
- proving the concept by dominating the niche and
- preparing for scalability.

Achieving all of these stages means marrying competences in marketing, people management and system design and implementation. However many people will only go one or two steps of the way – our early adopters only became fluent in a specific set of skills. The 'dawn of formality' requires someone who can manage a network; only when we get to the 'scalability' transition do we have anything that aligns with the 'official' demarcation line between users and professionals.

What has been lost is the engineering tradition that developed elegant structures through a combination of analytic thought

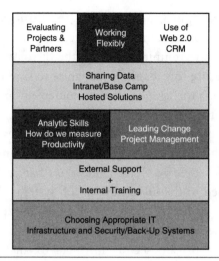

Diagram 5.4 Technologies for e-Enablement.

balanced with practical empirical experience which is necessary to create effective processes with 'just enough' structure. Just as Senge (1990) identified five core technologies needed to build a learning organisation, there are a core set of technologies that SMEs can adopt to fully e-enable their companies, as shown in Figure 5.4.

We believe that implementation projects can be developed around these blocks and that measures of improvement in productivity can be devised to suit these. 'Bite-sized chunks' of information to support this framework and contextualise these should be made available through integrated offers via - transfer partnerships between Universities, Development Agencies and Vendors. Particular topics that would deliver some real productivity gains to our prospective 'e-gazelles' might include:

- how to install and secure a wi-fi network with broadband,
- how to maintain a small business server network once it has been effectively installed,
- how to set up a secure VPN connection for remote working,
- backup, Security and Disaster recovery training,
- effective outsourcing,
- theory and practice of effective customer database systems,
- how to set up a secure area for collaborative working,

- effective use of Web 2.0 marketing techniques, and
- the leadership, analytic and project management skills needed to make innovations stick.

We believe that there is a real need to establish which approaches – be it training, advice or support – would help the rugged individualists who are directing and implementing the IT infrastructure of their companies without currently much in the way of support. Vendors in particular might capitalise on the growth of complexity in the infrastructure that the 'Abandoned Heroes' seek to manage by developing and bundling in 'IT Paramedic' training with the provision of technical support – as a kind of 'hybrid service'. Interestingly a recent study by the IOD reported a significant growth in hybrid arrangements of this type.

Our research shows that generally people seek advice from their peers followed by their trusted advisers. One approach to knowledge transfer might be a structured 'Ask the Expert' website. A precursor of this approach was successfully used in the list server set up to support UKOnline4 Business advisors. An excellent current example of this in action is the online-networking site Ecademy where people can ask a question of whoever is online in real time. This generally produces several usable suggestions in less than an hour.

Most of the early adopters we talked to during the 'Punch above your Weight' phase of the project had in fact learned most of the techniques they used by networking online and offline via social networking organisations such as Ecademy. If technical support individuals from key Telco and ICT vendors were available to supplement peer input this could prove to be a valuable resource (and might well lead to additional sales). Involvement of universities as 'honest brokers' as part of their technology-transfer role would maintain the image of impartiality which may be necessary to reassure the SMEs.

Bite-sized interactive information modules focused on practical case studies could be produced to benefit the SME sector. They need to contain sufficient technical content to allow a semi-technical responsible individual to 'pick up the ball and run with it'. In small companies the strategist often has to get his/her boots wet. One of the issues with UK Online for Business was that it erred in favour of the strategic rather than the detailed. In the corporate and public sector worlds strategy and tactics do not meet very much. In the SME domain integration of these two is the touchstone of success.

We believe that there is real scope to develop tools, courses and information that addresses the needs of the small business as it approaches the different levels of the hierarchy that was outlined above. While the transitions around the scalability issue will undoubtedly require professional IT support both within and without the organisation, much of the learning for the earlier transitions will be better if it sits in an informal environment. There may be some benefit in formal monitoring and accreditation, but few of the prospective clients will perceive much merit in it. It is perfectly possible to combine informality with rigour. It will just require a shift in the value systems of policy makers to achieve it.

Conclusion

If we start from the premise that a vibrant small business sector is a prerequisite of a successful modern economy, we need to ensure that support, guidance and implementation is there to allow them to grow effectively to whatever level is suitable for the owners and employees to fulfil their aspirations. We have seen that organisations have a choice in how far and how fast they grow along a clearly defined continuum of process and underlying support system. The best work that has been carried out in the area of small business support suggests that companies need to be encouraged to acquire a holistic view of how their business can progress.

However, if information and training is to be accepted and successful it needs to be:

- practical,
- detailed,
- structured,
- bite-sized,
- informal and non-accredited.

Where accreditation IS necessary it should be in line with industry-defined and hence widely accepted qualifications rather than confections of the LSC/SSC/educational complex developed in vacuo. We need to integrate analytic systems thinking with the practical day-to-day imperatives of acquiring and satisfying customers. The best features of what has been lost should be revived but integrated with a lively, moderated, online learning and networking environment which also supports offline networking in the way that the best practice social networks such as Ecademy do. Only then can the necessary overview be applied to the different styles of business model practised by twenty-first century entrepreneurs. This is a much more exciting and engaging vision than the aridities of the Leitch report, which sees nothing beyond remedial reading and writing and a limited set of SSC-approved training packages as the route to UK competitiveness in 2020.

Bibliography

Bloom, N. et al (2005) 'Management Practices across Firms and Nations', *Centre for Economic Performance*, London: School of Economics and McKinsey & Company.

Gerber, M. (1995) *The e-myth Revisited: Why most Small Businesses Don't Work and What to do about it*, New York: Harper Collins.

Harris, L., Rae, A. and Grewal, S. (2008) 'Out on the Pull: How Small Firms are Making Themselves Sexy with Online Promotional Techniques', *International Journal of Technology Marketing*, Vol. 3, No. 2.

Institute of Directors Policy Paper (2006) 'Small and Medium Enterprises: Successful Growth Through ICT Investment' at www.iod.com/ intershoproot/eCS/Store/en/pdfs/policy_paper_sme_dell.pdf.

Jones, P. and Hwang, J. (2002) 'Improving Business Performance in Service SMEs: Modelling Best Practice', 25th ISBA *National Small Firms Policy and Research Conference*.

Leitch Review of Skills (2006) 'Prosperity for All in the Global Economy – World Class Skills', *HM Treasury*.

Neely, A. (2002) 'Closing the Gap 3', *SBS/Cranfield Benchmarking Data*.

Olins, W. (2003) *Olins on Brand*, London: Thames and Hudson.

Rae, A. et al (2007) '*Abandoned Heroes*' available from www .westfocus.org.uk/ ICT/Home_3.aspx.

Senge, P. M. (1990) *The Fifth Discipline*, New York: Random House.

Strassner, P. (2000) 'Where are the Profits in e-Commerce?' Paper presented at the *World ICT Congress*.

6

COLLATERAL DAMAGE? THE IMPACT OF GOVERNMENT POLICY ON UK HIGHER EDUCATION

SIMRAN GREWAL

Introduction

The aim of this chapter is to explore the impact of UK government policy on higher education since the 1980s. The focal point for discussion will centre on the rationale that government policy to widen and increase student participation is a key factor driving UK universities to invest in e-Mediated learning technologies. Many higher institutions of learning in the UK believe that e-mediated learning technology can provide a panacea to meet the demands created through these policies by increasing efficiency and reducing work tasks. Yet, there is conflicting evidence on the extent to which such technologies can provide a blanket solution. As such, this chapter will present the findings from an empirical investigation, which highlights how such technologies redefine academic staff roles and restructure work tasks roles rather than reduce work tasks and thus bring the consequences of government policy on UK higher education to the forefront.

A useful way to present the raison d'être of this study is by drawing on the work of Giddens (1996). He suggests that 'although modern institutions have created greater opportunities than any other pre-modern systems there is also a dark side to these opportunities'. As such, it can be argued that he views modernity as a 'double-edged' sword, in that consequences are an inevitable outcome of opportunities. Whilst this chapter does not intend to provide an in-depth deliberation of sociological constructs, Gidden's notion of the consequences of modernity provides a useful framework which helps to put into context the impact of UK government policy on the UK higher education sector.

Market Forces

Grewal (2004) suggests that social, technical, economic and political factors create both an opportunity and a threat for UK higher education. Both external macro and internal micro pressures are driving fundamental changes to UK government policy on higher education. One of the key factors driving change is competition from other countries, for example global institutions of higher education are offering education via e-mediated learning technologies into those markets that have traditionally belonged to the UK. If UK higher education does not respond as efficiently it will lose not just the potential to develop new markets, but also its share of existing markets. Both the overseas and part-time markets for adult lifelong learning are amenable to e-Delivery and offer the capacity for rapid growth (CVCP HEFCE, 2000). If UK higher education does not keep adapting to meet these needs then others will. However, securing and sustaining such a position demands a considerable investment of funds, time and skills as demonstrated by the failure of the UKeU (UK eUniversities) project.

The UKeU project was backed by the UK government with £62m of funding. It was launched in January 2003 with the aim of bringing UK universities together to deliver university education online at a global level. However, the project was scrapped in 2004 as it faced a number of problems. Firstly, the project failed to attract any private investment. Funding of approximately £120 million was required. Secondly, UKeU only signed up 900 students against a target of over 5,000 in the second year. Thirdly, the Open University and London University's external degree program pulled back from involvement. It was estimated that these two institutions would bring in 100,000 students between them and the success of the UK's Open University could be emulated online. Fourthly, developing the platform from scratch meant that it was custom-built, inherently riskier and more expensive, since the platform would require constant updating and improvement in order to keep up with competition. Over a third of the total funds, (£20 million) were spent on developing this platform. Fifthly, according to UKeU staff, out of the 900 students recruited, only 215 were actually using the platform, the majority stayed with the systems used by their universities. Finally, staff felt that the project may have still been viable had it been properly managed. Some of the issues raised were a lack of marketing focus, a lack of documented business strategy and an autocratic management style (MacLeod, 2004). Nevertheless, the residual grant originally allocated for the UKeU project has been transferred to the UK government and the Higher Education Funding Council for England's (HEFCE) 10-year strategy for e-Learning project, which was announced in March 2005 (http://www.dfes.gov.uk/elearningstrategy).

Other key government policies acting as a catalyst for the introduction of e-Meditated learning technologies in UK higher education include increased access, widening participation and the introduction of tuition fees. Each of these areas will be discussed later on in the chapter.

Introduction of Private Sector Practices

Whilst external opportunities and threats are driving the implementation of e-Mediated learning technologies in the UK higher education sector, more critically, pressure from the state since the 1980s to introduce private sector practices into the public sector play a fundamental role in the shaping of UK higher education as we know it today. For instance, since the 1980s universities in the UK have been increasing the proportion of income generated from private sources and this is predicted to increase to 47 per cent by 2010. In addition, whilst total public expenditure on UK higher education and student support has increased in real terms since 2004–5, the UK currently spends 1.1 per cent of its GDP on higher education. Yet other countries all invest more in their higher education institutions than the UK. For instance, France, Germany and the Netherlands all contribute approximately 1.5 per cent of their GDP in public funding to higher education, whilst the USA contributes 2.9 per cent (Leitch Report, 2006). It is clear that other countries see that developing the knowledge economy requires better-trained people in the workforce. As such, UK higher education is being forced to adopt private sector practices. Yet, public sector organisations operate simultaneously in a political and public arena; this makes these organisations part of a larger system because of their responsibilities to the government and their citizens and therefore, inherently more difficult to manage.

At a surface level it is claimed that e-Mediated learning technology can provide a cost-efficient means of enhancing the teaching and learning process, and this is one of the key arguments used to support the implementation of the technology into UK higher education. However, exploring beneath the surface reveals that in fact UK government policy for higher education plays a much more substantial role in the shaping of e-mediated learning technology in UK higher education. As a growing number of higher education institutions are currently in the process of using e-Mediated learning technology to meet the external demands of government policy, it is important to understand the issues that the technology brings with it. Some of these issues will be brought to the fore through the empirical research presented later in the chapter, but before these issues can be addressed, it is important to set the context for the study. Thus, the following section will outline the changes taking place in UK higher education since the 1980s. This will be followed by a brief outline of research design and the case study under investigation, before the results from the empirical investigation are discussed and conclusions drawn.

UK Higher Education Post-1980

The 1980s signified a period of enormous change for UK higher education. This was partly to do with the ideology of the government at that time with its emphasis on introducing market forces wherever possible into the public sector. Williams (1991) states: 'There is no doubt that the higher education of the 1990s is much more consumer orientated than the 1970s.' He goes on to say: 'British Higher Educational Institutions are now operating largely as market orientated service enterprises.' (Williams, 1991; 24)

Increased Access

At the beginning of the 1980s there was concern that some universities may have had to close due to a lack of students, but government policy to increase and widen access led to large numbers of 18–30 year olds entering UK higher education. For instance, full-time home student numbers rose from 470,000 in 1979 to 560,000 in 1988 (Williams, 1991). Government reform to increase and widen access resulted in a growth in student numbers by 40 per cent and this number is set to increase to 50 per cent by 2010 (DfES, 2003). The number of students in full-time higher education in 2004/5 was 2,480,145 – this is an increase of 39,635 from 2003/2004 (www.ucas.co.uk, 2006). It signifies a transition from an elite system where in 1962 approximately 6 per cent of the UK population under 21 participated in higher education, to a mass system today where 43 per cent of the population aged between 18 and 30 attend university (DfES, 2006). The current percentage of 18-30 year olds of the UK population in higher education has remained at 43 per cent for the last three years. The expansion is aimed at meeting the demands of employers and the needs of the economy and students. The argument for increased and wider access was proposed in view of the declining numbers of 18-year-olds in the population, and to make these institutions accessible to people from a more diverse background. Growth has become a central aim of universities and the financial incentives attached to growth are becoming more transparent.

Widening Participation

With university income tied directly to student numbers, students are being actively recruited rather than passively selected. Widening access has meant that a more diverse body of students is being targeted. This is leading to different demands, such as part-time study, or e-Delivery. The number of part-time students in UK higher education studying for an undergraduate first degree increased by 82 per cent in 2003 compared to 2002, from 103,545 to 188,360. Part-timers constitute approximately a quarter of all undergraduates and 41.7 per cent of the total number of students in higher education (www.bbc.co.uk, 2005a).

In 2003 the government set a target of attracting a further 50,000 international students to the UK (exclusive of the EU) by 2005 (DfES, 2003). In the academic year beginning 2003/4 there were 213,000 international students in UK higher education institutions (www.bbc.co.uk, 2005b). This number increased to 300,055 in the academic year beginning 2004/5. The numbers of international students entering the UK higher education sector is forecast to increase by 20 per cent over the next two years.

Other initiatives introduced by the UK government to widen participation include 'University for Industry's Learn Direct' and the 'Digital Academy'. Since Learn Direct's inception in 2000, over 1 million people from England and Wales have enrolled on over 3 million courses. These include management, IT, skills for life and languages. Learn Direct was developed with a remit from the UK government to provide learning opportunities to post-16-year-olds with few or no skills and qualifications, and for those who are unlikely to participate in traditional forms of learning (www.learndirect.co.uk, 2005).

The Digital Academy was launched in 1999, with substantial private sector and UK government backing. The intention was to provide small and medium-sized enterprises (SMEs) with the benefits of cost savings and flexibility to up-skill their employees by introducing e-Mediated learning into the workplace. In 2005 the digital academy announced a new range of courses available to students, in collaboration with their partners, the Guilford College of Further and Higher Education and the Reading College and School of Art and Design, AGFA and Hewlett and Packard (www.digitalacademy.com, 2006).

Government policy towards widening access in UK universities has meant that e-Mediated learning technology may have the potential of meeting these needs. Therefore, it is envisioned that e-Mediated learning technology can offer heterogeneous social groups the opportunity to easily engage in lifelong learning. This is because new forms of higher education may be more suited to the needs of non-traditional students.

Decreased Funding

Despite government policy to increase student numbers, the initiative has not been matched by a rise in government funding. This has led to a decrease in the level of resources per student. The restriction of public expenditure (a 20 per cent cut since 1981) has been a major factor underpinning the changes in higher education (Williams, 1991). These cuts were the largest reductions in income ever forced on the UK higher education, but the numbers of students entering into the system has continued to increase since the 1980s. As such, higher education institutions have been searching for efficiency gains. Many higher education institutions view e-Mediated learning systems as a solution to achieving these gains. This is because the technology allows lecturers, administrators and researchers to reach a large and diverse body of students, particularly mature and overseas students, in a cost-efficient way. Nevertheless, research has shown that there is limited evidence of significant cost savings associated with the introduction of e-Mediated learning technology in higher education (HEFCE, 1999; Gladieux and Swail, 1999; CVCP HEFCE, 2000).

Students and teaching staff are also at the receiving end. Over the past three decades, the student to staff ratio in UK higher education has increased from nine students to one teacher, to 19 students to one teacher. This is a rise of more than 100 per cent. (University and College Union, 2006). It results in students having less face-to-face contact with academic staff and as a consequence, academic staff having to deal with larger class sizes.

Increasing Accountability

Expansion has brought about its own set of stresses for universities, one of which is the call for more accountability for public funds by the state. This has led to the increased dependence on research councils for funding and the development of the research assessment exercise (RAE) and the quality assurance assessment (QAA) to systematically evaluate research and teaching. In 2005 in collaboration with the Joint Information Systems Committee (JISC), Higher Education Academy (HEA) and the UK Government, HEFCE introduced their

10-year e-learning strategy: HEFCE strategy for e-learning. This strategy was developed in direct response to the government White paper 'The Future of Higher Education'. The preliminary stage of the e-Learning strategy was via a consultation on a national e-Learning strategy. This was developed by DfeS and was titled 'Towards a Unified e-Learning Strategy'. The results of this consultation were published in April 2004. The aim of the e-Learning strategy is to enable all universities and colleges to make the best use of information and communications technologies in their learning and teaching (www.dfes.gov.uk/elearningstrategy, 2005). The UK government has given in the region of £41 million to HEFCE to provide support for individual higher education institutions to invest in e-Learning which institutions have to competitively bid for.

The RAE was introduced in the UK in 1986 as a means of selectively funding research according to defined quality standards. The RAE directly determines the amount of funding the university receives and the best research performers are rewarded with appropriate incentives. Therefore, academics are under significant pressure to research in order to secure funding. As universities are under pressure to obtain funding for research activities in order to attract extra funding, tension exists between research and teaching activities. As a result, promotion for academics is based largely on research excellence rather than teaching ability.

Furthermore, members of teaching staff are being actively encouraged to join the Institute for Teaching and Learning as the growing professionalisation of university teaching represents a response to the demands for accountability. Internationally, universities are seeking to compete for non-EU high fee students and an international labour market. Universities are also in a much more competitive environment, competing for international research grants and contracts such as those from the European Commission. The connection between the objectives of the RAE and the adoption of e-Mediated learning is quite important. This is because the technology is often seen as a way of shifting the routine work of lecturers onto the technology, thus, freeing up staff time for interaction with students and research work in order to meet RAE objectives. This key issue will be discussed later in the chapter.

Tuition Fees

The introduction of tuition fees in 2006 has resulted in each university in the UK having the autonomy to set its own fees of up to £3,000 per year. This has made the relationship between the university and the student far more consumer-like and direct, and driven students to expect more efficiency within the university system as a whole. The relationship between the student and the university has shifted over a period of time, from one where the student was simply a passive receiver of information to one which Silver and Silver (1997) have termed a 'customer' or a 'consumer' of higher education. Increased student expectations, partly due to the introduction of tuition fees are prompting a move to a more service-based culture. Parallels are beginning to emerge with a 'culture of expectation' that is typical of the American higher education system since the 1970s, and which began to emerge in the UK from the late 1990s.

However, the extent to which e-Mediated learning technology can provide a blanket solution is a bone of contention amongst a growing body of academics. Cornford and Pollock (2003), Quinsee and Hurst (2005), Grewal (2006; 2004a; 2004b; 2003; 2002) Abrahams (2004), Groves and Zemel (2000); Jacobsen (2000) and Rogers (2000) question the rhetoric of the technology and argue that the implementation and adoption of e-Mediated learning technology into institutions of higher education is a complex process. This paints quite a different picture from the visionary rhetoric presented by advocates of the technology such as Shimabukaro (2005), Twigg (2003) and Laurillard (2001).

Case Study

This study has focused on a single case design and draws on empirical data obtained from a traditional campus-based university within the UK higher education sector. The material was gathered from an investigation of written documents, semi-structured interviews with 34 members of faculty, emails, steering group meetings and the observation of organisational settings and context.

The case study university has a student population of 14,000 including 3,000 post-graduate students and 1,700 academic staff. The university has experienced a significant increase in staff and student numbers over the last decade and as a result has trebled in size. External pressures such as UK government policy to increase and widen participation, together with the influence of the RAE and the QAA are significant drivers of this change. Consequently, these external pressures have significantly influenced the way in which the university currently operates, particularly within the areas of research, learning and teaching, widening participation and in strengthening its external links with businesses and the community.

In 2002, the university was repositioned as a research-led university. It can be argued that these changes are leading the institution towards the adoption of private sector practices, in that the university has to prove excellence in research and teaching in order to secure funding through grants. At the same time, the university understands that significant income can be generated through the intake of fee-paying students including home, EU and international students. Therefore, it is under pressure to compete with other institutions at both a national and an international level. Recruiting and retaining students has become one of the university's key strategic objectives, particularly fee-paying international students. For instance, the numbers of international undergraduate and postgraduate students at the university are predicted to rise from 12 to 20 per cent by 2008.

Striving towards the university's mission of becoming research-led, all academic schools are expected to provide high-quality teaching that is focused on student learning and to foster innovative teaching and learning practices including the implementation and development of e-Mediated learning technology. Herein lies a major paradox, on the one hand the university is attempting to increase and widen student participation by improving the quality and diverse forms of teaching it provides. At the same time, the strategic objective of the university is to become research-led. Hence, lecturers are expected to carry out research. However, the university has reduced the number of non-research active teaching staff whose strengths lay in teaching. Therefore, lecturers are expected to provide both high-quality teaching and produce high-quality research against increasing student numbers and a heterogeneous student group. As such, the implementation of e-Mediated learning technology is seen as a way of easing this pressure on lecturers. Or in other words, e-Mediated learning technology is seen as a panacea for effecting this change.

Technological Change

WebCT (an online virtual learning environment that aims to facilitate the teaching and learning process) was implemented campus-wide across the university in 2002. At this stage four different types of computing systems were being used simultaneously, but all on a voluntary basis. WebCT became the dominant e-Mediated learning system from the academic year beginning 2004/5, replacing the Intranet and other systems that were also being used. During the course of the change programme, problems began to surface as the proliferation of systems caused notable confusion amongst students in terms of having to use a number of different systems in order to access course materials for different modules. This was in addition to creating unrest amongst lecturers, as they had to make a decision about which technology to adopt. Subsequently, peer and student pressure played a large part in coercing lecturers to adopt WebCT. Lecturers were concerned about the large amounts of time they would have to spend learning to use an e-Mediated learning system, with the possibility looming that the system they learned may then be replaced by another system or an updated version. This meant that lecturers would have to invest additional time into learning either a whole new system or a different set of features, at a time when they were already faced with other competing pressures such as researching and assessing large groups of students. Upon adoption of WebCT, some lecturers were concerned about the design and navigational features of the technology, particularly ease of use.

Whilst the university has been experiencing changes across the board, the most notable change has been an increase in the numbers of students attracted at both an undergraduate and postgraduate level. This increase in student numbers placed extreme strain on the university and insufficient support was provided to lecturers who were already juggling a number of different responsibilities in a pressurised environment. Consequently there was an air of uncertainty and low morale within the university and significant numbers of non-research active teaching staff applied for voluntary redundancy. These staff members traditionally carried the burden of teaching large groups of students. The irony of the situation meant that the university was moving away from becoming a research-led institution. The findings of this study show how WebCT furthered this process by restructuring the work tasks of academic staff and redefining their roles.

Findings and Discussion

The Dual Role of the Lecturer

The research findings reveal that WebCT alters the traditional role of the lecturer and creates a separate hybrid role for the lecturer as an expert and as a lay person (a user who is operating the system at the access point). However, this hybrid academic role is not the same as the traditional academic role. In their hybrid academic role, lecturers are not experts in the sense that they have technological as well as subject-specific expertise. From a technological point of view, lecturers are simply operators or lay persons of WebCT; they may not be experts in WebCT. At an individual level in adopting, developing and using WebCT to deliver their expertise, the lecturer adopts the role of the lay person. This development work takes place in the background, out of the view of the student. When the lecturer uses WebCT to interact with students, their expertise is brought into public view of the student. In adopting WebCT, the traditional expertise of the lecturer is hidden behind WebCT, and consequently, their overall expertise becomes a potential source of vulnerability.

For instance, the case study findings revealed that students expected lecturers to facilitate their teaching and learning experience in more diverse ways than before. Lecturers commented on the negative student evaluations based on WebCT, in which the students commented less on the intellect of the subject area, but more on the multimedia aspects of the module, such as 'the slides should have more colour'. Lecturers also felt that students expected WebCT to provide 'pearls of wisdom', in that extensive detailed notes should be uploaded onto the system. This was instead of using WebCT as a support tool to illustrate the detailed concepts explained by the lecturer in their traditional role as an expert during the lecture. Figure 6.1 illustrates how the technology changes the role of the lecturer at two distinct levels.

1. *Lay Person*: The lecturer as a lay person (i.e. an operator of WebCT, not an expert) at an individual level and with the student at the access point to WebCT, which subsequently holds and supports their expert knowledge. The lecturer's role now changes from an 'expert' to a hybrid 'lay person and expert' as illustrated in Figure 6.1. The traditional role of the lecturer as an expert often leads to the presumption that the lecturer is also an expert in WebCT, rather than simply a lay person. Yet, as the findings from the study reveal, lecturers may not necessarily be technical experts in WebCT. As such, using the technology in

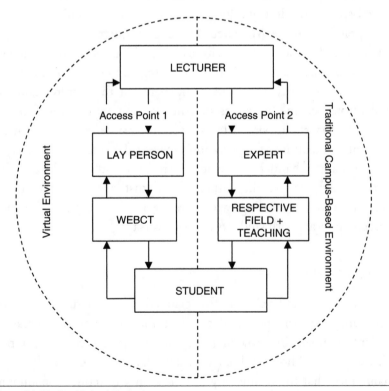

Figure 6.1 The Dual Role of the Lecturer.

the role of a lay person has the potential to significantly impact on the trust relations between the lecturer and the student. In other words, the lecturer as a lay person may have had training to use WebCT, which affords the lay person with a certain level of skills, but not the level of professional education as an expert.

2. *Expert*: The lecturer in a traditional role as an expert having gained the professional qualifications through a process of formal education. The lecturer is in the traditional role of an expert within their subject area and this professionalism is displayed via teaching and research. The trust relations are largely dependent on the lecturer displaying their expertise through face-to-face interactions with students during lectures and seminars in a campus-based environment, and to research colleagues at conferences.

e-Mediated learning technology has therefore changed the traditional relationship and recreated the student and lecturer interaction across virtual space. In addition, due to a lack of explicit guidelines about best practice and e-Mediated learning etiquette the boundaries between students and lecturers have blurred. This means that students can now contact lecturers via this technology 24 hours a day, 7 days a week. Consequently, the relationship between the lecturer and the student has become hybrid, as students can contact lecturers face-to-face and also virtually via e-Mediated learning systems. This is driving a heightened culture of expectation between the student and lecturer as the separate channel of interaction creates an additional role. This paradoxically changes the nature of the trust relationship with the lecturer, as well as creating two separate access points through which lecturers interact with students and vice versa.

Restructuring of Work Tasks

At an institutional level it is often claimed that e-Mediated learning technology has the potential to meet the demands of increasing student numbers by providing the means for lecturers to interact with students 24 hours a day, 7 days a week at a global level. It is also maintained that the technology has the ability to reduce the amount of time lecturers spend on administrative tasks, such as photocopying course materials for students. Additionally, it is posited that communication tools such as discussion boards inherent within the virtual learning environment allow students to interact independently of lecturers, thus relieving their burden and allowing them to spend more time on research related activities. To put the situation into perspective, the case study findings have identified that at an intrinsic level these claims are not entirely justified. The empirical research shows that adopting WebCT does not necessarily lead to a decrease in the work tasks of lecturers, as managing discussion boards can be extremely time-consuming and course materials require formatting so they can be placed online. It can therefore be argued that the technology does not reduce either the time lecturers spend on work tasks, nor relieve the burden, but instead the technology restructures the existing work tasks into new ones by simply transferring and repackaging the content.

Advocates of e-Mediated learning technology suggest that the technology can increase the efficiency of work tasks (Shimabukaro, 2005; Twigg, 2003; Laurillard, 2001). However, the findings drawn from this case study question such claims. It becomes clear how on the one hand WebCT enables work to be transferred between the stakeholders of the university. This allows the work tasks to be redistributed, transferring divisions of labour, theoretically saving the lecturer time to concentrate on other priorities such as research. However, on the other hand transferring the work task does not necessarily mean that time can be saved, or that the lecturer is relieved of a certain task. To illustrate this point, lecturers made the following comments:

> We get nothing by paper now and everything comes across by email. Everything you get, the calendar, the phone book, you have to print it out and you have to trot around. Add that all up and what does that make? It makes another task added onto all your other tasks. Reading all your emails takes an hour a day constantly going back in case you miss something. It's depressing especially when you come in on a Monday morning it could be more. It depends on what's coming up. It doesn't reduce your work. It increases your work. It changes the nature of your work. (Senior Lecturer)

You say ah, I must really answer my emails because people will be able to say I did send you an email. The problem is the more you reply to emails and this will be true to everybody, the more you create for everybody and the more they reply the more that comes back. So I had a meeting in Wimbledon yesterday, four of us generated about 18 emails just to decide where we were going to meet, what time, what date and what the items for discussion were. Had we just sat with our diaries at the last meeting and said we're meeting on these dates throughout the year. I think the emailing time was probably twice the length of the meeting. I think it's incredibly unproductive to do things in this way. (Lecturer)

What the above quotes summarise is that the work task is not reduced, but it is the method through which the task is carried out that changes. In many cases, the lecturer will have to learn a whole new set of skills in order to use the system in the first instance, and when the system is upgraded then the lecturer will be required to invest additional time into updating their skills. Yet adopting the technology at an advanced level requires a different set of skills. These can include the management of online seminars, because the dynamics of traditional face-to-face seminars and online seminars are entirely different. The findings also showed that the majority of lecturers interviewed who experimented with WebCT at an advanced level to hold online seminars did not continue to use the technology at such an advanced level because they simply did not possess the sufficient skills. This adversely affected their perception of the technology and as such, they went back to using WebCT at a more basic level (see Grewal, 2006 for a more detailed discussion of this aspect).

It can be argued that online seminars allow students who are less confident to communicate more openly via e-mediated learning technology. Yet, unlike a face-to-face environment it becomes difficult to gauge what the student is thinking without body language to support the non-verbal communication. One interviewee made the following comment with regard to his experience of conducting online seminars:

It's a bit frustrating, and if it's a consistent pattern and still not getting a response then I have to question whether it's something the students value. The other thing is the preparation – there is a degree of passivity here. It works well if you've got a student who questions, then fine but if you've got a student that logs on and waits for pearls of wisdom to pop through then I have very little idea of what they may be finding difficult, unless they tell me. Am I being too reactive here? Should I have constructed something? Should I have set the agenda? And if one is going to do that, then that's additional time and preparation and I really don't know what I would hope to achieve by it. (Senior Lecturer)

Redefinition of Academic Staff Roles

The emergence of the dual role of the lecturer has inadvertently changed the nature of the social relationship between the lecturer and student. This has created a greater culture of expectation and blurred the boundaries between students and lecturers. The findings suggest by taking on the role of a lay person, lecturers were increasingly concerned that the tacit consequences of adopting WebCT would have the potential to redefine their traditional roles as experts. Lecturers raised the critical issue of whether their job specification extended to also being technical experts in WebCT, as well as experts in their respective fields. Analysis of the case study findings shows that to adopt WebCT, lay persons required adequate training and support in order to use it at an advanced level. It can be argued that it would be beneficial for lay persons to receive training in using and managing WebCT, and that these skills would add to their staff development portfolio. However, at the same time lecturers questioned whether their traditional role as an expert extended to involve an element of technical expertise. Many lecturers argued that they did not consider themselves technical experts, but experts in academia and made the following comments with reference to adopting the role of lay persons:

> One of the points of discussion is should the technician be preparing materials to go online? I think lecturers are quite happy to write the material, the problem is to format it to get it compatible for WebCT. I don't think the lecturers should be doing it and the technicians don't want to do it. I think the question is who is responsible for doing that? I think that's partly why people aren't convinced you get a great deal of

benefit from using it. Unless people can see that there are some helpers who can take their standard documents and reformat it into an educationally effective way. If people are expected to do this themselves, they aren't going to be very happy about it. (Lecturer)

The issue for me at this point if I'm perfectly honest I don't see it as the role of the lecturer to have to be doing these things. That's where the School needs to get involved. There has to be a debate about what is the appropriate and proper role of a lecturer. There's no reason why it shouldn't change over time, but if we're going to require that kind of facility and input then there will probably have to be trade-offs. We can't keep expecting even more diverse skills from people. If being able to use WebCT and design the site and manipulate the technology is an integral part of what is expected as a lecturer, then it should be in the job description. It should be an integral consideration when you interview people. There should be sensitive training for people. When I started lecturing it was considered sophisticated even if you had OHPs that were typed, it was far more conventional to just write things down, and look where we are now. (Senior Lecturer)

Clearly, these quotes suggest that lecturers did not feel it was within their job remit to take on the additional role of a lay person without adequate support and training.

Trust

Lecturers took on the similar role of a lay person at the access points to WebCT and at a technical level they became very concerned about the robustness of WebCT. They indicated concern that if they placed their materials online, they would run the risk of losing their material. One interviewee summed up the feelings of lecturers quite well:

There are concerns about the robustness. Is it going to be up and running when I want to use it? If you've made a promise to students to make material available online on a specific date and time, it is very frustrating if the system is down. If I set up a multiple choice quiz and say it [WebCT] messed up the mark in some way and I hadn't noticed and some student said, I thought I got 65, actually I'm not really sure if we would have anyway of finding that out really protecting the integrity of student marks would be the most important thing WebCT could do. (Senior Lecturer)

Secondly, the amount of trust placed in WebCT by the lecturer is likely to be influenced by their early experiences of it. This places the lecturer in the role of a lay person in a vulnerable position as they attempt to illustrate their faith in WebCT, because they provide the connection between the technology and the student. The issue of trust tends to manifest when there is an element of scepticism regarding the knowledge claims of technical experts, or thoughts and intentions upon which an individual relies.

> WebCT is a much bigger operation. It's geared towards delivering at a distance. You can manage students, although it's ironic that students keep coming up and saying that's not working, this is not working, they can't get WebCT working at a distance, which is a bit of a condemnation of it, because that's what it was designed for. For example, in WebCT you think you've uploaded your lecture notes, but students can't view the notes until you click on 'update student view' and I'm sure that's a problem for a few people. (Lecturer)

With WebCT, there is a risk that the entire mechanism can falter affecting all those who use it. A carefully designed plan, together with training can help to minimise mistakes made. However, there is always an element of risk involved where both the technology and individual are concerned, regardless of how well WebCT is designed, or the efficiency of the lay person. The ramifications of its integration and functioning in relation to the operation of other systems and human activities in general cannot be entirely foreseen. Consequently it can be argued that e-Mediated learning technology is not currently living up to the rhetoric that has been written about it.

Conclusion

This chapter has explored how UK government policy to widen and increase student access together with the impact of market forces, plays a significant role in driving the implementation of e-Mediated learning technology in higher education. However, empirical research drawn from a case-study investigation into the diffusion of e-Mediated learning technology in UK higher education reveals that the technology does not reduce work tasks, but instead restructures the tasks. This is because e-Mediated learning technology creates a dual role for the lecturer as an expert and a layperson. As such, this chapter has brought to the fore some of the consequences of UK government policy on the UK higher education sector. At an organisational level these include the redefinition of academic staff roles and the restructuring of work tasks, but at a wider level and perhaps more critically, the falling standards of education as investment levels decrease, which are not matched by savings in cost.

Bibliography

Abrahams, D.A. (2004) *Technology Adoption in Higher Education: A Framework For Identifying and Prioritising Issues and Barriers to Adoption*, Doctoral Thesis, Cornell University, USA.

BBC News (2005a) *Big Rise in Part-Time Undergrads*, available at http://news.bbc.co.uk/go/pr/fr/-/1/hi/education/4462417.stm April 21.

BBC News (2005b) *Student Target 'Will Be Missed'*, available at http://news.bbc.co.uk/go/pr/fr/-/1/hi/education/4680313.stm July 14.

Committee for Vice Chancellors and Principals and Higher Education Funding Council for England (CVCP HEFCE) (2000) *The Business of Borderless Education: UK Perspectives*, Cheltenham: HEFCE, available at http://bookshop.universitiesuk.ac.uk/downloads/BorderlessSummary.pdf.

Cornford, J. and Pollock, N. (2003) *Putting the University Online: Information Technology and Organisational Change*, The Society for Research into Higher Education and Open University Press.

Department for Education and Skills (2003) *The Future of Higher Education*, London: Stationery Office, available at www.dcfs.gov.uk/hegateway/strategy/foreword.shtml.

Department of Education and Skills (2004) *Towards a Unified e-Learning Strategy*, HEFCE, available at www.dfes.gov.uk.

Giddens, A. (1996) *The Consequences of Modernity*, Cambridge: Polity Press.

Gladieux, L.E. and Swail, W.S. (1999) *The Virtual University and Educational Opportunities: Issues of Equality and Access for the Next Generation*, Washington, DC: The College Board.

Glaser, B.G. and Strauss, A.L. (1967) *The Discovery of Grounded Theory: Strategies for Qualitative Research*, Chicago: Aldine Publishing Company.

Grewal, S.K. (2006) *The Diffusion of e-Mediated Learning Technology in UK Higher Education*, PhD Thesis, Brunel University, UK.

Grewal, S.K. (2004a) 'Coerced Evolution: Integrating e-Learning into Traditional UK Universities'. In Budd, L. and Harris, L., *e-Economy: Rhetoric or Business Reality*, London: Routledge, pp. 106–22.

Grewal, S.K. (2004b) 'E-Mediated Learning in Traditional UK Universities: A Panacea for Change?' *Conference Proceedings ED MEDIA World Conference on Educational Multimedia, Hypermedia and Telecommunications 2004*, Vol. 1. pp. 2883–9.

Grewal, S.K. (2003) 'The Social Dynamics of Integrating e-Mediated Learning into Traditional UK Universities', *Conference Proceedings E-LEARN-World Conference on E-Learning in Corporate, Government, Health and Higher Education, 2003*, Issue 1, pp. 503–6.

Grewal, S.K. (2002) 'E-Learning in Higher Education', *European Union E-Learning Best Practices Conference Proceedings*, Luxembourg, available at http://www.spi.pt/innoelearning/results/project_seminar_proceedings. pdf.

Groves, M.M. and Zemel, P.C. (2000) 'Instructional Technology Adoption in Higher Education: An Action Research Case Study', *International Journal of Instructional Media*, Vol. 27, No. 1.

HEFCE (1999) *Communications and Information Technology Materials for Learning and Teaching in HE and FE: Summary Report*. HEFCE report 99/60, October, available at http://www.hefce.ac.uk/pubs/hefce/1999/99_60a.htm.

Higher Education Funding Council for England, Joint Information Systems Committee and Higher Education Academy (2005) *HEFCE Strategy for e-Learning, Policy Development*, available at www.dfes.co.uk/elearningstrategy.

Jacobsen, D.M. (2000) 'Examining Technology Adoption Patterns by Faculty in Higher Education', *Proceedings of Ace 2000, Learning Technologies, Teaching and the Future of Schools*, Melbourne, Australia.

Laurillard, D. (2001) 'The e-University: What have we Learned?' *The International Journal of Management Education*, Vol. 1, No. 2, pp. 3–7. Spring Edition.

Leitch Report 2006, available at www.hm-treasury.gov.uk/independent_reviews/leitch_review/review_leitch_index.cfm.

MacLeod, D. (2004) 'The Online Revolution', Mark II, *The Guardian*, April 13, available at: www.guardian.co.uk/education/2004/apr/13/highereducation.elearning.

Quinsee, S., and Hurst, J. (2005) 'Blurring the Boundaries? Supporting Students and Staff within an Online Learning Environment', *Turkish Online Journal of Distance Education-TOJDE*, January, Vol. 6, No.1. pp. 1–8.

Rogers, P.L. (2000) 'Barriers to Adopting Emerging Technologies in Education', *Journal of Educational Computing Research*, Vol. 2, No. 4, pp. 455–72.

Shimabukaro, J. (2005) 'Freedom and Empowerment: An Essay on the Next Step for Education and Technology', *Journal of Online Education*, June–July, Vol. 1, No. 5, pp. 1–6.

Silver, H. and Silver, P. (1997) *Students: Changing Roles, Changing Lives*, Buckingham: Open University Press.

Twigg, C. (2003) 'Improving Learning and Reducing Costs. Lessons Learned from Round 1 of the Pew Grant Program in Course Redesign'. *Centre for Academic Transformation*, available at www.thencat.org/PCR/Rd1Lessons.pdf.

University and College Union (2006) 'Further, Higher, Better' Submission to the Government's Second Comprehensive Spending Review, Section 26, available at: http://www.ucu.org.uk/csrdocs/csrsection26.pdf.

Williams, G., in Schuller, T. (1991) *The Future of Higher Education*, The Society for Research into Higher Education, Open University Press.

PART III

FUNCTIONAL FIELDS FOR e-GOVERNANCE

7

e-GOVERNANCE ISSUES IN SMALL AND MEDIUM-SIZED ENTERPRISES

COLIN GRAY

Introduction

Recent increased public policy interest in small and medium enterprises (SMEs), the 20 million or so EU firms employing less than 250 people, springs from three perceived SME strengths:

1. Their role in promoting flexibility and innovation.
2. Their labour market function in creating jobs and absorbing unemployment.
3. The enormous size of the sector (99 per cent of EU firms and 70 per cent of EU jobs).

For these three points alone, it is clear that SMEs need to be taken into account when issues concerning citizenship, democracy and governance are considered. However, there are more compelling reasons to include SMEs, especially with information and communication technologies (ICT) now improving communication and offering enhanced participation outside traditional structures and channels of communication. SMEs are not only diffused through every community and locality and, indeed, are often the mainstays of many small communities, they also form a major part of the marginalised sections of society with the lowest rates of participation in political processes. The largest SME segment, the self-employed, are generally from a *milieu* where personal independence and autonomy are prized. SMEs often organise themselves informally in structures that lie outside official organisations, as networks that address a mix of business, social and political needs. In fact, it is through these networks that many SMEs interface with the larger firms and government organisations that dominate our economies. Because of their importance, and their potential for mediating the participation of SMEs in the e-society, the different types of SME networks require some attention.

Another dimension concerning the power relations between SMEs and large organisations is crucial to a proper understanding of SME participation and governance issues, internal and external to the SME networks. Power relations affect governance issues in SME networks in four major areas:

1. Transactions costs and vertical disintegration of larger firms.
2. Local clusters of complementary SMEs.
3. Communities of practice.
4. Family and community ties.

This chapter describes the key issues in each area and the potential that ICT holds for increasing the participation of SMEs in discussion and decision making at a local, regional and national level.

In recent years, there has been an upsurge in interest in small and medium enterprises (SMEs) and the potential role they are expected to play in promoting innovation, productivity improvements and the necessary flexibility to ensure the effective and efficient working of networks and clusters. Public competition and innovation policies aimed at promoting SMEs in order to achieve these goals tend to adopt a top-down or 'hub and spoke' perspective that subordinates the role of SMEs to that of large firms, especially those seen as national 'champions' in an era of global competition. This contrasts with earlier policies when most of Europe faced mass unemployment and SMEs were promoted because of their capacity for generating new jobs. This labour market approach survives in Western Europe mainly as social policies aimed at combating social exclusion of different kinds and in a number of local regional development policies. In both these public policy approaches, SMEs are treated instrumentally.

There are very few initiatives or directives that are designed to address the current needs of the SME sector as opposed to the hoped-for future benefits. There are also few policies that take into account the everyday importance of SMEs as a social, cultural and economic sector. At the Lisbon European Council in 2000, the EC launched the Charter for Small Enterprises as part of a wider drive to make the EU 'the most dynamic economy by 2010' through stimulating entrepreneurship. These are laudable aims but will only apply to a minority of SMEs. It is left to the activities of SME lobby and representative organisations to raise the concerns that the majority of SMEs feel affect them – or at least the SMEs that belong to these business association networks. The smallest and least successful SMEs generally remain unrepresented at policy level. Given the huge size of the sector and the tendency for SMEs to network, this is somewhat surprising.

SME Sector in the EU

Of more than 20 million firms in the European Union, less than 40,000 employed more than 250 people (the dividing line between SMEs and large firms) (EC, 2003). Some 99 per cent of all EU firms are SMEs and, before the recent accession of 10 new Member States, they accounted for 70 per cent of Europe's 122 million jobs. They also accounted for 57 per cent of Europe's €25 trillion sales. Roughly half are self-employed who employ no one other than themselves. The rest divide rather unevenly between microfirms with less than 10 employees (42 per cent), small firms of 10–49 employees (6 per cent) and medium firms of 50–249 employees (1 per cent). There are strong size effects in relation to productivity, export activities and propensity to engage in initiatives that are designed to boost their economic potential. The SME sector is very heterogeneous with significant differences between different industries, regions and sizes of firms.

In addition, and possibly more importantly, there are also huge differences in capabilities, resources capacities, management abilities and styles, inter-firm linkages and strategic objectives. Indeed, it is the main purpose of this chapter to show that the very heterogeneity and dispersal of the sector through many different smaller economic segments and community groups implies that SMEs are an indispensable element in democracy at all levels. Furthermore, it is the disparities of concentration and power between SMEs and other elements in the political economy that bring governance issues to the fore when considering the wider socioeconomic role of SMEs and what part the adoption of more advanced information and communication technologies (ICT) might play. Certainly, timely access to better-quality information is very important though there is then a further challenge of ensuring that the SMEs know how to make best use of the information. To better understand this, and to provide a clue as to why SMEs – especially the microfirms – appear to be reluctant to engage in public initiatives, it is important to be aware of the dominant work motivations that drive most SME owners and of the precarious nature of their relations with the economy and other firms. A special EU report on cooperation between SMEs revealed a surprising degree of stability in the network relationships formed by SMEs but also showed that the cooperating firms were a minority (EC, 2002).

SME Behaviour in the UK

The number of businesses in Britain has been increasing steadily for more than a decade. The total topped 4 million for the first time in 2003 and, by 2006, had exceeded 4.5 million – an increase of 3 per cent on the previous year and the highest recorded level (DBERR, 2007). Apart from some 27,000 medium-sized firms (50–249 employees) and 6,000 large firms (250 or more employees), all these were small firms, including 3.3 million own account self-employed without any employees (73 per cent of all firms, an increase of 9 per cent on 2002). Some 13 per cent of these are partnerships, 24 per cent are companies and 62 per cent are sole proprietors. As a whole, the SME sector accounts for 59 per cent of all private sector employment in Britain and 52 per cent of all sales turnover.

Most of the SMEs in Britain, as in the rest of the EU, are self-employed, accounting for some 13 per cent of all employment. There has been a sharp increase in self-employment since 2001, mainly in business services and construction. Some self-employed are technically employees of their own companies as sole directors. When responding to Labour Force Surveys, however, most classify themselves as self-employed '. . . because of the flexibility and control they have over their employment', even though many work for agencies or as sub-contractors where there is often strong external control over their work (Lindsay and McCauley, 2004). This is not just a statistical point but a significant indicator of the culture that pervades the SME sector, especially the self-employed. One of the main reasons for SMEs across Europe not opening themselves up to working with other firms is a fear of loss of independence (EC, 2003b). That the desire for autonomy and independence is the main career motivator of SME owners in Britain has been known for a long time, as Small Enterprise Research Team (SERTeam) findings over time demonstrate (see Table 7.1).

There is little doubt that where the desire for independence equates to a resistance to 'being told what to do' or to sharing, then co-operation, sharing and openness will be seriously impeded. Gray (1999) found that 78 per cent of 'lifestyle' owner-managers were reluctant to delegate and had a directive management style. The owner-managers with clearer business/economic objectives are more likely to delegate, but 59 per cent still described themselves as having directive and non-participative management styles (Zhang et al, 2004). Fortunately, it is clear that many SME owners, especially those with employees, are driven more by a need for autonomy in decision making and in responsibility, which is very compatible with the over-

Table 7.1 SME Main Personal Career Motivation 1990–2004 (column %)

	1990	1996	1999	2004	2006
Independence/be own boss	50	52	46	42	52
Make money	19	16	17	15	13
Security for future	9	10	14	13	11
No alternative/avoid unemployment	6	11	8	6	7
Family tradition	5	5	5	6	6
Other	11	8	10	9	8
Sample size (n)	1,349	753	1,121	808	638

Source: Small Enterprise Research Team – Quarterly Survey of Small Business in Britain, Vol. 22, No.2.

all objectives of good governance, rather than a need to be in control or to be left alone. Furthermore, in their external relations other than business, large proportions of the self-employed, if not always a majority, do engage in political processes which is another important element of good governance in society.

The British Social Attitudes Survey of 2002 (a large-scale annual survey of 2,290 households conducted by the UK government which includes a self-employed sub-sample of 245) found that two-thirds of UK citizens believe that they have no influence on government and that the most alienated included 14 per cent of self-employed (compared with 10 per cent overall). However, as Table 7.2 shows, the self-employed are only a little less likely than other citizens to engage.

If most SMEs believe they have little direct impact on government, some 40 per cent of the self-employed are interested in political involvement and more than one-third (37 per cent) are happy to go on protests or demonstrations to support their positions. In general, politically and socially engaged people appear to be more inclined to use the Internet to gather information. In political terms, the self-employed do tend to vote centre-right (35 per cent Conservative), particularly those who have employees.

However, a similar proportion (30 per cent) tends to vote centre-left (Labour) with around 11 per cent preferring liberals and 4 per cent environmental (green) parties. In all these non-conservative or minority party options, it is the self-employed without employees

Table 7.2 SME Community/Political Involvement 2002 (row per cent)

Action/Attitude	With Employees	No Employees	Sample (n)	%
Interest in political issues	37	63	64	40
Go on protest/demonstration	30	70	34	37
Not go on protest/demonstration	38	61	125	63
Not involved in campaigns	40	60	127	80
No impact on government	34	65	112	70
All	59	100	159	100
% (n= 159)	35	65	100	

Source: British Social Attitudes Survey 2002.

who are strongest in their affiliations. This may be another reflection of a non-conformity associated with their need for independence and autonomy (which, it could be argued, is an essential element of democracy and good governance in society). It may also reflect a feeling among the self-employed and owners of microfirms (less than 10 employees) of being marginalised from the mainstream.

However, for SMEs governance issues have less to do with political issues and more with how they relate to their stakeholders – investors, staff, customers and suppliers. It has also been long recognised that a serious barrier to SME development and participation with other firms has been poor management capabilities compounded by reluctance to engage in systematic management or staff development (Gray, 1998; EC, 2003a). Once again, the main exceptions seem to be those SMEs that have a clear growth strategy and link their development of internal competences to that strategy (Thomson and Gray, 1999; Gray, 2004). To some extent, this is linked to educational levels and the type of industry.

There is a tendency for graduates to be more likely than non-graduate owner-managers to offer systematic staff and management training (though they do not always feel a need for it themselves). One important implication of this is that firms with a more systematic approach to staff and management development also appear to have structures in place for consultation and information sharing with staff and they appear to be more open to engaging in business networks and public initiatives aimed at improving business performance and local economic development. This openness, participation and acceptance of responsibility for staff development are not only signs of good management but also characteristics of good governance. Although such SMEs also appear to have a stronger tendency to grow, however, there are plenty of SMEs with very direct management styles that also grow. Performance is not necessarily a sign of good governance and good-governance SMEs are very much a minority (Gray, 1998, 2002).

Key Issues

The purpose of this chapter is to explore what governance means in the SME context and whether more widespread use of ICT may offer wider and more effective SME participation in society. EU policy on governance sees the role of networks as crucial. The EC White Article on governance points out that (2001, p. 18) 'new technologies, cultural changes and global interdependence have led to the creation of a tremendous variety of European and international networks, focused on specific objectives. Some have been supported by Community funding. These networks link businesses, communities, research centres, and regional and local authorities. They provide new foundations for integration within the Union and for building bridges to the applicant countries and to the world.' However, the White Article also recognized that 'many of these networks, whose roots reach down deep into society, feel disconnected from the EU policy process. By making them more open and structuring better their relation with the Institutions, networks could make a more effective contribution to EU policies.' (emphasis in the original). Before examining how SMEs network it is first necessary to examine the concept of governance as it relates to SMEs.

Management and Governance Issues

In 2001, the EC published a White Article on governance in order to address the increasing problem of non-participation by EU citizens in EC decisions and to stimulate debate on the main issues. The EC sees that there are five main governance issues – openness, participation, accountability, effectiveness and coherence – and has stated that each 'principle is important for establishing more democratic governance. They underpin democracy and the rule of law in the Member States, but they apply to all levels of government – global, European, national, regional and local'. The White Article stressed the importance of good governance for effective democracy which it noted (p. 11) 'depends on people being able to take part in public debate. To do this, they must have access to reliable information on European issues and be able to scrutinise the policy process in its various stages'. However, the focus of the White article was on institutions, not on the role of businesses, and even less on the role of SMEs.

More recently, in an article on governance issues among SMEs in the new Accession States, Smallbone (2004) notes that governance 'is concerned with the rules, procedures and practices affecting how power is exercised. These issues are central to the democratic process, because they influence the legitimacy and effectiveness of institutions, which . . . can have major impact on entrepreneurship development'. This implies that there is both an internal and external dimension to governance when applied to SMEs. It is clear that the internal dimension is linked to good management, especially the management of human resources (in the sense of consultation and clear communication), information, quality and effective compliance with regulations. This is linked to the external dimension where sound practices in relation to regulations and standards, as well as respect for the environment and participation in the political process, are also very important. Given the huge size of the SME sector (including the related contribution to national revenues from the associated direct and indirect taxation), therefore, issues concerning good governance within and between SMEs form an important part of a functioning democracy in a modern industrial society.

However, information gathering and regulatory compliance can pose problems for many very small firms, not necessarily because of a desire to evade the regulation but often because of higher resource and time costs associated with search and compliance (Bannock and Peacock, 1989; Gray and Bannock, 2005). Conformance with regulations and other aspects of good governance practice generally involves not only the completion of work to high and transparent standards but also the management of various stakeholders inside and outside the firm. Nevertheless, most SMEs take the trouble to conform to regulations that they perceive as relevant and those that have employees try to keep them informed and involved in decisions that affect them. The May 2004 final report of the EC forum on fostering corporate social responsibility among SMEs, a very important dimension of good external governance, observed that:

... many SMEs are committed to environmental, social and community responsibility is certainly clear. Much of this will not be called 'CSR' by those who are doing it! Successful SMEs are regularly providing excellent goods and service. They provide employment. They engage their employees and harness their motivation and skills for the long-term success of the enterprise. They recognise the value of informing and consulting employees, and of creating participative workplaces. They are intensely alert to human rights issues and to health and safety considerations; they encourage staff to acquire new skills; help them achieve better work-life balance; recruit and promote on merit – irrespective of gender, race, disability, age, sexual orientation. Many SMEs are striving to operate sustainably: conscious of their use of natural resources; mindful of their sourcing; seeking ways to reduce their energy and water consumption and their excess packaging and waste. Many SMEs are also putting something tangible back into their local communities: such as providing work experience for local schools, sponsoring local community organisations, supporting environmental clean-up drives.

Clearly, the economic, political and social impact of SMEs is further strengthened when they operate through networks and it seems reasonable to suppose that the effective use of ICT will enhance those impacts. As there are many different types of SME, however, they also belong to different types of networks. It is important to have a clearer understanding of the role of different types of SME networks and how they mediate the behaviour of SMEs.

SME Network Typologies and Effects

In a 2003 EU study on cooperation between SMEs, networks are described as 'nodes and branches where the enterprises form the nodes and the relationships between the enterprises form the branches. The relationships are described in qualitative terms, the most important being trust, and as transactions or flows' (EC, 2003b). This is similar to the communications model of networks used by many ICT providers and, although this particular definition envisages that 'co-operation in the network is assumed to generate synergy', the model seems rather mechanistic. In the OUBS-led NEWTIME study of the impact of broadband on networks of microfirms in the EU (Gray, 2003), it became apparent that the social dimension of networking was as important for many firms (especially the smaller microfirms) as the business dimension. It was also clear that, as the EU study also acknowledges, not all nodes are equal (some are more central anchors whilst others are more peripheral) and the branches or lines joining them are of varying strengths and represent different frequencies of contact. Furthermore the network structure and links can be formal (contractual), informal or a mix of both.

In the context of this chapter, this is very important because stronger ties between nodes or SMEs often imply the firms and the network itself are more deeply embedded in local communities, but often more resistant to change and new entrants, while weaker ties imply more openness and flexibility. Both these dimensions are important with respect to effective and wider governance. Furthermore, variations in the strength of ties and the 'anchoredness' of nodes implies an unevenness in the power relations between firms, an unevenness that needs to be considered when discussing governance issues in relation to SMEs. Taking into account the social/business and formality/informality dimensions, NEWTIME identified four broad network types that involve SMEs – supply chains/production systems, business associations, industry clusters and local/regional clusters. The later overlaps with more social networks, especially those covering the self-employed and microfirms.

Supply Chains

The emergence of supply chains or production systems, as large firms began to contract out previously internal operations, has been widespread for more than 30 years. Following the seminal work of US economist Ronald Coase (1937), Oliver Williamson (1975) popularised the 'transactions costs' approach with its strong focus on supply chain management. The underlying rationale is that large firms developed and grew to enormous size in the ninteenth and first half of the twentieth centuries because they faced such a risky and uncertain external business environment that they found it more economic and safer to control, as much as possible, all their transactions in-house. As the rule of law and trade regulation became more established, large corporations found it more economic to focus on their core activities and to sub-contract or outsource components, distribution, and services. In some cases the contracted firms were the original internal departments set up as new small firms, but often they are existing SMEs that offer the particular product or service. However, this approach makes very clear that it is always the competitive position of the larger, core (or focal) firm that is dominant.

Relations between small and large firms is more complex than a simple jobs substitution or a 'simple slimming down during recession' by large firms, though this unintentional large-firm disintegration played, and still does, a key role in the rise of self-employment. Much of the rise in new small-firm formation rates during the 1980s was due to a number of large-firm fragmentation strategies as they 'vertically disintegrated', a process that was seen by some as ultimately favourable to the interests of large firms and of international capital (Shutt and Whittington, 1987; Storey, 1994; Rainnie, 1991). This process certainly exposed unequal power relations between large and small firms, and within firms between owners, managers and workers. This does not create a climate conducive to democracy, participation or good governance. Indeed, in various parts of the SME sector with its traditional milieux of family firms and self-employment where independence and autonomy are prized, the following differences emerged as many newer and more specialist SMEs were drawn into large-firm strategies:

- *traditional* – independent and well established locally (mainly survival, not growth-oriented);
- *independent competitor* – use their flexibility to grow through competing with other small firms, large and small;
- *dependent* – sub-contracting and supply chain relations;
- *independent niche* – compete in specialised or very local markets; and
- *innovators* – exploiting a new field or technology to compete or be acquired by a large firm or investors.

During the 1980s, many key governance issues appeared in attempts to encourage SMEs to adopt 'total quality management' (TQM) systems and international standards such as ISO 9000. Although the main EC standard-setting bodies, CEN and CENELEC, attempt to involve SME networks and representative bodies, standards such as ISO 9000 are seen by many SMEs as applying mainly to large firms (hence not relevant to them) or as an extension of the control from focal large. As global competition intensified and supply chains began to be seen more as production and distribution systems, the mechanistic and formal relations gave way to more collaborative relations (albeit, in many cases, still dominated by larger focal firms). The 1990s has seen renewed local and regional development interest in clusters.

Clusters

The special EU report on cluster and network policies in Member States (EC, 2002) noted that firms are 'often concentrated in small geographic areas where the business environment seems to be more favourable and where companies can get access to qualified manpower and expert knowledge . . .'. Such geographic concentrations of competing and cooperating firms, suppliers, services, research institutions and associated organisations are defined as clusters. The clusters that link SMEs, networking and innovation can be traced back to Marshall (1891) and his 'industrial districts', where independent firms and workers are linked together through their shared specialisations which they trade – almost as commodities – regionally, nationally and, increasingly, internationally. Successful industrial districts are characterised by their capacity to transmit, exchange and react to new information extremely rapidly. Marshall talked of his industrial districts having a 'special atmosphere' that encouraged participation, cooperation and innovation.

The industry clusters of northern Italy have been studied and held up as local economic development models since the 1970s (Piore and Sabel, 1984) albeit with critical reservations. Unlike the unidirectional power relations that characterise supply chains and contracting-out arrangements, the power and information relations between firms is more balanced, dynamic and open.

The real boost to the cluster network model of wider economic development came from Michael Porter (1990, 1998) who views clusters in the context of global competition where different clusters that enjoy particular comparative advantages tend to specialise and trade their expertise in an analogous way to the many individual firms in a single cluster. Although very influential in current local economic development policies, Porter's approach to clusters has been criticised for conceptual imprecision and for not recognising that effective clusters are embedded in their local or regional economies through cultural and social ties (Martin and Sunley, 2001). The defining feature of Porter's clusters is their capacity for boosting local and national business competitiveness through drawing on local skill specialisations and other factor advantages, and both the competitive and cooperative relations between firms in related industries, usually driven by prevalent supply-demand conditions. With respect to governance issues, clusters offer more open and mutually constructed systems of shared attitudes, behaviours and norms that can replace, on one hand, the informality and lack of structure found among many individual microfirms and small firms and, on the other, the formal, legalistic and rule-driven relations found in earlier supply chains and contracting-out relations between focal firms and SMEs. However, there is not a clear-cut dichotomy between the open and closed systems of relations between firms because many recent clusters have emerged from the same processes of vertical disintegration that created supply chains with their less even power relations (Scase, 2002). Table 7.3 summarises network membership from a 2002 national survey of 1,168 SMEs in Britain and shows clearly the more dynamic nature of cluster networks, compared with supply chains and business associations.

The first point to note is that a large majority of respondents (85 per cent) belong to a business network of one type or another and they all derive significant benefits from their networks. The second point, as might be expected from cluster theory (Porter, 1998) and Marshall's (1891) earlier concept of the 'industrial district', is the high value placed on social contact as well as on cooperative business behaviour (and, in regional clusters, help in recruitment – a classic industrial district effect). Thirdly, networks are used widely as sources of business and technology advice. Increased use of broadband and mobile technologies has significantly improved this function, as well

Table 7.3 SMEs Network Use 2002 (%)

Network Use	Supply Chain	Association	Industry Cluster	Local Cluster	All Networks	All SMEs
Social contact	37	41	64	70	41	46
Business advice	43	53	58	69	50	42
Technology advice	30	31	39	38	29	25
New customers	25	20	32	47	23	20
New suppliers	18	15	25	30	15	14
Joint marketing	12	13	20	18	11	10
Joint purchasing	8	9	12	12	8	7
Recruiting staff	3	3	4	6	3	3
Sample (n)	343	810	291	125	992	1,168
%	29	69	25	11	85	100

Source: NatWest Quarterly Survey of Small Business in Britain., 18:2

as communication between firms, an important element in establishing more effective governance in the SME sector.

Another important point of interest is the comparatively low value placed on social contact and business advice in the supply chains, where the ties between participants are often more formal and reflect the stronger power of the focal firms. Indeed, in many cases, this takes form as a preferred suppliers list, with SME suppliers sometimes being obliged to furnish financial details to the focal firms and often having to bear the burden of standards compliance (such as ISO 9000) and holding stocks so that the larger focal firm's just-in-time systems function effectively. Potentially, this can improve regulations and standards compliance in the supplier SMEs, one of the EU's governance objectives, but possibly at the expense of real participation, another key objective.

Associations

The most common form of network, where issues concerning regulations awareness and compliance are communicated and discussed by SMEs, is an association. These are mainly membership bodies and include organisations like chambers of commerce, industry associations, professional institutes and business clubs. In many EU

Member States, membership of chambers of commerce is part of the official registration system and is obligatory. In Britain, membership of chambers and trade associations is voluntary yet a high proportion of firms – especially small and medium firms – do join these networks as Table 7.2 reveals. Indeed, it is the associations and various lobby groups that are also membership organisations through which policy makers and government attempts to communicate and consult with SME Association networks, therefore, are important channels of communication and an essential element in the development of good governance in the SME sector. Increasingly, however, these forms of association – both formal and informal – are based on shared knowledge and professionalism, as communities of practice.

Communities of Practice

The professions such as law, accountancy, medicine, architects, engineers and other knowledge-based specialists are often members of professional institutes and other bodies. In part, these function like other business associations but they can also have a part to play in maintaining and developing the skills and competences base of their community. Network members are bound together by their collectively developed understanding of what their community is about and a wider sense of common purpose. Members build their community through various interactions with each other, establishing norms and relationships of mutuality that reflect these interactions. Communities of practice develop shared communal resources – language, routines, competences, sensibilities, artefacts, tools, stories, styles and so on (Wenger, 2000). With new business, communications and organisational opportunities emerging as a result of vertical disintegration and ICT-based innovations, communities of practice are becoming more frequent in the industries most affected directly (business services such as finance, employment agencies; the media and publishing; creative industries; computer services; and so on).

In general, SMEs prefer informal contacts from within their business community as information sources in preference to external or formal sources. Transactions and relationships with other SME owner/managers, provide a significant means of learning and knowledge, particularly when), these are clustered into communities of practice (Wenger, 1998). Work in small and medium firms is increasingly project-driven so it is important that specialists are able to work together, pooling their talents and skills in creative and productive ways. Trust relations – a key element in good governance – become more important, developed through working in ever-changing and fluid work teams. Work expectations are often stretched beyond specific personal technical and creative competences. Team members become interdependent upon each other for the success of shared goals (Scase, 2002). It is this interdependence of skills that is the key integrative mechanism which because of their external client and professional orientations – might fragment because of other conflicting pressures from customers and individual firm's strategies (Mintzberg, 1983).

Earlier work on organisational learning (Argyris and Schoen, 1978) re-emerged during the 1990s in concepts such as the learning organisation (Senge, 1990) and knowledge management (Amidon and Skyrme, 1997). Essentially, the model is one based upon knowledge sharing and, through constant and open communication, the making explicit of often buried or tacit knowledge held by all employees. The drawing together of experiential knowledge of key employees (including the owner/manager) and the making explicit the effective routines developed within the firm in order to share, combine knowledge and create new knowledge is the innovative process that lies at the heart of knowledge management. ICT is seen as providing support for this process both internally and also in relations externally with other firms. However, the British Social Attitudes Survey 2002 revealed that only 16 per cent of the self-employed would be willing to form a group with like-minded people and those with employees were less likely to. Clearly, for some SME owners this could still be a problem, but for many it reflects existing participative management styles. As communication and access to information improves with the increased diffusion and use of ICT applications, this role in support of good governance is also likely to develop.

Role of ICT

Since 1985, there has been a marked increase in the use of ICT, especially the Internet, websites and networked computers by SMEs as Table 7.4 shows.

The European Foundation Centre (EFC, 2002), commenting on the EC White Article on governance (2001), sees a vital role to be played by the increased communication and access to information offered by ICT and strongly welcomed 'the Commission's proposal to provide up-to-date, on-line information on the preparation of policy through all stages of decision-making'. However, the EFC also noted that more clarity and transparency was needed on establishing the credentials, provenance and representativeness of bodies that purport to represent elements of civil society, including SMEs. In particular the ESF concluded that information of bodies consulted by the EC 'should be made available, and should document who they represent, in particular for national and European umbrella organisations and networks, and what is their specific expertise/competence in the field(s) concerned'. In Britain, the SERTeam quarterly survey in the first quarter of 2002 revealed (Table 7.5) that SMEs were beginning to overcome some lack of trust and are using web-based search engines plus business and government websites to obtain information of relevance to their business and social lives as citizens.

Personal contact is still preferred by most SMEs but there is a growing interest in ICT-mediated communication to obtain

Table 7.4 SME Adoption of ICT in Britain 1985–2003 (column %)

	1985	1991	1996	1999	2001	2003	2005	2007
Computer	36	68	81	81	88	92	92	96
Internet	0	5	14	45	77	86	87	83
e-mail	0	3	17	46	75	82	87	81
Website	0	0	6	26	49	58	63	63
e-Commerce	0	0	0	0	7	8	11	10
wireless	–	–	–	–	–	14	29	38
Sample (n)	1,090	984	1,099	601	720	808	670	528

Source: Small Enterprise Research Team: Quarterly Surveys of Small Business in Britain.
Vol 23, No. 2

Table 7.5 Business Information and Communication by Type of Technology

Source	face2face	Internet	Telephone	e-Mail
Professional advisor	274	188	139	119
Government service	135	114	70	79
Business associations	90	92	153	86
Trade links	233	190	123	121
All	408	301	218	190
% (n = 654)	62	46	33	29

Source: Small Enterprise Research Team: NatWest/SERTeam Quarterly Surveys of Small Business in Britain

information (there were multiple mentions). Although SMEs are generally reluctant to use external advice they do make use of professional advice when it is relevant and clearly outside their areas of competence (most commonly accountants). There is a strong preference for face-to-face contact for this sort of information. For more business-related advice and information, they overwhelmingly prefer their trading partners (customers, suppliers, partners in joint projects and so on). These are cluster-type contacts and there is a stronger preference for using the Internet and websites for communication with strong evidence of an increasing use of mobile, wireless (hand-held) connections. Many belong to trade and business associations but do not use them for business advice or information (except on specific matters). There is also a reluctance to use government sources of advice except for specific information often related to compliance with regulations (and this appears to often be information taken from government websites). This pattern of a remaining strong preference for face-to-face communication with a growing use of the Internet and websites by SMEs reflects the findings from the British Social Attitudes Survey of 2002. This revealed positive links between political and social involvement and the use of the Internet to gather general information (in that more than one-third of the 29 per cent of UK households that reported a lot of interest in such issues used the Internet for information compared with less than one in five of the 12 per cent who had no interest at all). Table 7.6 summarises SME Internet usage patterns with respect to information gathering among SMEs.

Table 7.6 SME Use of Internet for Information and Communication 2002

Internet use	With Employees	No Employees	All
Home access to Internet	69	66	67
Internet e-mail	45	41	43
General information	36	43	40
Shopping	24	26	25
News + current affairs	17	14	15
Training + education	14	16	15
Chat rooms	1	3	2
Do not *use* Internet	47	45	45
All	89	156	245
% (n = 245)	35	65	100

Source: British Social Attitudes Survey 2002.

This is slightly more interesting from a governance perspective because this is a survey of households, not businesses, so the respondents are individual citizens who happen to be self-employed, some with and some without employees. The first point to note is that the reported access to the Internet and use of Internet e-mail is lower for households in 2002 than for small firms in 2001 (see Table 7.3). Secondly, although more than half the self-employed do use the Internet, the usage rate is lower than the access rate. Even so, a large proportion of self-employed sole traders without employees use the Internet for general information (43 per cent) and around one-quarter of all self-employed use the Internet for shopping as consumers (far more than those who currently have a business use for the Internet as vendors). The use of the Internet for training and education (e-Learning) was quite low in 2002 and the use of chat rooms was almost non-existent among the self-employed.

Conclusion

The SME sector is extremely heterogeneous, split not only into different industries and different sizes, but also distinct in their career aspirations, business strategies and their propensity to engage and network with other firms. Initiatives and policies designed to promote good governance need to take these different factors into account.

Some SMEs, especially the larger ones and those founded on know-ledge and technology specialisations, do have clear growth strategies and generally have no problems in complying with regulations, quality systems and staff development. This minority of SMEs often have management and organisational systems that meet the five criteria of good governance, both internally with staff and externally with other stakeholders – openness, participation, accountability, effectiveness and coherence.

However, most SMEs, even those that are active in several net-works, do not have the inclination, knowledge or resources to comply. They clearly need support and policy targets that are shorter term and more directly related to outcomes that will benefit their busi-nesses in clear and obvious ways. They will also want reassurance that regulations and the demands of good governance will not threaten their independence. As policy does involve government influence and both normal business relations and networking often reflect the unequal power enjoyed by large and focal firms, this poses severe policy and communication challenges.

Turning to the opportunities that ICT may offer in bridging these gaps, the picture is not yet clear. Most firms already use computers and the adoption of the Internet, broadband and websites is already high and growing. Furthermore, SMEs are using the Internet, websites and e-mail to access business and regulatory information. However, there are fewer signs that SMEs have increased significantly their collaboration with each other – except in certain creative, financial and media industries – or are engaging in the determination of policies that affect them. It is the participation side of good govern-ance that poses a major problem with regard to the SME sector. Although SMEs make good business use of the increased communi-cation capacity offered by ICT applications, they are not yet using these to engage in political and policy setting debates. No doubt time is a key factor in this but so too are deeply entrenched SME attitudes and suspicion of government. This has to be addressed in a political, not technological, arena.

Medium-sized firms and larger small firms may have the resources and capabilities for engaging in this process. However, the very small microfirms and self-employed in the main do not. Although ICT adoption studies and surveys, such as those from the SERTeam reported in Table 7.4, show almost universal adoption of computers by SMEs there is, in fact, a small proportion of microfirms and self-employed (4 per cent in the 2007 SERTeam survey) that do not have a computer or know how to use them. Indeed, the proportion of these firms may be under-reported. Because of time, communication, cultural and, in some cases, educational constraints, these firms do not respond to surveys. It is hard to see how the adoption of new ICT applications can directly improve the participation of these firms. Even among the smallest SMEs that do have computers, the low take-up of e-Learning and low use of informal chat rooms suggests that these self-employed and SME owner/managers are reluctant to engage and use the Internet unless they have a clear purpose and can obtain relevant information. The business value of ICT know-how needs to be related to their circumstances as does any targeted developmental support if they are not to be further marginalised. The adoption and effective use of ICT programmes and services that support good governance among small firms are likely to flow from the relevance and value of ICT applications to the successful achievement of their business and quality-of-life objectives.

Bibliography

Amidon, D. and Skyrme, D. (1997) *Creating the Knowledge Based Business*, London: Business Intelligence Ltd.

Argyris, C. and Schoen, D. (1978) *Organizational Learning*, Harlow: Addison-Wesley.

Bannock, G. and Peacock, A. (1989) *Governments and Small Business*, London: Paul Chapman.

Centre for Strategy and Evaluation Services (2002) 'Benchmarking the Administration of Business Start-Ups: Final report', European Commission Enterprise Directorate General.

Coase, R. (1937) 'The Nature of the Firm', *Econometrica*, 4 (November) pp. 386–405.

Department for Business, Enterprise and Regulatory Reform (2007) *Small and Medium-sized Enterprise (SME) Statistics for the UK 2006*, DBERR. August 2007.

Commission of the European Communities (2001) *European Governance: A White Article*, EC July, COM(2001), 428 final, Brussels.

(EC) Commission of the European Communities (2002) *Final Report of the Expert Group on Enterprise Clusters and Networks*, Enterprise Directorate. Brussels.

(EC) Commission of the European Communities (2003a) *Competence Development in SMEs*. Observatory of European SMEs. Report 1. EC/ENSR 2003/No 1. Luxembourg.

(EC) Commission of the European Communities (2003b) *2003 Observatory of European SMEs: SMEs and Cooperation*, Report 5. EC. Enterprise Directorate. Brussels.

(EC) Commission of the European Communities (2003c) *SMEs in Focus: Main Results from the 2003 Observatory of European SMEs*, Report 8. EC. Enterprise Directorate. Brussels.

European Foundation Centre (2002) *European Commission White Article on Governance: The EFC View*, Brussels: EFC.

Gray, C. (1998) *Enterprise and Culture*, London: Routledge.

Gray, C. (1999) 'Stages of Growth and Entrepreneurial Growth Career Motivation', Working Article Series, Small and Medium Enterprises Research Unit, Open University Business School, 99/1SMERU.

Gray, C. (2002) 'Entrepreneurship, Resistance to Change and Growth in the Small Firm', *Journal of Small Business and Enterprise Development*, Vol. 9, No. 1, pp. 61–72.

Gray, C. (2003) *Broadband, Networking and Small Firm Development*, Buckingham: Open University.

Gray, C. (2004) 'Management Development and Organisational Growth in European Small and Medium Enterprises', *Advances in Developing Human Resources*, Vol. 6, No. 4, Invited Special Issue November, 2004.

Gray, C. and Bannock, G. (eds) (2005) *Government Regulation and the Small Firm*, Institute for Small Business and Entrepreneurship/Small Enterpise Research Team, Milton Keynes.

Gray, C. Langkjaer, K. and Oliveira, A. (2002) 'SME Networks: Broadening their Reach and Success'. In Stanford-Smith, B. Chiozza, E. and Edin, M. (eds.), *Challenges and Achievements in e-Business and e-Work*, Amsterdam: IOS Press, pp. 987–94.

Lindsay, C. and McCauley, C. (2004) 'Growth in Self-employment in the UK', Labour Market Trends, October, Vol. 112, No. 12, London: Office of National Statistics (ONS).

Marshall, A. (1891) *Principles of Economics* (2nd edn), London: Macmillan.

Martin, R. and Sunley, P. (2001) 'Deconstructing Clusters: Chaotic Concept or Policy Panacea?', Cambridge Working Article 244, University of Cambridge.

Mintzberg, H. (1983) *Structures in Fives: Designing Effective Organisations*, Englewood Cliffs, NJ: Prentice Hall.

Piore, M. and Sabel, C. (1984) *The Second Industrial Divide: Possibilities for Prosperity*, Basic Books: New York.

Porter, M. (1990) *The Competitive Advantage of Nations*, Basingstoke: Macmillan.

Porter, M. (1998), 'Clusters and the New Economics Competition', *Harvard Business Review*, November–December pp. 77–90.

Rainnie, A. (1991) 'Just-in Time, Subcontracting and the Small Firm', *Work, Employment and Society*, Vol. 5, No. 3. pp. 353–75.

Scase, R. (2002), *Living in the Corporate Zoo*, Oxford: Capstone Publishing.

Senge, P. (1990) *The Fifth Discipline: The Art and Practice of the Learning Organisation*. New York: Doubleday.

Shutt, J. and Whittington, R. (1987) 'Fragmentation Strategies and the Rise of Small Units: Cases from the North-West'. *Regional Studies*, Vol. 21, No. 1 pp. 13–23.

Smallbone, D. (2004) 'Institutions, Governance and SME Development in Transition Economies', Article 5. Working Party on Industry and Enterprise Development, Expert meeting on Good Governance for SMEs, April. European Commission for Europe.

Storey, D. (1994) *Understanding the Small Business Sector*, London: Routledge.

Thomson, A. and Gray, C. (1999) 'Determinants of Management Development in Small Businesses', *Journal of Small Business and Enterprise Development*, Vol. 6, No. 2 pp. 113–27.

Wenger, E. (1998) *Communities of Practice: Learning, Meaning and Identity*, Cambridge: Cambridge University Press.

Wenger, E. (2000) 'Communities of Practice and Social Learning Systems', *Organization*, Vol. 7, No. 2, pp. 225–46.

Williamson, O. (1975) *Markets and Hierarchies: Analysis and Antitrust Implications*, New York: Free Press.

Windrum, P., de Berranger, P. and Meldrum, M. (2003) UK SME-Internet Tracking Study, MMUBS.

Zhang, M., Macpherson, A., Taylor, D. and Jones, O. (2004) *Networks of Learning: SME Managerial Approaches and Responses*, Manchester: Manchester Metropolitan University Business School.

8

e-GOVERNANCE AND LOCAL GOVERNMENT

JANICE MORPHET

Introduction

This chapter sets out ways in which the United Nations Educational Scientific and Cultural Organisation (UNESCO) goals of e-Governance through e-Administration, e-Services and e-Democracy have been used as a means of developing an e-Government delivery programme for local authorities in England from the period 2000 onwards. Since the 1997 election, much of the government's attention has been focused on how to turn policy into action. A variety of different approaches have been used and there has also been a more critical look at civil service implementation skills and an increase in external recruitment. There seems to be an impatience to find a cadre of deliverers rather than thinkers. One of the teams which was set up which did not conform to any of these patterns was the Local Government Modernisation Team, set up in the Government department responsible for local government and made up of those with senior experience of local government. It had the combined roles of developing policy and ensuring delivery in a particular policy area – that of local e-Government.

In 1999, the Prime Minister set a target for local government to e-enable 100 per cent of transactions by December 2005 (Cabinet Office 1999). e-Government is about using technology to provide services in ways which people prefer. In the *Modernising Government* White Paper (1999), the Prime Minster established a target for all government services to be e-enabled for the citizen by December 2005. This approach was based on a stated wish to move from central to local delivery, with government as a whole being seen to being 'convenient, customised and cost-effective' (Byrne 1997). Finally, the Central Government lead department was given £675m capital funding to support local authorities in delivering on e-Government 2000–2006.

The same 2005 e-Government target was applied to local and central government although the means of measurement of the achievement of that target were different. For Central Government, the emphasis was on the development of e-Business plans which concentrated on the services provided by Whitehall Departments and Agencies directly to the public. These services were seen as the main way to achieve the highest percentages of e-enabled services by volume (e.g. Inland Revenue's online tax return service). The success of local authorities in achieving this target was to be measured by a Best Value Performance Indicator, which was operational from April 2001.

Local e-Government Delivery Strategy

The immediate delivery concern was to use the funding to achieve defined e-Government targets but in a way that would be of positive value to local authorities and the communities they served. Priority was given to the development of e-Enabled services, improved e-Administration and the development of e-Democracy. To support local authorities to achieve these outcomes by 2005, an approach was developed that used two complementary methods. The first was based on building capacity within local government, through joint working and partnerships. The second was the identification of clear and measurable targets which were self-assessed annually and externally checked by auditors at fixed points. It was agreed that outcome measures would be used as far as possible leaving each local authority to determine the means and timescales for delivery within the overall time horizon. This was to prevent an artificial increase in supplier prices, as over 300 local authorities seeking to implement e-payment or CRM systems at the same time would create an artificial demand such as happened in 2000. It would also enable local authorities to implement business change programmes as part of their overall workload, rather than seeing e-Government as a separate activity.

Identifying Operational e-Government Targets

In order to support e-Government delivery at the local level, local authorities were asked to prepare their own action plans, known as Implementing Electronic Government (IEG) statements. Although some common content was requested, councils were asked to demonstrate how they intended to reach the e-Government target by using locally set programmes and targets. This approach was much criticised by suppliers and some other parts of government. However, there was a willing acceptance of the target from local government.

Local e-Government was set seven critical tests of success by Central Government in providing e-Services, which were:

- joined-up in ways that make sense to the customer,
- accessible,
- delivered (or supported) electronically,
- delivered jointly,
- delivered seamlessly,
- open and accountable,
- used by citizens (e-gov@local DTLR 2002).

In return for preparing a satisfactory IEG statement, funding for individual local authorities was made from the £675m funding, and over the five-year period each local authority in England received £900,000. This funding was allocated on a flat-rate basis to all local authorities regardless of size. This was innovative and based on recognition that smaller local authorities would need a disproportionate amount of funding as they deal with the greater proportion of citizen transactions. It was also considered that larger councils could generate more efficiencies from improving processes.

Local authorities were encouraged to work together to seek benefits from joint procurement and shared expertise. A partnership fund for joined-up approaches across local authorities was also established and the Audit Commission report 'Message beyond the medium' (Audit Commission 2002) demonstrated that within a year of IEGs being submitted for the first time, over 90 per cent of councils were working together, which represented a significant change in working practices.

Despite this, many local authorities considered the e-Government agenda to be costly and risky in technological terms. A series of early projects provided live models with software or systems for councils to use. In all, 25 projects were developed including smart cards, electronic planning application processes and e-procurement, customer relationship management systems (CRM) and knowledge management systems. These projects were set a tight timescale for delivery in 12 months and they were required to disseminate their learning and their products to local government as a condition of funding and over 150 proposals for funding were submitted with private sector partners. Although there was some expectation that not all projects would deliver given these time constraints, the only real issues were faced by projects that had to deal with changes in the digital TV market place, which was particularly vulnerable in 2001/2002. The outcome of these projects was a series of products that were developed by and for local government, were operationally successful and reshaped the supply market.

Access to e-Services

The use of e-Government to deliver e-Services has generally been set within the debate about digital inclusion, with many arguing that e-enabled services are exclusionary to those who do not have access to digital services. It is important to review this issue before considering the delivery of e-Services because it can become a barrier to debate about the role of e-Services and their contribution to the majority of the population. In England, household broadband access was 63% in 2006 (www.statistics.gov.uk) and is still rising each year. The use of the web to buy goods and services in the UK is the second highest in the world after the US, and UK businesses received the second highest numbers of orders via electronic means in Europe. This includes access to member-only website services provided by leading football clubs such as Manchester United (e.g. www.manutd.com and www.liverpoolfc.tv) that have a wide cross-section of membership.

This development in the use of web-enabled services has also been supported by the digital switchover for television, local digital TV services and mobile phone development. Hence although not everyone has web access at home, the vast majority of people have access at work, through a publicly provided facility, a private corner shop Internet café or through a proxy – generally a friend or relation. The evidence of use and acceptance of the web as part of daily life in England is now accepted.

However, this means that those without access may feel excluded from peer groups and others, although for younger people access at school or college is good. The greatest increase in the use of the web is from those who are aged over 80. For those communities that are digitally excluded, a number of initiatives are in train such as those in East Manchester and Newham. In these, whole areas are provided with wifi, access and training. Also for those in social housing, tenant training schemes are also being provided. So although some people remain excluded from the web channel, other channels remain for use. It is also important to consider that those who do not use the web also include a high proportion of 'web refusers', who will never have any interest in accessing information or services in this way.

The high level of take-up of purchasing online in Britain has also led to the question of why public service take-up is lower that in other countries in Europe and North America. One of the obvious responses to this issue is the geography of distance, with web services in Canada and the US holding records for the highest take-up although their population density may be much lower than in a more urbanised country such as Britain. Web take-up in Europe is also greater in Finland and Sweden, where distance and climate do not support face-to-face access. In Latvia, web take-up is high because new services have been able to build on existing citizen registration processes and new services have been designed for web delivery.

In Britain access to public services online has been the subject of repeated campaigns by central government. The government website, (www.directgov.gov.uk) provides a generalised access to many services, although there are also many additional government websites outside this system. The success of some Government services online including personal taxation and car tax have demonstrated that it is possible to attract high usage if the service can be accessed quickly, it is accurate and supported by strong systems. This has led to the proposals to streamline all Government websites into this service

(Varney 2006). The digital exclusion argument would also have more force if other channels were closed once web channels were opened. However, local government has always kept all channels open and has made strong efforts to develop the interoperability of channels by users. So, the use of e-Government can change the means of interaction (Flinders 2002) whilst not seeking to replace existing means of interaction.

Supporting Citizen Engagement and Delivery

The contract between the citizen and the state, whether in the existing or new forms, is likely to be seen from the citizen's perspective in the ways in which their public service interactions work. This will include how easy they are to operationalise, the credibility of their outcome and the security of their use:

- Form of interaction – is it easy to use?
- Issues to be considered – how meaningful are they?
- Decisions – are they at least in part dependent on the interaction?
- Organisational cultures – are these amenable to the interaction and its potential outcome?
- Administrative silos – are these preventing access? Do organisations treat me as the same person without multiple provision of the same information?
- Professionalism – are boundaries preventing joined-up delivery?
- Tracking – can I always find out where my concerns are in the process as I can on Amazon?
- Citizens or subjects – am I central to the process or am I lucky to get what is given?

e-Services

Local authorities in England were required to deliver e-Services through ten generic transaction types against which their performance was measured:

1. Providing information.
2. Collecting revenue.

3. Providing benefits and grants.
4. Consultation.
5. Regulation.
6. Application for services.
7. Booking venues, courses and resources.
8. Paying for goods and services.
9. Providing access to community, professional or business networks.
10. Procurement. ((Department of Environment Transport and the Regions (DETR, 2000a)

The ability to join up services around citizens at the local level now can be more rapidly operationalised using e-Government tools than has been possible before. These tools provide the means to provide citizens with their entitlements rather than expect each individual to pursue claims from a plethora of agencies. These entitlements can be generated either personally or through intermediaries. e-Government can change 'the relationship between the governors and the governed and will be more complex, direct and immediate' (DETR 2000a, 33), leading to greater transparency and disclosure (Flinders 2002).

Although ensuring that entitlement details are correct remains a key concern, the ability to improve take-up in under-claiming households, to change payments as soon as circumstances change and to switch on new services at the point of immediate need such as free school meals is a prize worth considering. Such entitlement approaches can remove the dependency relationship between the citizen and the state, which currently is seen to persist. Entitlement can be seen as less emotive than 'benefit' although all words can be overladen with new meanings in time (Varney 2006; Lyons 2006).

e-Administration

Local authorities also quickly saw that e-enablement could help to streamline the back office to provide more joined-up citizen services. Although there is an efficiency driver in this approach, it is primarily focused on resolution of all issues at the first contact and using multi-service contact centres. This develops the notion of the individual citizen or business account – a concept that is growing into delivery (Varney 2006).

The immediate contact with citizens, regardless of the channel, is increasingly likely to be supported by the use of a customer relations management system (CRM), which can track customers or citizens through these different points of contact. A CRM can ensure that the organisation knows that it is dealing with the same person. Personal needs can be profiled to ensure that people receive the best service. This process can be extended so that a call or email, which is automatically put into the back office system, can be performance managed, and commitment accounted. The process can be transparent throughout its passage through the system by the citizen on the website, at home or in the library or through digital TV. The same information can be used by staff engaged in face-to-face processes or on the phone, using the same technology.

In order to deliver in ways that are joined-up to the citizen, local authorities also took the view that they could go further. Not only would it be helpful if all services within the local authority could be delivered jointly but these should also be joined in some way to those public services which are delivered by other organisations – notably central government departments. For planning matters, this was seen to provide far greater integration with other agencies such as the Environment Agency, Fire Service, Health and Safety Executive. This could also be extended across neighbouring areas to reduce the impact of administrative and geographical boundaries where this made sense to the user. In planning, there are obvious benefits and user synergies in a joined-up regulatory and enforcement process where often a number of organisations are involved at different points in the process. This also extends to consultees on planning policy and application matters.

Encouraging e-Democracy – The Debate

The continuing debates and concerns about the engagement of citizens with government generate considerable theoretical and applied discussion on understanding this 'problem'. Overall, there is an assumption that a 'healthy' democracy is one in which 'there are major opportunities for the mass of ordinary people actively to participate' (Crouch 2000; 1). Much of this debate relies on improving models of engagement between citizens and the state based on a traditional relationship which primarily revolves around the producer's view and the ballot box. Additionally, there are some who would argue that this effort to improve engagement is largely illusory, with professionals, politicians and administrators preferring to maintain the status quo. In terms of solutions to this 'problem' of democratic engagement, there are those who have argued or hoped that e-Government could make a significant contribution.

The Citizen/State Contract

The more recent shift in the debate from issues of government to those of governance marks a new way of demonstrating equality in the contractual relationship between government and the citizen. It also represents a move away from subject to citizen (Magnette 2003). This transfer has been engendered by a number of issues. Firstly, the concept of governmental legitimacy is being seen as one of considerable concern (Parkinson 2003) in the context of notional 'democratic deficits' being defined by low voter turnout. Other issues have centred on the increase of the appointed 'quangocracy' and the privatisation of services. In seeking to overcome these democratic deficits, a number of approaches have been adopted. One approach has been widening the areas and organisation involved in the political process into the voluntary and business movements. A further approach has been to widen the means of citizen engagement through citizens' juries, focus groups, telephone polls, etc. Finally, new methods to improve citizen engagement in traditionally legitimating ways have been introduced such as the ballot box through new e-Voting methods (Representation of the People Act 2000).

Yet active citizenship, through participation is not always viewed positively. Where citizen engagement reaches higher levels of participation, particularly at the local level of governance, there are often concerns that the process can be taken over by local elites. Attempts to increase citizen engagement often show that it is where people are against proposed government actions that they rise up and organise e.g. fuel protests (Doherty et al 2003) rather than where they support the general run of policy. As active participation is being encouraged, the concerns about active participation by the articulate are being balanced by a return to evidence-based policy making in such processes as the development of Community Strategies. Evidence about the progress of citizens in educational attainment, about road deaths or low health levels are expected to be used to target policies for improvement across all the public sector agencies at the local level.

Other approaches to changing this relationship concentrate on the failure of participation amongst specific groups related to age or class. There has been particular concern about the loss of interest in young people, which is seen to have considerable implications for the future of voting behaviours, thus fundamentally questioning the basis of future political legitimacy (Henn et al 2002). As Henn et al found, there is no evidence of a lack of interest in political issues from young people but rather a concern that traditional means of participation do not seem to affect outcomes. However, this research did show that varying the form of elections as enabled by the Representation of the People Act 2000 would encourage more participation in the electoral process. Such approaches offered included voting by phone and internet or in a public place. The greatest interest was generated by being able to vote over more than one day. Young people were also interested in compulsory voting as a means of encouraging participation – a means which is found to be successful in Australia (Hill 2002). Other research has shown that participation in planning exercises has been made more useful where all responses and comments were made available on the web over the period of consultation (Murray and Greer 2002).

Has Local e-Government Been Successful?

e-Government provides local tools of governance and delivery, which can begin to overcome barriers although these need to be combined with organisational and political will. Easier transactions do not improve the experience if they remain separate or low in relevance. The combination of channels can improve the *means* as citizens can use the method they prefer on each occasion. At the same time, the citizen should be able to obtain added value from each transaction regardless of the means, so that requests for one service can lead to the offer of others which could be available or relevant.

The provision of e-Government creates more transparency (Flinders 2002) with less ability to withhold information. Issues that have also been primarily regarded as *'professional'* can also be opened to wider participation through e-Government. This can occur in a variety of ways – through greater provision of information about entitlement rules, viewing progress of applications and cases and also through the development of one-stop delivery for services, which can expose specific services to more detached performance monitoring. e-Government can also provide more information not only on the issue but also during the process of decision making (Murray and Greer 2002).

e-Government cannot remove all the barriers to joint working between professionals, but the ability to join case records or track those in the system changes the parameters of potential delivery. One recent example of this is the system being developed for children at potential risk. Joined-up systems encourage an open debate between different professional groups on differing but similar application forms, differing protocols for similar reasons or services. These joined-up approaches also allow for all appropriate staff to be able to access and contribute to records, enabling case-tracking regardless of child movements and multiple agency involvement.

e-Government cannot change the nature of the content of *decisions* and this remains a matter for political determination. However, it can assist in changing the climate of what can be considered and how this can be done. The same is true of organisational cultures although the openness of e-Government can create a context within which internally driven producer cultures are less acceptable. Reforms including Business Process Re-engineering (BPR) may assist in removing long-established working practices where these persist. The same is true of administrative silos where these are preventing access to service and entitlement. Organisations can now treat citizens as the same person without multiple provision of the same information. Services again can be offered proactively rather than the weight of responsibility for service access being primarily on the citizen. Citizens can track the progress of their own business and organisations will be more exposed to dealing with the causes of delay. Poor access to service will no longer be able to be used as a means of rationing service delivery.

Finally, e-Government can encourage the transition from people being 'citizens' rather than 'subjects'. Entitlement can be clearer and more accessible. It can be related to individual circumstances and public service can start to provide added value. The reduced distance between the service and the responsible organisation can help improve accountability. Increased expectations of citizen-centred delivery methods, which are transparent, participative and clearly monitored can all serve to change this state/citizen contract. Citizens can be central to the process rather than feel lucky with what they are given.

The EU Approach

In addition to the Prime Minister's target for e-Government achievement in local and central government, the EU has also identified e-Government as one of their major fields of activity in e-Europe (Council of the European Commission, (CEC 2003)). In this programme, which was formally adopted on 21 February 2003, the Action Plan has identified a common list of basic public services which list twenty transactions which the Member State governments have agreed should be benchmarked across the EU. This list of services includes applications for building permission which we can assume is planning consent. The other transactions deal with issues such as change of address, car registration, enrolment in higher education. Achievement of the these targets is to be benchmarked (CEC 2002) and includes the number of services available on the web, but also the use of the web for four monitored transactions – obtaining information, obtaining forms, returning completed forms. There is also a supplementary indicator which each Member State is asked to identify how many public transactions are integrated with the back office. The focus on the use of the web and emphasis on back office integration probably goes further than the Best Value Performance Indicator (BVPI) requirements as they stand for England. Nevertheless considerable progress is being encouraged in this direction

through the annual process of each authority producing an Implementing Electronic Government Statement (Office of the Deputy
Prime Minister (2002d) and the national strategy on local
e-Government (ODPM 2002b).

Conclusions

The approach adopted to introduce e-Government in local government was very different from a more traditional approach to policy
making and delivery in central government. Firstly, it was citizen
focused from the outset and did not use a fully prescriptive style.
Secondly, it has encouraged local authorities to use their own
priorities to drive implementation. Thirdly, it encouraged local
authorities to generate their own solutions rather than use 'single
bullet' products developed for them. By using dedicated funding to
develop capacity and to use the implementation and problem-solving
skills of local authorities, the e-Government agenda has been one that
has been able to release the positive energy within local government.
It has been an outcome-focused approach, not input driven.

For the private sector, this approach has provided some impetus
to change. It has provided larger contracts; it has benefited from participating in the creation of new products; it has provided incentives
to innovate and finally the use of flat-rate funding demonstrated a
commitment from government to delivery which has given some
security to providers.

Finally the team which developed e-Government policy for the
local level policy was also directly involved in its delivery. Thus feed-
back is immediately considered and many minor changes were
accommodated to ensure that approaches fit with changes in local
government including best value, e-Democracy, and the CPA processes. Local authorities were encouraged to work together in ways
which they did not finding threatening; they were able to share
problems and solutions as they tackle delivery in locally determined
programmes. Progress has been fast and yet there has been recognition that joining up services around citizens is beneficial if achieved.
It is the cultural challenges within local authorities which need to be
tackled now and not the technical ones (ODPM 2002 a, b, c).

In all of this, working with the grain of local government, under-standing the operational climate, knowing about the pressure of initia-tive overload and avoiding some the usual resentment which is felt by the imposition of top-down solutions is generating innovative change. However, if the level of activity is an indication of the changes that are being brought about in citizen focus, changing and reducing depart-mental boundaries and offering new ways to work then local govern-ment seems to have a good chance of success. There are few other programmes to compare with the delivery of e-Government at the local level. As yet the approach used has not been copied elsewhere. It will be useful for all in central and local government to see how this delivers in the longer term. At present from a later start, e-Government readi-ness in local government is seen to be making significant progress.

Bibliography

Audit Commission (2002) *Message Beyond the Medium*: *Improving Local Government Services through e-Government in England* London: Audit Commission.

Audit Commission (2003) *Connecting with Users and Citizens* London: Audit Commission.

Balls, E. (2003) 'Foreword'. In *New Localism* D. Corry and G. Stoker London: IPPR.

Blair, T. (2002) 'The Courage of Our Convictions: Why Reform of the Public Services is the Route to Social Justice' *Fabian Ideas* 603 London: The Fabian Society.

Blaug, R. (2002) 'Engineering Democracy' *Political Studies* Vol. 50 pp. 102–16.

Byrne, L. (1997) *Information Age Government: Delivering the Blair Revolution* London: Fabian Society.

Cabinet Office (1999) *Modernising Government* London: HMSO.

Cabinet Office (2000) *e.gov: Electronic Government Services for the 21st Century* London: PIU/Cabinet Office.

Cabinet Office (2001) *Better Policy Delivery and Design: A Discussion Paper* London: PIU/Cabinet Office.

CEC (2002) *Draft Paper on Benchmarking Citizen Transactions* Brussels: European Commission.

CEC (2003) *e-Europe* Brussels: European Commission.

Copus, C. (2001) 'New Political Management Arrangements and the Party Group: New Models of Political Behaviour' *Local Governance* Vol. 27 No. 1 pp. 53–63.

Corry, D. and Stoker, G. (2003) *New Localism Refashioning the Centre-local Relationship* London: New Local Government Network.

Cross, M. (2003) 'Spoke in the Wheel' *The Guardian Inside* IT p. 18 10th April.

Crouch, C. (2000) 'Coping with Post-Democracy' *Fabian Ideas* 598 London: The Fabian Society.

Crouch, C. (2003) 'Commercialisation or Citizenship Education Policy and the Future of Public Services' *Fabian Ideas* 606 London: The Fabian Society.

DETR (2000a) *Best Value Performance Indicators* London: DETR.

DETR (2000b) *Local Government Act* London: DETR.

Doherty, B., Paterson, M., Plows, P. and Wall, D. (2003) 'Explaining the Fuel Protests' *British Journal of Politics and International Relations* Vol. 5 No. 1 pp. 1–23.

DTLR (1999) *Local Government Act* London: DTLR.

DTLR (2001a) *Access for all Modern Councils Modern Services* London: DTLR.

DTLR (2001b) *Community Strategy Guidance* London: DTLR.

DTLR (2002) e-gov@local *Draft National Strategy for Local e-Government* London: DTLR.

Flinders, M. (2002) 'Shifting the Balance?: Parliament, the Executive and the British Constitution' *Political Studies* Vol. 50 No. 1 pp. 23–42.

Graham, S. (2002) 'Bridging Urban Digital Divides? Urban Polarisation and Information and Communication Technologies' (ICTs) *Urban Studies* Vol. 39 No. 1 pp. 33–56.

Grieco, M. (2000) 'Intelligent Urban Development: The Emergence of "Wired" Government and Administration Guest Editor's Introduction' *Urban Studies* Vol. 37 No. 10 pp. 1719–21.

Henn, M., Weinstein, M. and Wring, D. (2002) 'A Generation Apart? Youth and Political Participation in Britain' *British Journal of Politics and International Relations* Vol. 4 No. 2 pp. 167–92.

Hill, L. (2002) 'On the Reasonableness of Compelling Citizens to "Vote": The Australian Case' *Political Studies* Vol. 50 pp. 80–101.

Illsley, B., Lloyd, M.G. and Lynch, B. (1999) 'One Stop Shops in Scotland: Diversity in Co-ordination and Integration?' *Local Governance* Vol. 25 No. 4 pp. 201–10.

Leach, S. (2002) 'Is there a Future for Overview and Scrutiny?' *Local Governance* Vol. 28 No. 2 pp. 83–9.

Ling, T. (2002) 'Delivering Joined Up Government in the UK: Dimensions, Issues and Problems' *Public Administration* Vol. 80 No. 4 pp. 615–42.

Lyons, M. (2006) *National Priority, Local Choice and Civic Engagement* London: Her Majesty's Treasury.

Magnette, P. (2003) 'European Governance and Civic Participation: Beyond Elitist Citizenship?' *Political Studies* Vol. 51 pp. 144–60.

Marchington M., Cooke, F.L. and Hebson, G. (2003) 'Performing for the "customer": Managing Housing Benefit Operation across Organisational Boundaries' *Local Government Studies* Vol. 29 No. 1 pp. 51–74.

Margetts, H. and Dunleavy, P. (2002) *Better Public Services through e-Government* London: National Audit Office.

Moreira, G. (2003) *e-Government in Local Level in Portugal* Planning Research Conference Oxford Brookes University.

Morphet, J. (2003a) 'Joining Policy with Implementation in Central Government: The Approach to e-Government' *Local Government Studies* Vol. 29 No. 1 Spring pp. 111–16.

Morphet, J. (2003b) *Understanding e-Government* London: Chadwick House.

Murray, M. and Greer, J. (2002) 'Participatory Planning as Dialogue: The Northern Ireland Regional Strategic Framework and its Public Examination Process' *Policy Studies* Vol. 23 No. 3/4 pp. 191–209.

National Audit Office (2001) *Joining Up to Improve Public Services* London: Her Majesty's Stationery Office.

ODPM (2002a) *Councils Freed from Whitehall Controls* Press Notice 26 November London: ODPM.

ODPM (2002b) *Local e-Government National Strategy for Local e-Government* London: ODPM.

ODPM (2002c) *Sustainable Communities Delivering Through Planning* London: ODPM.

ODPM (2002d) *Implementing Electronic Government Statements Guidance* London: ODPM.

ODPM (2002f) *Plans Rationalisation Study Report* London: ODPM.

Office for Public Sector Reform (2002) *Reforming our Public Services Principles into Practice* London Cabinet Office.

Parkinson, J. (2003) 'Legitimacy Problems in Deliberative Democracy' *Political Studies* Vol. 51 No. 1 pp. 180–96.

Performance and Innovation Unit (2001) *Joining up to Improve Public Services*

Pollitt, C. (2003) *Joined Up Government: A Survey Political Studies Review* Vol. 1 pp. 34–49.

Portfolio Communications (2003) *The Take Up of e-Government Services* ICM.

Rushmer, R. and Pallis, G. (2002) 'Inter-Professional Working: The Wisdom of Integrated Working and the Disaster of Blurred Boundaries' *Public Money and Management* October–December pp. 59–66.

Snape, S. and Taylor, F. (2000) 'Scrutiny' *Local Governance* Vol. 26 No. 3 pp. 187–203.

Sweeting, D. and Ball, H. (2002) 'Overview and Scrutiny of Leadership: The Experience of Bristol City Council' *Local Governance* Vol. 28 No. 3 pp. 201–12.

Varney, D. (2006) *Service Transformation: A Better Service for Citizens and Businesses, A Better Deal for the Taxpayer* London: Her Majesty's Treasury.

Webb, P. and Fisher, J. (2003) 'Professionalism and the Millbank Tendency: The Political Sociology of New Labour's Employees' *Politicks* Vol. 23(1) pp. 10–20.

Wright, S. (2002) 'Dogma or Dialogue? The Politics of the Downing Street Website' *Politics* Vol. 22(3) pp. 135–42.

Woodman, C. (1999) 'The Evolving Role of Professionals in Local Government' *Local Governance* Vol. 25 No. 4 pp. 211–19.

9

e-GOVERNMENT, DISABILITY AND INCLUSION

FINTAN CLEAR AND CHARLES DENNIS

Introduction

When the World Wide Web Consortium (W3C) launched its initiative to develop guidelines promoting accessible website design for people with disabilities, Berners-Lee, father of the Web, observed that 'The power of the Web is in its universality. Access by everyone regardless of disability is an essential aspect' (W3C, 1997). Similarly, commentators in government, education, medicine, charitable agencies and society at large have lauded the Web as a means of allowing people with disabilities some level of independence and social inclusion that might otherwise be difficult and perhaps impossible to achieve in the offline world. Thus receipt of state benefits, organisation of healthcare, delivery of education, communication with local and national government, and the exercise of democratic rights, let alone increased opportunities to work, shop and be entertained, can all be enabled for those with disabilities, so the proponents argue, by use of the Web. While there is undoubtedly truth in these contentions, such enabling is not without complexity. Thus this chapter seeks to explore the issues that promote and inhibit use of the Web for these ends.

This chapter begins with a brief examination of forces that strove for a paradigmatic shift in societal thinking in regard to the disabled, and goes on to catalogue policy development and legislation that sought to outlaw discrimination on the basis of disability in the UK. After examining the 'digital divide' and how this can affect people with disabilities, concepts of website accessibility are examined along with the development of guidelines that seek to promote such usability. The chapter goes on to note critiques of policy and accessibility guidelines from empirical and theoretical perspectives. This is then followed by concluding remarks.

Disability and the Rise of Social Constructivism

'In the 1960s, the dominant view of an individual with an impairment was that life was a personal tragedy' (Barnes and Mercer, 2005). Citing Oliver (1983), these writers observe that a 'functional limitations perspective' encouraged politicians, professionals and practitioners to view disabled people as a 'problem' who were dependent, and in need either of 'cure' or 'care'. Such views however were increasingly criticised by self-help groups of disabled people that sprung up in the 1970s and rejected this apparent 'clinical' or 'medical model'. Their charge was voiced by the 'Union of Physically Impaired Against Segregation' (UPIAS) amongst others, which argued that disability was an artificial and exclusionary social construction that penalised people with impairments who do not conform to mainstream expectations of appearance, behaviour and/or economic performance (Tregaskis, 2002). Finkelstein (1980) and Oliver (1983) supported this charge by advancing theoretical positions that challenged contemporary norms, arguing instead that it was society itself, not disabled people, which has impairments.

Thus Oliver, for example, contended that the medical view in which 'disability' was seen as incapacity should be replaced by a 'social model' of disability which directs focus away from individual functional limitations, and instead to the barriers to social inclusion created by disabling environments, attitudes and cultures. He argued for a holistic approach that would focus on a multiplicity of barriers to service delivery in everyday life, including inaccessible education, working environments, and information and communication systems, inadequate disability benefits, discriminatory health and social support services, inaccessible transport, housing, public buildings and amenities, and negative cultural and media representations. Citing Bickenbach et al (1999) and Van Oorschot and Hvinden (2001), Barnes and Mercer (2005) argue that such analyses gained a growing influence on social policy at both the national and international levels, and thus helped contribute to a paradigm shift at societal levels in which normative approaches to service delivery began to be replaced by differential and inclusive approaches to disability. Ultimately such sentiments have been reflected in legislative process such that, amongst other national efforts, the US passed into law the 'Americans with Disabilities Act' in 1990, Australia the 'Disability Discrimination Act' in 1992 and the UK the 'Disability Discrimination Act' in 1995. As the Web has evolved, these legal instruments, allied by policy developments at international, regional and national levels, have been interpreted to include discrimination in an online form. This has led in turn to the promotion of 'accessible' website design through which such discrimination may be minimised.

Legislation: The Disability Discrimination Act (1995)

Riddell (2003) argues that the incumbent Conservative government was initially resistant to disability legislation, but finally passed the Disability Discrimination Act (DDA) in 1995. To the disappointment of disability campaigners, education was excluded in part due to the cost to the public purse of making schools subject to the legislation. Nevertheless the DDA established 'comprehensive and enforceable civil rights for people with disabilities, granting statutory rights in the areas of employment; access to goods, services and facilities; and the buying and renting of property' (Schmidt et al, 2005).

Enacted in three parts, Part I, which came into force in 1996, made it unlawful to treat a disabled person less favourably for a reason related to their disability. Part II, which came into force in 1999, required service providers to make reasonable adjustments to prevent their arrangements or premises from discriminating against disabled people using their services. Part II also required the establishment of an independent body called the 'Disability Rights Commission' (DRC); created in 2000, the DRC acts as an independent body upholding rights for the disabled, and plays a critical role in the formulation of codes of practice and encouragement of the advancement of disability rights (Sloan, 2001). Part III, which came into force in 2004, focuses on physical adjustments and 'requires providers of goods, facilities and services to . . . make reasonable adjustments, including the provision of auxiliary aids and services, to any practices, policies or procedures which make it unreasonably difficult for disabled people to make use of the services they provide' (DRC, 2004). The act applies to all service providers in the public, private and voluntary sectors, and for their free or paid-for services.

Taking a more expansive view of disability rights, implies Riddell (2003), the incoming Labour government in 1997 created a 'Disability Rights Task Force' which, reporting in 1999 (DfEE, 1999), recommended extensions to the DDA. This ultimately led to the 2001 Special Educational Needs and Disability Act (SENDA) which removed education institutions from exemption under the DDA. Thus Part IV of the DDA came into force in England, Scotland and Wales in 2002, with Northern Ireland enacting separate legislation at this point.

According to the DDA, 'A disabled person is someone who has a physical or mental impairment which has an effect on his or her ability to carry out normal day-to-day activities. That effect must be . . . substantial adverse, and long-term . . .' (DDA, 1995).

The heterogeneity of disabilities makes precise classification illusory, but Bohman and Anderson (2004) cite a number of 'major categories' including 'visual disabilities' (blindness, low vision, colour blindness), 'deafness', 'motor disabilities' (slow movement, inability to use a mouse, etc.), 'cognitive disabilities' (reading disorders, attention deficit disorders, etc.) and 'seizure disorders' (such as epilepsy). Disabilities have spectrums of severity so that, as cited, visual impairments include colour blindness and range from near- or far-sighted conditions all the way to full blindness. Additionally some individuals have lifelong conditions, while others suffer disability as the result of accidents or illness, with the incidence of the latter increasing, as noted above, as a consequence of age. Studies that examine the impact that specific disabilities have for web page use include Anderson et al (2004) and Poulson and Nicolle (2004) who look at cognitive impairments, Berry (1999) who looks at visual impairment, the RNIB (2002) who look at blindness, and Gybels (2004) who looks at deafness.

The multi-dimensional and dynamic nature of disability makes measurement elusive, but across the world one estimate shows that there are around 750 million people with disabilities (Larkin, 2000). Some 8.5 million of the UK adult population are thought by the Disability Rights Commission (based on 2001 census returns) to have disabilities covered by legislation, though the UK Government's 'Regulatory Impact Assessment' works on the basis of 11.7 million people being so affected (Schmidt et al, 2005). Comparative statistics show 54 million people in the United States (Paciello, 2000) and 3.7 million Australians (ABS, 1998) with disabilities. Burnett (1996) argues that there is a strong correlation between the needs of disabled people and the elderly, with Paciello citing one in two Americans of 65 years and older as having a disability, a much higher rate of disability than the average for the American population. Research with older people in the USA who are attempting to maintain independent lifestyles suggests that computers may extend autonomy and independence, helping successful adaptation to late life disability (Kahana et al, 2006).

Arguing a universal perspective, Darzentas and Miesenberger (2005) point out that providing support for visual, auditory and tactile (e.g touchscreen) access will also benefit users with small display screens (such as in mobile phones), Web TV and kiosks. Application of accessibility concepts also increases usability of websites when there is low bandwidth (where images, for example, are slow to load), when an 'unusual browser or operating system' is used and when there is a lack of fluency in the language a site is written in (Dunn, 2003). Larkin (2000) adds to this list noisy environments when it is difficult to hear audio. Thus Anderson et al, (2004) and Dunn (2003) observe that making a site accessible in this manner makes access easier for all users, whatever their circumstances. This highlights the value of concepts such as 'Design for All' (Darzentas and Miesenberger, 2005), 'universal usability' (Shneiderman, 2000) and 'universal design' (Mace et al, 1991). So quite apart from accommodating the needs of disabled users, policy and legislation that attempts to promote website accessibility will naturally be inclusive, for example, of a host of situations in which people are 'temporarily disabled' or incapacitated in some manner.

Although access to websites is never explicitly mentioned in the DDA, the form of words used in the Act does not exclude website accessibility (Kelly et al, 2005) as it refers to 'access to and use of means of communication . . . and information services' as examples of services covered by DDA provisions (DRC, 2004). Any ambiguity in these terms is resolved by explicit reference to accessibility issues in regard to websites by the DRC's Code of Practice published in 2002. Additionally the DRC (2004) report notes a pronouncement by an earlier Secretary of State for Education and Employment that 'includes commentary and examples that create a very strong anticipation that any future case law will support this interpretation of the Act' (DRC, 2004). Sloan (2001) asserts that it is common for UK courts to consider practice in other jurisdictions when dealing with 'new technology' problems, and that the UK DDA is very similar in content to the Australian DDA. When Australian legislation was tested in court in the case of 'Maguire v. The Sydney Organising Committee for the Olympic Games' (SOCOG), web accessibility was accepted as being within the scope of the Act. Bruce Maguire, a blind man, had argued successfully that the Olympics website was inaccessible due to a failure in the provision of 'ALT' tags amongst other failings. 'ALT' tags (noted above) are HTML attributes that allow images to be described in textual form, and if they are missing or contain deficient information, then it may be impossible to navigate for someone depending, for example, on screenreader software. To date, however, UK DDA legislation remains to be tested in court.

Digital Equality

As part of an e-Government discourse, UK government policy seeks to improve accessibility to technology and its ease of use for the digitally-excluded, a group that includes people with disabilities (Cabinet Office, 2005). This is enabled in part by a nationwide network of 'UK Online centres', often located in local libraries, where access to the Internet is available, and where there are opportunities for training in its use. Seen as offering a significant role in supporting e-Government policy, some success is cited in access terms with 74 per cent of otherwise digitally excluded individuals able to use these centres, and 34 per cent of citizens stating they would be able to access or learn to access e-Government services at UK Online centres (Cabinet Office, 2005). While low-cost access (in relative terms) is available at these centres and Internet cafés, most people prefer to access the Internet from home (Citizens Online, 2006). Naturally people with mobility issues will be amongst these. Not all UK Online centres have facilities for disabled people in any event: Bradbrook and Fisher (2004) note, for example, that 21 per cent of such centres do not provide wheelchair access.

Rogers (1995) argues that people who are slowest to take up an innovation such as the Internet are likely to be older with lower education levels and lower socioeconomic status (SES) than the average – i.e. the demographic characteristics most prone to social exclusion and commonly including people with disabilities. These characteristics are borne out in an analysis of the British Household Panel Study (carried out for the Future Foundation and British Telecom (BT, 2004)). Many poor and disabled inner city residents are already disadvantaged by not possessing suitable forms of transport so that, for example, accessing UK Online centres and local government offices is problematic. Fitch and Fernie (2002) demonstrated that the socially excluded tended to have low levels of computer ownership and Internet access. Whilst 40 per cent of owner occupied households had computers, only 16 per cent of renters did, falling to 13 per cent for social housing. Internet access for the lower income households was less than one-tenth of the level of the highest income ones.

Fitch (2004) drew attention to 'an extremely strong link between social exclusion and digital exclusion' based on the Scottish Household Survey. Households who found local food provision 'very convenient' were almost 50 per cent more likely to have a home computer than those who considered it 'very inconvenient'. Households who found food shopping least convenient were least likely to have a home computer with an Internet connection. The picture is similar across the UK as a whole, where the Oxford Internet Survey found a 'clear [positive] relationship between economic status and Internet use' (OxIS, 2005) Across the UK, 7 per cent of households are involuntarily excluded from the use of the Internet (Citizens Online, 2007). A report for the Joseph Rowntree Foundation (Kingston,

2001) demonstrated that though there have been many government initiatives to increase the variety of services and shopping available online, nevertheless, the report suggested that insufficient attention was being paid to access issues, including cost.

One set of Internet adoption figures for the population at large show that, of non-adopters, 57 per cent gave the response 'Don't want to' when asked about why they did not use the Internet (ONS, 2003). This contrasts with a figure of 15 per cent for disabled people. Even though large numbers of disabled people may be interested in using the Internet, 2.4 million of them are digitally excluded (Bradbrook and Fisher, 2004). In addition to economic factors, research identifies disability as one of the primary barriers to using the Internet (Senior Canada Online, 2001). It is forecast that by 2025, the number of registered disabled will increase as a proportion of the total digitally excluded from 10 per cent in 2004 to 16 per cent by 2025 (BT, 2004). In 2001, over 23,000 telephone enquiries were made by disabled people to AbilityNet's telephone helpline. Pilling et al (2004) surveyed a sample of these (n = 196) and reported that 29 per cent of these enquirers did not use the Internet. By far the most common reason for this was cost (40 per cent). The other principal reasons were the need for training and having the right adaptations. Nearly nine out of ten (89 per cent) of the disabled respondents stated that they would be more likely to use the Internet if they had more funding, adaptations or training. Only one-third had heard of the government's 'UK Online' campaign. Only 10 per cent knew where their local UK Online Centre was and over 85 per cent thought that it would be a good idea for the Government to make all of its services available online.

A graphic illustration of the possibilities of the Internet for disabled people is given by one quote: 'Internet is the only method for a tetra-plegic for private [remote] communication [and] . . . the only way for a tetraplegic to shop.' (Bradbrook and Fisher, 2004). Apart from access to the technology per se, digital equality implies the ability for someone with complex needs such as a tetraplegic to gain efficacious use of that technology. Di Maggio and Hargittai (2001) note that as technology now 'penetrates into every crevice of society', the question of access should not be restricted therefore to connectivity and 'who can . . . log on?' but should also include 'what are people doing, and what are they able to do when they are online?' Critical of UK government policy which appears to hinge on avoiding a spectre of division between the 'connected' and the 'unconnected', Adam and Kreps (2006) argue that access to the Web needs to be examined through four discourses: the 'digital divide', the 'social construction of disability', the 'legal' and the 'web accessibility' discourse. Di Maggio and Hargittai (2001) create a taxonomy of universal usability factors that qualify concepts of Web access, and which therefore offer potential for inequality: technical means; autonomy of use; skill; social support; and purposes for which the technology is employed. All of these have their own dimensions that taken together reveal depths of relative equality. Thus training intervention is required to add to skill levels and autonomy of use. Social support implies the network of people that help can be sought from when problems are met. Equipment implies all the hardware, software and associated tools through which the Internet is used. In terms of purpose for which it is employed, the Internet offers a host of applications by which to work, study and enjoy leisure. If there were true 'digital equality', then a tetraplegic would be able to pursue their interests in the same way as any other Internet user.

There are a number of technologies that aid those with disabilities in use of the Internet. Over eight million people in the UK suffer from some form of disability causing them to have difficulty using the standard PC and keyboard (SOCITM, 2005). So Foley et al (2005) cite alternatives to the mouse and keyboard operated by feet, elbows or mouth. They cite other technologies with the blind and partially-sighted in mind such as voice activated speech recognition, synthesised speech and Braille printers. Sponsored by the government's Social Exclusion Unit, they argue that such hardware and software should be made available free of VAT (Value Added Tax) to disabled people. However while pointing to extra costs faced by disabled people in gaining efficacious use of the Internet, Foley et al (2005) also point to adaptations which are cost-free if little known such as the accessibility options in Microsoft products. Nevertheless in a dynamic marketplace, complexity is ever at hand given the rapid developments in technology, and this has implications for users. For example, advances in chip technology which enable greater processing capacities are then matched by the demands of software developers for that greater processing power in their applications. Such spiralling demands can render obsolete – to all intents and purposes – information and communications technology (ICT) in only a few years. While this has financial implications for all, the costs felt by those with restricted resources are much more acute.

Usability

As Rowan et al (2000) contend, 'Many web developers continue to hold the view that the Web is, by nature, a graphical medium and therefore is the domain of the graphic designer'. However they and the World Wide Web Consortium argue that the web can offer a means of delivering content whatever its format but that graphic representation should ultimately be under the control of the user. In this vein Chisholm et al (2001) point out a number of scenarios that need to be taken into account by website developers when considering users:

- They may not be able to see, hear, move, or may not be able to process some types of information easily or at all.
- They may have difficulty reading or comprehending text.
- They may not have or be able to use a keyboard or mouse.
- They may have a text-only screen, a small screen, or a slow Internet connection.
- They may not speak or understand fluently the language in which the document is written.
- They may be in a situation where their eyes, ears, or hands are busy or interfered with (e.g. driving to work, working in a loud environment, etc.).
- They may have an early version of a browser, a different browser entirely, a voice browser, or a different operating system.

Consideration of these different situations by website developers means that 'each accessible design choice generally benefits several disability groups at once and the Web community as a whole' (Chisholm et al, 2001).

W3C Web Accessibility Guidelines

The World Wide Web Consortium, which sees itself as an international, vendor-neutral consortium of 300 members, seeks to promote the 'evolution, interoperability, and universality of the Web' in four domains: 'Architecture', 'Interaction', 'Technology and Society', and the 'Web Accessibility Initiative' (WAI). The object of the WAI is to 'actively promote inclusive design practice for those with disabilities'. To this end in the last few years the W3C has worked with disability organisations, research centres and governments to help identify web design problems for people with particular disabilities (see www.w3c.org/WAI) in order to refine the guidelines. Separating into three 'components', the WAI contains provisions for (a) web content (Web Content Accessibility Guidelines 1.0 or WCAG 1.0), (b) web authoring tools (Authoring Tool Accessibility Guidelines 1.0 or ATAG 1.0), and (c) web browsers, media players and assistive technology (User Agent Accessibility Guidelines 1.0 or UAAG 1.0). The WAI is viewed by the W3C as a dominant instrument around which national guidelines for accessibility can be harmonised. Chisholm (noted above) is one of a number of prominent academics that have contributed to the work. As with all W3C recommendations, compliance is voluntary.

The Web Content Accessibility Guidelines have 14 points which summarise essential elements of accessible web design:

1. Provide equivalent alternatives to auditory and visual content.
2. Don't rely on colour alone.
3. Use mark-up and style sheets and do so properly.
4. Clarify natural language usage.
5. Create tables that transform gracefully.
6. Ensure that pages featuring new technologies transform gracefully.
7. Ensure user control of time-sensitive content changes.
8. Ensure direct accessibility of embedded user interfaces.
9. Design for device independence.
10. Use interim solutions.
11. Use W3C technologies and guidelines.
12. Provide context and orientation information.

13. Provide clear navigation mechanisms.

14. Ensure that documents are clear and simple.

There are 65 checkpoints (16 of which are designated as Priority 1, 30 as Priority 2 and 19 as Priority 3) which interpret and specify the application of the guidelines in website design. These checkpoints are graded in priority rankings:

- *Priority 1* is for checkpoints that 'a developer must satisfy other-wise some groups of people will be unable to access information on a site'.
- *Priority 2* is for checkpoints that 'a developer should satisfy or else it will be very difficult to access information'.
- *Priority 3* is for checkpoints that 'a developer may satisfy other-wise some people will find it difficult to access information'.

The checkpoints can benefit all users. For example, web access for people with visual disabilities can also help people accessing the web from mobile phones, hand-held devices, or car-based computers (i.e. when connection speed is too slow to support viewing images or video, or when a person's eyes are 'busy' with other tasks). Check-points such as captions support access for people with hearing impairments and also help people who are using the web in noisy environments (Pilling et al, 2004).

UK Cabinet Office guidelines (2002) stress the need for 'depart-ments and agencies to make their services as accessible to disabled people as is reasonably possible'. Thus the guidelines require compli-ance of central government websites with the 'Priority 1' checkpoints and some from 'Priority 2' and 'Priority 3'. Guidelines also require design to be professional and attractive, with content plainly written, broken up into lists and easily scanned (e-Envoy, 2003). Even so, many central government websites are not following the guidelines (Cuddy, 2003). Further attempts to consolidate good practice in webpage design terms have seen guidelines produced in 2006 by the British Standards Institution (BSI) called 'Publicly Available Specification' (PAS78) which was commissioned by the DRC in the light of the report 'The Web. Access and Inclusion for Disabled People' (DRC, 2004). PAS78 is not a BSI standard but offers advice on how to commission, plan, implement and maintain accessible websites.

Validation and Testing

There are a number of automatic software tools that when submitted with a webpage address or URL (Uniform Resource Locator) will generate non-conformance errors against WCAG guidelines. These include 'Page Valet', 'A-Prompt Toolkit' and 'Wave' but the most well-known tool according to the literature appears to be 'Bobby' even though it has now been replaced by 'WebExact'. After inputting the website address or Uniform Resource Locator (URL), such a tool scans the page and automatically generates a report which 'highlights areas of concern and suggesting what can be done to rectify them' (UK Cabinet Office, 2002). Use of such automated tools makes for rapid conformance checking, though the length of reports and quantity of detail can be 'daunting' (ibid). However as DRC (2004) analysis points out, 'Automatic testing tools alone cannot . . . verify effective compliance'. Echoing the views of Adam and Kreps (2006), Witt and McDermott (2004) observe that 'Software tools cannot evaluate a site for layout consistency, ease of navigation, provision of contextual and orientation information, and use of clear and easy-to-understand language'. The Cabinet Office guidelines point out limitations of such a tool and the fact that a successful test and any W3C WAI validation does not necessarily guarantee that the site is, for example, accessible via a screen reader, or that text used in ALT attributes for images (i.e. descriptive text that explains what the image represents) is appropriate.

Website Accessibility in the UK: The Confluence of Theory and Practice

In Feb 2001, the e-Minister, Patricia Hewitt, made a public commitment that all new government websites should be accessible. This was matched by Cabinet Office guidelines (Cabinet Office, 2002). However a National Audit Office report (NAO, 2003) showed that many government websites still did not incorporate design features that would make it easier for older people to use them. An examination of 65 websites likely to be of interest to many older people revealed that none complied with all the criteria, and only 25 per cent passed tests involving software to check adherence with worldwide standards. The Office of the e-Envoy has now begun to review government websites and discuss improvements with the relevant departments and agencies. Many are making improvements as they update their sites.

Whatever the legal strictures now in place in the UK, a comprehensive investigation into website accessibility sponsored by the DRC, entitled 'The Web. Access and Inclusion for Disabled People' (2004) makes clear that 'Despite the obligations created by the DDA, domestic research suggests that compliance, let alone the achievement of best practice on accessibility, has been rare'. The DRC report showed that an automatic conformance checking of 1,000 public websites revealed that only 19 per cent reached a minimum level of accessibility as defined by World Wide Web Consortium (W3C). Further in-depth analysis highlighted the fact that the automatic tools only picked up 45 per cent of the access problems with manual checking revealing the remainder.

The DRC (2004) report used notes evidence of issues and obstacles for website users from the perspective of a series of disabilities. Overall results for a set of tasks undertaken by the user group of 50 people who had different disabilities including blindness, being partially-sighted, hearing-impaired, physically-impaired, and dyslexic are shown in Table 9.1 (DRC, 2004).

Table 9.1 Task Success Rate by Impairment User Group

Impairment Group	Tasks Succeeded	Tasks Failed
Blind	53 per cent	47 per cent
Partially sighted	76 per cent	24 per cent
Dyslexic	83 per cent	17 per cent
Physically impaired	85 per cent	15 per cent
Hearing impaired	85 per cent	15 per cent
All impairments	76 per cent	24 per cent

Source: DRC, 2004

The most common refrain from the user group was the 'unclear and confusing layout of pages'. Many found compatibility problems between assistive technology and webpages so that, for example, screen reading software failed to detect certain links or invented non-existent ones. With the obvious exception of blind users, all found 'inappropriate use of colours and poor contrast between content and background' to be an issue, while hearing-impaired users found that 'lack of alternative media for audio-based information and complex terms/language' to be a problem particular to them. Overall the most disadvantaged group according to the report were blind users who, apart from confusing page structures and layouts which made screen reading and website navigation difficult, also suffered through 'ALT' tags for images with non-existent or unhelpful ALT tags for images. One of the report's conclusions is that accessibility is not just an issue for those with disabilities as all users benefit from clear and well-structured layout and other measures that make sites accessible and usable by blind people. The DRC report makes a broad range of recommendations for changes to accessibility guidelines used by the UK government.

Looking at public sector provision, the DRC (2004) cited evidence from other studies such as Kelly (2002) who described the level of compliance by UK universities with website industry guidance as 'disappointing' and a report by 'Interactive Bureau' (2002) into 20 key 'flagship' government websites which found that 75 per cent were 'in need of immediate attention in one area or another'. Criticism of the private sector included a study by the Royal National Institute of the Blind (2000) of 17 websites which concluded that the performance of high street stores and banks was 'extremely disappointing'; conformance audits by AbilityNet of popular UK airline and newspaper websites reported wholly poor accessibility with only one responding positively to a request to make a public commitment to accessibility. Among issues raised by other studies, Witt and McDermott (2004) note that some webpages which claim 'A1 status' are shown to be incorrect, for example, as the result of webpage amendments which had been made without thinking about accessibility. Though the DRC (2004) found that the websites of large firms generally performed better than those of SMEs (Small and Medium-sized

Enterprises), nevertheless there was evidence that barriers to accessibility appeared to be the product of unsupported assumptions about what is required to make a website accessible, and of ignorance about how to go about tackling access issues even where there is a will to do so. The DRC also pointed out the lack of formal mechanisms within firms to take up issues in relation to website accessibility.

The general failure to understand either the spirit or the 'letter of the law' as defined by DDA requirements was one element that lead to the introduction of the 'Disability Equality Duty' (DED) (OSI, 2006). Aimed at the public sector, 'The DED is meant to ensure that all public bodies – such as central or local government, schools, health trusts or emergency services – pay "due regard" to the promotion of equality for disabled people in every area of their work' (DRC, 2006). As with the DDA Act itself, the DED is not explicit in regard to website accessibility (though in any event it is hard to imagine any process seeking to maximise policy dissemination without use of the Web). The DED places a legal duty on all public sector organisations in Britain (some 45,000 bodies including libraries, hospitals, NHS Trusts, schools and colleges, police forces, central and local government) to promote equality of opportunity for disabled people. Thus since December 2006 public bodies have had to publish a 'Disability Equality Scheme' which must demonstrate how concepts of equality under the DDA are to be put into practice.

The criticisms of practice must also help to explain a UK Cabinet Office response in December 2005 when it set up the 'Office for Disability Issues' (ODI), a body that strives for 'joined-up thinking' in service delivery by a number of central government departments. Evidence of difficulties are noted when the ODI (2007) observes that 'greater cooperative working between central government departments is urged by many disabled people, particularly between the Department of Health and the Department for Work and Pensions'. The ODI publish a set of 'Guidelines for UK Government websites' based on the W3C's 'Web Accessibility Initiative' (WAI) which promotes inclusive design practice for those with disabilities. Referenced in national accessibility guidelines of a number of countries including the UK, the WAI can therefore be regarded as a global source of best practice.

Nevertheless there have been a number of criticisms of the WCAG 1.0 (web content) guidelines element of the WAI. The rapid evolution of the Web leads Kelly et al (2005) to assert that such guidelines reflect W3C theoretical perspectives more than 'real world' experience. A focus on 'xHTML' mark-up languages (such as HTML), for example, by which website content is laid out has meant that any non-HTML-related content such as Adobe Acrobat documents and (Macromedia) Flash media are ignored in these guidelines. Abou-Zahra (W3C, undated) implies that devices with screens that are much smaller than that of a standard desktop computer – such as mobile phones and PDAs (Personal Digital Assistants) – are also not accounted for in the guidelines. Apart from specific criticisms of WCAG 1.0, Kelly et al (2005) argue that 'the WAI model does not reflect the diverse uses made of Web technologies and the diversity of the end user environment'. Additionally, they observe that the WAI the model is reliant on developments in technologies such as user agents (e.g. browsers) and authoring tools (e.g. Dreamweaver) over which Web authors have no control, forcing them to wait for market forces and user awareness to influence the deployment of UAAG-conformant browsers. Kelly et al further argue that guidelines are ambiguous in places, and are also too complex, causing others to write further documents to explain them.

A changing world and criticisms of guidelines originally drawn up in 1999 led to work starting on an updated set of guidelines called WCAG 2.0. Expected to come into force during 2007, WCAG 2.0 retains much of WCAG 1.0 but shows some accommodation for criticisms. Thus, for example, the WCAG 2.0 design approach is 'format neutral'. Based on four broad principles under which the more specific guidelines and techniques are to be subsumed, WCAG 2.0 advocates website content that is (a) 'perceivable' (the user should be able to get at the content), (b) 'operable' (interface elements must be usable), (c) 'understandable' (the content must be organised and presented in a way that makes sense to the user), and (d) 'robust' (the content can be used with current and future technologies) (Bohman and Anderson, 2004). So whereas WCAG 1.0 presented developers with a list of 'do's and don'ts' that are restricted mostly to HTML technology, WCAG 2.0, they argue, takes a more holistic and less prescriptive approach that attempts to span current and future technologies with 'broadly applicable principles, rather than isolated techniques' which by definition should shift website developers' focus away from a 'compliance' mentality to a 'usability' one (Bohman and Anderson, 2005). Nevertheless Abou-Zahra contends that draft WCAG 2.0 guidelines have greater 'testability' of website conformance given criteria that are more clear and precise. Simpler to understand they are also therefore easier to translate into languages other than English. Product of an approach that is open and consensus-based, WCAG 2.0 has been the subject of several published drafts which have received responses from disability organisations, developers, practitioners, researchers, policy makers and other standards bodies around the world (Abou-Zahra, undated).

W3C argue that web accessibility is dependent upon the development and interaction of a number of 'actors': website content; web browsers and media players; assistive technology; users' knowledge and experience; developers; authoring tools; and evaluation tools. All of these need to be considered for the websites to be accessible for people with disabilities. Thus when accessibility features are effectively implemented in one component, then the other components are more likely to follow suit; if any one of these is weak, then there may be little motivation for the other components to implement features when they do not result in an accessible user experience (WCAG 2.0, 2000). Thus W3C highlights a danger that 'Fragmentation of the market makes it increasingly difficult for website and tool developers to comply with partially competing standards and thus to provide accessibility for people with disabilities'. They argue therefore for the harmonisation of web accessibility standards and see WCAG 2.0 as 'a potential convergence target in the effort of diminishing this fragmentation'. However not all are convinced. Though the rapid pace of technological development in Web technologies meant that version 1.0 became outdated 'rather quickly', attempts to be technology-neutral has meant that version 2.0 guidelines are 'extremely vague' and 'verbose and full of jargon-filled language' to the point where they are 'almost unusable' (Webcredible, 2006). This trenchant criticism from a practitioner underlines the fact that standards regimes seeking to remain applicable in a dynamic market will see tensions generated amongst stakeholders. How such tensions are resolved (or not) will have a direct impact on Web accessibility.

Conclusion

This chapter sought to explore issues that promote and inhibit the use of the Web for e-Government. Following a brief examination of forces that strived for a paradigmatic shift in societal thinking in regard to disability, legislation that sought to outlaw discrimination on the basis of disability in the UK was enacted in 1995. This Disability Discrimination Act was enabled over a period of ten years. Though the DDA does not explicitly mention website accessibility, policy intentions for web use are made clear through a DRC (2002) 'code of practice' in which website accessibility receives explicit treatment. Accessibility guidelines aimed at the public sector then serve to explain in some detail what is required of websites in order to ensure that those with disabilities are not excluded. These guidelines reference international standards produced by W3C whose WAI is a source of 'best practice' in website design for accessibility. The under-pinning concept of usability inherent in this 'accessibility' means that the needs of those with disabilities – whose incidence increases with age – and those with temporary incapacities (such as while driving) can be accommodated to some level.

The evidence set out in this chapter however suggests that although a legislative framework and supporting 'codes of practice' exist to promote accessibility of websites produced in the UK, there is little evidence that accessibility is an ingrained design norm as yet. Findings such as those sponsored by the DRC (2004), for example, effectively condemn the performance of public websites in the UK. Thus, even if disabled people want to use the Web and can meet the cost for basic technology by which to gain web access, and perhaps too the cost of assistive technology, these are only the first steps in a chain of potential hurdles that can be experienced by disabled users interacting with websites of variable accessibility attributes. So rather than enabling inclusion, websites that are partially or wholly inaccessible would only serve to add to inequalities felt by disabled users.

While use of the Web does offer the means of attempting greater inclusion of marginalised groups such as those with disabilities, the quality – or otherwise – of web access is critical and likely to 'shape significantly the experience that users have online, the uses to which they can put the Internet and the satisfactions they draw from it, and their returns to Internet use in the form of such outcomes as human capital, earnings or political efficacy' (Di Maggio and Hargittai, 2001). Clearly the concept of 'access' requires a variegated level of consideration that goes beyond dichotomous availability of technology on the demand side and apparent technical conformance to accessibility guidelines on the supply side. If the concept of 'inclusion' is to be meaningful therefore and not an 'empty shell' (Adam and Kreps, 2006 after Hoque and Noon, 2004), greater effort needs to be devoted to public website design, implementation and the user experience they engender. As things stand therefore any wholesale rush to the use of electronic channels by which to deliver e-Government to disabled people would appear ill-advised.

Bibliography

Abou-Zahra, WCAG 2.0: A Convergence Target,

Adam, A. and Kreps, D. (2006), 'Web Accessibility: A Digital Divide for Disabled People?' IFIP 8.2 Social Inclusion: Societal & Organizational Implications for Information Systems, Limerick, Ireland, July.

Anderson, S., Bohman, P., Burmeister, O. and Sampson-Wild, G. (2004), 'User Needs and e-Government Accessibility: The Future Impact of WCAG 2.0'. In Stary, C. and Stephanidis, C. (eds), VI4A11 2004, LNCS 3196, pp. 289–304.

ATAG 2.0 http://www.w3.org/TR/ATAG20/.

Australian Bureau of Statistics (ABS) (1998), (http://www.abs.gov.au/ausstats/).

Barnes, C. and Mercer, G. (2005), *Work, Employment and Society*, Vol. 19(3), pp. 525–527.

Berry, J. (1999), 'Apart or a Part? Access to the Internet by Visually Impaired and Blind People, with Particular Emphasis on Assistive Enabling Technology and User Perceptions.' *Information Technology and Disabilities*, 6(3), pp. 1–16. http://www.rit.edu/~easi/itd/itdv06n3/article2.htm Access date: 23/04/07.

Bickenbach, J., Chatterji, S. Badley, E. and Ustun, T. (1999), '. . . disabilities and handicap', *Soc Sci Med.*, Vol. 48(9), pp. 1173–87 http//:ncbi.nlm.nih.gov.

Bohman, P. and Anderson, S. (2004), 'Toward User-Centered, Scenario-Based Planning and Evaluation Tools'. In Miesenberger, K. et al (eds): ICCHP 2004, LNCS 3118, pp. 355–60, Berlin Heidelberg: Springer-Verlag.

Bradbrook, G. and Fisher, J. (2004) *Digital Equality: Reviewing Digital Inclusion Activity and Mapping the Way Forwards*, Citizens Online, Swindon.

British Standards Institute (BSI) PAS 78.

BT (British Telecom) (2004), *The Digital Divide in 2025*, London: British Telecom.

Burnett, J. (1996), 'What Service Marketers Need to Know about the Mobility-disabled Consumer', *Journal of Services Marketing*, Vol. 10(3), pp. 3–20.

Chisholm, W., Vanderheiden, G. and Jacobs, I. (2001), 'Web Content Accessibility Guidelines 1.0', *Interactions*, July–August, 2001.

Citizens Online (2007), *Statistics*, available from: http://www.citizens online.org.uk/statistics (accessed 7 February, 2007).

Cuddy, I. (2003) 'Disability Laws Force Redesign of almost 800 Government Websites', *eGov monitor Weekly*, available at: http://www.egov monitor.com/newsletter/w73/ln01.html.

Darzentas, J. and Miesenberger, K. (2005), 'Design for All in Information Technology: A Universal Concern', in Anderson, K., Debenham, J. and Wagner, R. (eds.), Database and Expert Systems Applications: 16th International Conference Proceedings, DEXA 2005, Copenhagen, Denmark, August 22–26.

DfEE (2001), Towards Inclusion – Civil Rights for Disabled People, London: HMSO.

DfEE (1999), What the Disability Discrimination Act (DDA) 1995 means for schools and LEAs: DfEE Circular 20/99.

Disibility Discrimination Act (DDA), (1995), HMSO http://www. opsi.gov.uk/acts/acts1995/1995050.htm.

Disability Rights Commission (DRC) (2002), Code of Practice: Rights of Access Goods, Facilities, Services and Premises.

Disability Rights Commission (DRC) (2004), 'The Web. Access and Inclusion for Disabled People. A Formal Investigation conducted by the the Disability Rights Commission', London: TSO.

Disability Rights Commission (DRC) (2006), Disability Equality Duty (DED) http://www.drc.org.uk/employers_and_service_provider/ disability_equality_duty.aspx (accessed 27.01.07).

Dunn, S. (2003), Return to SENDA? 'Implementing Accessibility for Disabled Students in Virtual Learning Environments in UK Further and Higher Education', City University.

e-Envoy (2003), *Illustrated Handbook for Web Management Teams*, available from: www.eenvoy.gov.uk/Resources/WebHandbookIndex1Article/fs/ en?CONTENT_ID=4000092&chk=XHiT3L.

Finkelstein, V. (1980), 'Attitudes and Disability: Issues for Discussions', New York: World Rehabilitation Fund.

Fitch, D. and Fernie, J. (2002), 'Local Stores in Scotland: Opinions, Prospects',

9th *International Conference on Recent Advances in Retailing and Services Science*, Heidelberg, EIRASS.

Fitch, D. (2004), 'Measuring Convenience: Scots' Perceptions of Local Food and Retail Provision', *International Journal of Retail and Distribution Management*, 32(2) pp. 100–8.

Foley, P. Alfonso, X. Fisher, J. and Bradbrook, G. (2005), *e-Government: Reaching Socially Excluded Groups?* International Electronic Commerce Research Centre.

Gybels, G. (2004), *Deaf and Hard of Hearing Users and Web Accessibility*, The Royal National Institute for Deaf people (RNID).

Interactive Bureau (2002), A Report into Key Government Websites.

Kahana, B., Kahana, E., Lovegreen, L. and Secin, G. (2006), 'Compensatory Use of Computers by Disabled Older Adults', *Lecture Notes in Computer Science*, 4061 pp. 766–69.

Kelly, B. (2002), Web Watch: An Accessibility Analysis of UK University Entry Points.

Kelly, B., Sloan, D., Phipps, L., Petrie, H., and Hamilton, F. (2005), 'Forcing Standardization or Accommodating Diversity?: A Framework for Applying the WCAG in the Real World.' Proceedings of the 2005 International Cross-Disciplinary Workshop on Web Accessibility (W4A), ACM International Conference Proceeding Series, Vol. 88, pp. 46–54.

Kingston, R. (2001) *The Social Implications of E-Commerce: A Review of Policy and Research*, York: Joseph Rowntree Foundation.

Klironomos, I., Antona, M., Basdekis, I. and Stephanidis, C. (2006), 'White Paper: Promoting Design for All and e-Accessibility in Europe', *Universal Access in the Information Society*, Vol. 5(1), pp. 105–19.

Larkin, M. (2000), 'Web Gears up for People with Disabilities', *The Lancet*, Vol. 356, Issue 9224, 8 July 2000, p. 142.

Mace, R., Hardie, G. and Place, J. (1991), 'Accessible Environments: Towards Universal Design'. In Preiser, W., Visher, J. and White, E. (eds), *Design Intervention: Towards a More Humane Architecture*, New York: Van Nostrand Reinhold.

Mankoff, J., Fait, H. and Tran, T. (2005), 'Is Your Web Page Accessible? A Comparative Study of Methods for Assessing Web Page Accessibility for the Blind'. In Proceedings of the SIGCHI Conference on Human Factors in Computing Systems, Portland, Oregon: ACM Press.

Marincu, C. and McMullin, B. (2004), 'A Comparative Assessment of Web Accessibility and Technical Standards Conformance in Four EU states', First Monday, Vol. 9(7) http://firstmonday.org/issues/issue9_7/marincu/index.html.

MRQSA Accredited Supplier (2003), *Mobility Survey*, London: John Grooms.

Nielsen, J. (2001), 'Beyond Accessibility: Treating Users with Disabilities as People', Alertbox, November 11, http://www.useit.com/alertbox/20011111.html.

Office for Disability Issues (2006), 'Disability Equality: A Priority for All', ODI.

Office for National Statistics (2003), 'Internet Access 2003', www.statistics. gov.uk.

Oliver, M. (1983), *Social Work with Disabled People*, Basingstoke: MacMillan.

OxIS (2005), Oxford Internet Survey, Results of a Nationwide Survey of Britons Aged 14 and Older, Number of Respondents: 2185, Oxford Internet Institute.

Paciello, M. (2000), *Web Accessibility for People with Disabilities*, Berkeley, CA: CMP Books.

Pilling, D. Barrett, P. and Floyd, M. (2004), *Disabled People and the Internet: Experiences, Barriers and Opportunities*, York: Joseph Rowntree Foundation.

Poulson, D. and Nicolle, C. (2004), 'Making the Internet Accessible for People with Cognitive and Communication Impairments', *Universal Access in the Information Society*, Vol. 3(1), pp. 48–56.

Riddell, S. (2003), 'Devolution and Disability Equality Legislation: The Implementation of Part 4 of the Disability Discrimination Act 1995', *British Journal of Special Education*, Vol. 30(2), pp. 63–70.

Rogers, E. M. (1995), *The Diffusion of Innovations*, 4th edn, New York: Free Press.

Rowan, M., Gregor, P., Sloan, D. and Booth, P. (2000), 'Evaluating Web Resources for Disability Access', ASSETS'00, November 13–15, ACM: Arlington, Virginia.

Schmidt, R., Jones, P. and Oldfield, B. (1995), 'Implementing the Disability Discrimination Act 1995: A Comparison of Manchester City Centre and Out-of-Town Retailer Responses', *International Journal of Retail & Distribution Management*, Vol. 33(9), pp. 669–84.

Shneiderman, B. (2000), Universal Usability. Communications of the ACM, Vol. 43(5), pp. 84–91.

Sloan, M. (2001), 'Web Accessibility and the DDA', *Journal of Information, Law and Technology*, 2, http://elj.warwick.ac.uk/jilt/01-2/sloan.html.

SOCITM (2005), *Better Connected 2005: A Snapshot of Local Authority Websites*, Society of Information Technology Management.

Tregaskis, C. (2002), 'Social Model Theory: The Story so Far . . .', *Disability and Society* Vol. 17(4), pp. 457–70.

UK Cabinet Office (2002), Web Handbook – Building in Universal Accessibility, www.cabinetoffice.gov.uk/e-Government/resources/handbook/html/2-4.asp.

UPIAS (1976) *The Fundamental Principles of Disability*, London: UPIAS/ Disability Alliance.

Van Oorschot, W. and Hvinden, B. (eds) (2001), *Disability Policies in European Countries*, Kluwer Law International.

W3C (1997), World Wide Web Consortium Launches International Program Office for Web Accessibility Initiative Press Release Government, Industry, Research and Disability Organizations Join Forces to Promote Accessibility of the Web http://www.w3.org/Press/IPO-announce.

W3C (1999), *WCAG 1.0* Web Content Accessibility Guidelines http://www.w3.org/TR/WAI-WEBCONTENT/.

W3C (2000), *ATAG 1.0* Authoring Tool Accessibility Guidelines http://www.w3.org/TR/WAI-AUTOOLS/.

W3C (2002), Web Accessibility Initiative (WAI) www.w3.org/wai.

W3C (2002), *UAAG 1.0* User Agent Accessibility Guidelines http://www.w3.org/TR/UAAG10/.

W3C (2004), *WCAG 2.0* Web Content Accessibility Guidelines http://www.w3.org/WAI/GL/.

W3C (2004), How People with Disabilities Use the Web, www.w3.org/WAI/EO/Drafts/PWD-Use-Web/.

Webcredible (2006), WCAG 2.0: The New W3C Accessibility Guidelines Evaluated.

Witt, N. and McDermott, A. (2004), 'Website Accessibility: What Logo will we use Today?', *British Journal of Educational Technology*, Vol. 35(1), pp. 45–56.

10

e-GOVERNANCE IN TRANSITION ECONOMIES

ANTOANETA SERGUIEVA AND KAMEN SPASSOV

Introduction

Established European democracies implement the principles of e-Governance as further development at the new technological level. Countries in Central and Eastern Europe, on the other hand, experience political, economic and social changes, coinciding with a constant process of reinventing governance. The introduction of e-Governance in transition economies enables and drives the process of democratisation. The focus of discussion here is Bulgaria, where the specialisation in the field of information technology within the former Soviet Bloc and the tradition of the education system has contributed to the eighth place worldwide in the number of computer science graduates and IT certified professionals (Trifonov, 2006). In its priorities for 2006, the Bulgarian Ministry of State Administration and Administrative Reform envisage that 'The increase in electronic communication will eliminate administrative barriers and promote the development of the economy and society, will raise the effectiveness of the state governance and improve the interaction and dialogue between institutions, private sector and citizens. The service delivery by electronic means will diminish the conditions for corruption.' (Vassilev, 2006). The e-Governance strategy has been developed and implemented through the participation of Bulgaria in the EC Programmes IDA, IDA II and IDABC. Bulgarian Universities, NGOs and private companies have further taken part in projects within the Framework Programmes FP5 and FP6, within e-Content and e-Ten. We evaluate the implementation of the overall strategy, consider some of the projects in detail, and identify further challenges.

The ICT Perspective

Bulgaria is located in South Eastern Europe, with a population of 7.72 million in 3 million households. The private sector constitutes 75 per cent of the economy. The GDP is $28 billion, growing at above 5 per cent over the last five years, while the inflation rate approaches 4 per cent (NSI, 2006). The total number of government administrative structures is 521, in December 2005, including 193 central administration units, and 327 regional and municipal administrations. An estimated 70 per cent of the employees in state administration use computers. The country is an EU member since January 2007.

Over a third of the population has computer access in 2006 (NSI, 2007). There is a PC in 40 per cent of the households with children, and a further 11 per cent are planning to buy within a year. There is a PC in 13.5 per cent of the households without children, and a further 3 per cent are planning to buy. A survey among 11th grade students, conducted in January 2006 in the Centre for Control and Quality Assurance at the Ministry of Education and Science, indicates that 58.5 per cent of students claim to have a computer at home. In another survey, conducted by Vitosha Research among 10th grade students, more than 80 per cent of the respondents declare using the Internet (Yalamov and Mirski, 2006). The share of Internet users in different types of schools is similar, in evidence that the school type is not essential for the students' access to the Internet. New technologies are becoming an imperative in students' life.

Companies also understand the role of the Internet as a line of communication and as a marketing platform. Effectively all companies with more than 100 employees, and 83 per cent of the companies with 51 to 100 employees, had an Internet connection by the end of 2005. The number of firms with less than 10 employees and Internet access doubled over two years and reached 62 per cent in 2005. The overall share of companies that offer and sell their products and services online increased from 12.2 per cent in 2004 to 19 per cent in 2005.

How do individuals use the Internet? More than 8 per cent of users work intensively in software development, and 60 per cent of those spend more than 40 hours per week. This is an indication of working remotely, and in most cases on international software development projects. A further 40 per cent of users spend more than 20 hours per week and target other job related activities and educational purposes. In Sofia, more than 60 per cent of households have Internet access and 35 per cent of those without access are planning to connect, according to a study by Gfk Bulgaria (Yalamov and Mirski, 2006). The quality of the connection is also improving. In October 2005, the share of broadband users reached 70 per cent of home Internet users in the country and 92 per cent in Sofia. This corresponds to 10.6 per cent of the population, and represents a growth of 22 per cent to the previous year. It is also close to the average of 10.8 per cent for the EU in July 2005.

The Bulgarian Government declares the ICT development as one of its top priorities, though the overall constraints on the budget allow for a moderate share. The factors contributing to the process include the tradition in technical education, the background of the ICT industry in the country, and the determined effort of private ICT companies to attract foreign investors. There are more than 1,000 small and medium-sized firms in the country; 100 of them are certified under ISO 9001 and 15 under ISO 14,000. Major activities include developing computer system software, networking software, web design, telecommunications and wireless development software, and application software. Bulgaria is ranked third in the world for certified IT professionals per capita, and eighth in the world in terms of absolute numbers. In addition to the college and university IT education, there are 110 CISCO academies in the country, and their students often win world CISCO annual awards. Bulgaria is a leader in outsourcing among Eastern European countries, according to a study by CIO and Meta Group Inc. (Trifonov, 2006). Two of the major foreign investors in the software development sector, SAP and Tumbleweed Communications (NASDAQ:TMWD), are expanding their operations in the country.

Another important factor in the ICT development was ceasing the monopoly of the Bulgarian Telecommunication Company (BTC) in landline communications in 2003, and further opening to competition in the area of mobile communications. The end-user demand stimulated companies from other sectors to enter the telecommunications market. The liberalisation of the market led to the licensing of 13 more companies. Cable TV operators are moving to triple play service – TV, Internet, and Voice over IP (VoIP). About 54 per cent of the households in the country subscribe to cable TV. Utility companies, e.g. Vestitel BG subsidiary of Overgas, are delivering voice and data transfer and using the infrastructure they already have in place. The competition is improving the communication services: BTC introduced Asymmetric Digital Subscriber Line services in 2004, and further opportunities are opening with the tender of High Definition TV (HDTV) licenses. The telecommunications sector also attracts foreign direct investment, amounting to $1.049 billion and 14 per cent of the total FDI, between 1998 and June 2004 (Trifonov, 2006). A larger deal was the $1.94 billion buyout of one of the Bulgarian mobile operators, Mobiltel, by Telekom Austria in July 2005. The same year, three 3G operators were licensed.

The tradition and recent developments in the ICT sector are expected to contribute to a better digital opportunity index (DOI) for the country. Table 10.1 presents the DOI rank and the GDP rank for eight countries, including Korea (highest DOI) and Luxembourg (highest GDP), as well as neighbouring countries in the Balkans (ITU, 2006). A higher GDP contributes to a better DOI rank, as the

Table 10.1 World Digital Opportunity Index, 2005

Country	GDP Rank	DOI Rank
Republic of Korea	37	1
Luxembourg	1	18
Greece	30	42
Bulgaria	80	46
Romania	78	53
Turkey	70	58
Macedonia	89	63
Serbia and Montene-Gro	83	70

Source: World Information Society Report 2006, International Telecommunication Union (ITU)

relatively high position of Luxembourg indicates. However, this is not the only factor, and Korea is the example of a strategic policy towards the information society. In comparison, the countries in South Eastern Europe have relatively low GDPs, and operate under budgetary constraints on their strategic decision, or such a strategy is not of high priority (Spassov, 2006). In this scene, the relative position of Bulgaria indicates an economic struggle, along with a good progress towards the information society.

e-Governance: Background and Strategy

Legal and Administrative Framework

The legal framework on e-Governance in Bulgaria is in line with the EC directives. The Administration Law passed through Parliament in 1998, introducing an organisational model and internal rules for state administrative units (SG, 1998). The Law was implemented in 80 per cent of the administrative units and functions by 2000, targeting a clear separation of political and administrative levels and an improved internal administrative control in preventing corruption. In response to the expectations for improved governance, reliability, transparency and openness, the Council of Ministers (CM) adopted in 2002 and updated in 2003, a strategy for further modernisation of state administration (CM, 2003). An action plan was endorsed for the period 2003–2006, and a transparency and anti-corruption strategy was approved in 2006 (CM, 2006).

The Electronic Document and Electronic Signature Law passed through Parliament in 2001 (SG, 2001). A set of regulations treating practical aspects of the implementation of the law were developed in the following years. Since 2004 all administrative units must accept documents submitted electronically and signed with a universal electronic signature. In 2006, more than 2,000 state employees authorised to sign official documents received their electronic signatures. The Electronic Trade Law was approved by the Parliament in 2006, including anti-spam regulations (SG, 2006). The e-Governance Law passed the first reading in year 2006 and is pending the final reading this year (MSAAR, 2006). With its approval, it is expected that the administrative services for citizens and businesses will improve dramatically. Inter-administrative electronic data exchange will be regulated, and state employees will not be able to require from citizens and businesses data already collected in other state administration units. The available data will have to be accessed electronically, saving time and taxpayers' money.

The Ministry of State Administration and Administrative Reform (MSAAR) is planning to further update in 2007, the strategy for modernisation and the action plan, the e-Government strategy and the strategy for state administration training. Legal Acts on privacy, personal identification documents, e-Health, information society, etc. are also closely related to e-Governance, though we are not able to provide details due to the limited space.

The e-Government strategy was adopted by the Council of Ministers on 28 December, 2002. It states that:

> The e-Government in Bulgaria is an element of the transition from industrial to information society and serves to accelerate the European integration process. It is a process of change that helps expand the means of citizens and businesses to participate in a new knowledge-based economy. In order to have the full potential of e-Government enforced, it is necessary to reform the administration, the management of business processes and information. (CM, 2002)

The strategy underlines the role of e-Government in meeting the general public needs for high-quality and accessible public services, as well as in increasing the transparency and minimising the corruption practices in the state administration. The overall objective is to provide services at places and times that are most convenient to citizens and businesses, through integrated and continuous electronic services. The vision for e-Government, according to the Strategy, is to provide modern and efficient governance, while using the means of contemporary information technologies in order to meet the real needs of citizens and businesses. The Government has formulated strategic objectives, which include the expansion of the technological capabilities of citizens and businesses for participation in the government decision-making process, and the development of organisational, communication and information environment for the effective and transparent functioning of the public administration according to the principles, standards and best practices of the European Union. The implementation of the strategic objectives is expected to reduce the maintenance cost of public administration, to improve service quality, and decrease corruption, as prerequisites for sustainable economic and social development. Four major aspects of communication and services are considered in the strategy, as summarised in Table 10.2.

The Action Plan was developed within a year of the adoption of the e-Government strategy. The actions and measures included in the plan ensure the implementation of the strategy with regard to electronic services (with an emphasis on the 20 services monitored by the EU), connectivity and infrastructure, information environment, operational environment, centralised services, e-Democracy, financing of e-Government projects, risk analysis, and public control over the action plan management. More than 200 e-Government projects were identified while developing the action plan. To avoid overlaps and optimise the use of resources, a methodology for project prioritisation is established and disseminated. A tool for monitoring and management of the e-Government strategy was further developed, using the Balanced Scorecard methodology.

Table 10.2 Aspects of Communication and Services

---

administration–citizens: modern Internet and Intranet Web-based solutions coupled with conventional means for ensuring broad access, which will lead to qualitative changes in terms of communication and provision of services to citizens;

administration–businesses: modern solutions for optimisation of processes and business relationships between the public administration and various business entities;

administration–administration: IT development at the national and interstate levels with a view of ensuring effective interaction of various administrative structures;

internal institutional efficiency and effectiveness: organisation and optimisation of business processes, administration-employee relations and communication processes within the administrative structures.

Source: Council of Ministers Decree No 866 of 28/12/2002

Interoperability

Following the action plan, a Working Group was created to propose a solution of the interoperability problems. The main goal of the Working Group is to establish a framework of measures and a real mechanism to achieve system integration and interoperability of the e-Government information systems. The Working Group has elaborated documents considering the favourable circumstances, the general approach to standardisation, the elements of implementation, and the conformity testing procedures. The favourable circumstances refer to:

- the overcoming of the opposition between standardisation bodies, such as UN/CEFACT, OASIS, Rosetta Net, Open Application Group, Open Management Group, OBI, etc.;
- the unprecedented speed of the adoption of the ebXML standards by ISO;
- the unification of the presentation of Web services through affirmation of BPEL, supported by ORACLE;
- the development of the European e-Government Inter-operability Framework (EGIF) by IDA;
- the development of the key principles of an interoperability architecture by the European Public Administration Network (EPAN); and
- the adoption of e-GIF in several European countries.

The general approach to standardisation of system integration and interoperability in the Bulgarian EGIF refers to a combination of:

- the classical Reference Model for Open Distributed Processing, ISO/IEC 1076:1998, which defines the infrastructure for distributed information processing between heterogeneous technological resources and multiple organisational domains; and
- the last stage in the evolution of the standards for system integration, the Service-oriented Architecture (SOA), when loosely-coupled modules of application functionality are combined and used for creation of new applications in the network.

Under this approach, all procedures of information exchange and processing in the e-Government infrastructure must be represented and parameterised as services, and each service forms a hierarchical structure.

Next, the elements of the implementation refer to the practical implementation of the above approach, which is realised by three centralised registers, with logical and operational connections between them:

- the Register of Standards, with four classification schemes;
- the Register of Electronic Services, including XML- and graphical description of the structure of services, as well as BPEL-description of the messages for the request/answer, the point of access, etc.;
- the Register of Information Objects, including XML, UML and graphical description of the structure of electronic documents, segments and data elements.

Finally, the conformity testing procedures refer to ensuring the conformity to the Bulgarian EGIF of all new e-Government information systems. The certification procedure is based on the ETSI Recommendations.

Implementation: Bulgarian Participation in International Initiatives

The adoption of legal acts is the start of the process, followed by the broader acceptance of the ideas and encouraging people to work systematically on their implementation. National and international contests are effective tools to create a stimulating environment for development and recognition of achievements in the area of e-Governance. It is essential to involve, along the state administrative structures, also NGOs, academic circles and private companies. Some international initiatives that motivated organisations in Bulgaria include the World Summit on the Information Society (WSIS) endorsed with Resolution 56/183 of the UN General Assembly, the World Summit Awards (WSA) as an initiative to promote the best e-Content worldwide, and the e-Europe Awards giving recognition of good practice among EU Member States and candidate countries. Complementary national events involve the Bulgarian

Online Services Awards, the Best Bulgarian Website Awards introduced as yearly awards since 1999 and currently organised by the Bulgarian Web Organisation, the Computer Space Competition as the most popular computer art event in the country carried out under the patronage of the Bulgarian President, etc.

Due to the limited space, we only discuss projects presented to the World Summit Awards. WSA is a global competition for selection of the best projects in the area of e-Content and applications. The initiative is targeting to bridge the digital divide and to fill the international e-Content gap, providing a forum for 168 countries to present their achievements. The contest is organised in the framework of and in collaboration with the World Summit on the Information Society.

WSA 2003

Bulgarian projects and best practices at WSA 2003 included nominations in a number of categories. The system for Internet Access to Court Information and Trade Registry Information in the Varna Region, in the category of e-Government; and the multimedia applications facilitating the Re-socialisation Process of Juvenile Prisoners, in the e-Inclusion category. The Medicine and Health Portal, in the e-Health category; and the Art and Culture Server Cult.bg, in the e-Culture category. In e-Learning, the Interactive Biochemistry web-based system at the Medical University of Sofia; and in e-Science, the interactive system Flora Bulgarica and in e-Business, the innovative mobile product CoMobi. The system nominated in e-Government provides access to Court information and Trade Registry information (www.is-vn.bg) and includes three components:

- Internet access to the court cases in the Varna Regional Court and Varna Court of Appeal, where the access to the document workflow systems provides detailed information about Court cases circulation.
- Internet access to data and information regarding the companies registered in the Trade Registry.

- Internet access to administrative services provided by the Court, including capabilities for requesting, accepting and registering of the following administrative services – the issuance of a certificate for the actual state of a company, the express service for changing the actual state of a company in the Trade Registry, the information request about a company from the Trade registry, the request to read a case in the library of the Varna Regional Court, etc.

The software nominated in e-Inclusion facilitates the re-socialisation process of juvenile prisoners and consists of three multimedia applications for independent work at the Penitentiary for young offenders at the town of Boychinovcy. The aim is to assist the tutorial process in the regular school at the Penitentiary, particularly in literacy and mathematics, geography and history, and computer literacy. The three applications are developed on the basis of modern web interface with interactive capabilities for independent work.

The e-Health application, the Medicine and Health Portal (www.med.primasoft.bg) contains useful scientific, reference and popular information. The rubric 'medical science' contains medical articles, online publications, manuals and reference books; while the rubric 'advice for everyone' contains popular information and recommendations in the areas of infections, dentistry, child health, psychology, homeopathy, alternative medicine, sport and health, etc. The section 'InterMed' includes links to valuable databases, periodicals, ftp-servers, discussion forums, mailing lists, medical yellow pages and other international content. The section 'medical companies' is an online tool for business offers, and the section 'medical services' contains lists of hospitals, sanatoriums, pharmacies, dental and medical practices, health centres, sport centres, and other institutions.

The e-Culture application, the art and culture server (www.cult.bg) is an Internet portal and server, developed with the purpose to provide a comprehensive presentation of contemporary Bulgarian art and culture, as well as to create a systematic archive and multimedia database of art collections and documentation. The responsibilities of the Editor-in-Chief for the portal involve content development and administration, and the members of the editorial team are in charge of various areas such as visual arts, music, cinema, etc. The portal is further maintained by a system administrator and a code developer. In addition, a number of free services are offered, e.g. free hosting for cultural projects and organisations, as well as weblogs, mailing lists, and free email. The portal has a stable audience of about 500 visitors per day.

The e-Learning application, the Web-based system Interactive Biochemistry (biochemistry.orbitel.bg) allows lecturers at the Medical University – Sofia to create Web-based courses, containing lectures, tests, clinical case simulations and other resources. The resources include coloured illustrations, animations, clinical correlations, interactive programs for visualisation of macromolecules, and virtual animated models of complex processes and experiments. The tests allow automatic (self)-assessment of knowledge, and simultaneous analysis of test questions discrimination and difficulty levels. Original interactive clinical case simulations integrate biochemistry with clinical disciplines, and help developing further professional skills. As a result, a problem-solving oriented Web-based platform is introduced to facilitate regular and distance learning in Biochemistry. The platform serves as a basis for creating a University portal for e-Learning in other disciplines.

In e-Science, Flora Bulgarica is an interactive compact disk on the Bulgarian Flora. It is the most comprehensive electronic issue of this kind. Flora Bulgarica includes all the 3,850 species of Bulgarian plants, represented with rich information on each of them and an enormous collection of 3,787 high-quality colour images, which can be used in identifying the plants. The information is systematised and organised in a way that allows a quick and easy access through intuitive and user-friendly instruments. Flora Bulgarica has been developed by the Bulgarian-Swiss Biodiversity Conservation Programme (www.bsbcp.biodiversity.bg), with the financial support of Pro Natura – Switzerland and the Swiss Agency for Development and Cooperation.

In e-Business, CoMobi (comobi.webgate.bg) is an innovative product based on a unique technology protected with a patent application 108042/29.07.03. The product provides direct data exchange between two Symbian OS based mobile phones through the data channel, and the technology ensures smooth migration to 3G.

WSA 2005

Following the success at WSA 2003, 21 Bulgarian projects were submitted in seven of the categories in 2005. The National WSA Contest Committee selected six projects and presented them to the WSA Office in Salzburg. The following of the nominated projects refer to the categories of e-Government, e-Inclusion, e-Culture, e-Learning, and e-Business. In e-Government, the Management Information System at the Ministry of Finance (ispa.minfin.bg) is financed by the European Commission under the EC Programme Instrument for Structural Policies for Pre-Accession (ISPA). In e-Inclusion, the i-Centres project (www.icentres.net) is a joint project between the Bulgaria Government and the United Nations Development Programme (UNDP). In e-Culture, the Discover Bulgaria Portal (www.discover-bulgaria.com) provides a wealth of information on Bulgarian life, history, traditions, nature, etc. In e-Learning, the e-Learning Portal of the Medical University – Sofia (www. mu-sofia.bg); the MUS Portal also won the IT Innovations 2004 competition organised as part of the largest Bulgarian exhibition for information and communication technologies (BAIT Expo). In e-Business, the mobile phone software Advanced Call Manager, with the unique feature of ultra-fast recognition of remote callers and automatic personalised reply options. Further information regarding the Bulgarian participation in WSA 2005 is available at www.i-space.org/wsabg.

Implementation: Case Studies

In this section, we present three e-Governance projects as case studies for the implementation of policy and principles. Transparency and public control are essential in good governance principles. The three case studies consider the practical implementation of these principles in e-Governance at the district, national and European level respectively.

OPEN Administration Varna Project

We start with a case study at district level. The Regional Administration Centre of Varna has identified an innovative tool and then on the basis of consensus among local institutions decided on its implementation. This has ensured a transparent and predictable process and allowed for public monitoring and debate. The initial problem can be described as follows. The public is mostly unfamiliar with the internal administrative rules that ensure precision in providing services and minimise the probability of wrong decisions. Thus the impression is that the administration intentionally delays services. In some cases, as the transactions in state-owned property – sale, exchange, renting – the public suspects that the delay is due to corruption pressures. The solution should allow for public access to information, showing in detail the tasks involved in providing a service, identifying the administration staff in charge of each task, indicating the time limits to complete every task, and specifying the reasons in case of delay.

What would be the effective solution? As was shown in Table 10.1, South Korea has the highest digital opportunity index worldwide. In the spring of 2003, an Agreement for Technical Cooperation and Assistance was signed between Korea and Bulgaria. Within the framework of the agreement, a number of Bulgarian officials participated in Korea-sponsored training courses, including members of the Regional Government of Varna. During the visits to Korea, the participants were also introduced to the Online Procedures Enhancement for Civil Applications System (OPEN System) of Seoul. The system has functioned successfully since April 1999, and it provides services to citizens in a transparent way and hence fights corruption. Furthermore, the Division of Public Economics and Public Administration of the United Nations recommends UN member countries to implement systems based on the OPEN System of Seoul, and related software is available free of cost. As a result, a decision has been taken to implement the OPEN system in line with the Bulgarian e-Government Strategy, and to develop and implement OPEN Administration Varna on a pilot basis. Prof Kyoung Bae, Sang-Myung University, Seoul, has rendered his support in the development of the system. Prof Bae is the former Director of

Information and Communication Technologies at the Seoul City Government, and leader of the team that developed and implemented the OPEN System of Seoul.

The OPEN Administration Varna has been developed as a web-based dynamic system for provision and public monitoring of services (Trifonov, 2006). The system allows free real-time public access and monitoring of the status of current requests and their track in the administration structure until completion. This results in improved quality of services, reduced time for service completion, reduced costs to citizens and businesses, increased transparency and accountability of service procedures, and decreased corruption pressure. The specific objective is providing a portal solution on regional level in Varna and integrating existing information systems of local government. This specific objective is in line with the guiding principle of the Bulgarian e-Government strategy, which is citizen-centric.

Though using the main ideas and principles of the OPEN System of Seoul, the OPEN Administration Varna is a new development and considers the specifics of Bulgarian Administration. The system was launched in early September 2004, with six services in the category of 'hot' procedures:

- real property exchange, i.e. the exchange of private state-owned property for real properties owned by physical or legal persons;
- issuing statements of public state-owned property to institutions, ministries, etc.;
- issuing statements of private state-owned property to institutions, ministries, etc.;
- issuing statements of state ownership to sole proprietors with state-owned property;
- issuing statements of private state ownership of state-owned land with conceded building right for purchase;
- issuing statements of state ownership of land plots included in the layouts of farming yards.

The information on an application is presented in its depth structure, e.g. an application contains several procedures, each procedure contains sub-procedures, and the sub-procedures involve individual steps with a designated administrator in charge and a specified completion deadline. The applicants can compare the progress of their cases to similar cases in the system, without breaching the Personal Data Protection Act. Furthermore, access to relevant information is granted to anybody, not just to applicants for services. This ensures transparency and eliminates doubts of privileged service. Internet access is provided through a link on the Local Government Website (www.vn.government.bg) or directly at (open.vn.government.bg).

What is the impact of the system? Along with improved quality of services, reduced time and cost, increased transparency and accountability, and decreased corruption pressure, the system also contributes to increased public participation and increased productivity of the administration. Importantly, a competence centre has been developed, and the acquired knowledge and skills can be transferred to similar projects in other regions of Bulgaria. Preliminary discussions have been held between the Local Authorities in Varna and Sofia, and a strong interest has been expressed by the Sofia City Council. Business processes in all local administrations in Bulgaria should be the same, as they are written as procedures in the law. Technically it is feasible to use the same application in all districts in the country, while the transfer of the organisation that supports the efficient function of the application further depends on the political will of the Governors and the motivation of state employees.

Balanced Scorecard Project

The second case study considers the management information system for the implementation of the e-Government strategy at national level (Gueorguiev et al, 2005). The main purpose of the management information system is to support the decision-making process through reliable monitoring and strategy management tools.

> The Government of the Republic of Bulgaria will provide modern and efficient governance, while using the means of contemporary information technologies in order to meet the real needs of citizens and businesses at any time and any place is the vision statement in the Strategy (CM, 2002).

The mission of the Government is conveyed through three strategic goals, which in turn are presented by a set of objectives included in the management model. The strategic map (Kaplan and Norton, 2004) consists of four perspectives that, according to the Balanced Scorecard methodology (BSI) and for the purposes of the Balanced Scorecard project (obs.is-bg.net), reflect the viewpoints of all groups of stakeholders.

- The management and development perspective reflects the viewpoint of employees and operations managers in State Administration who are actively involved in the improvement of administrative services. It outlines the opportunities for their professional development and training, focused on establishing the new organisational culture. This perspective stands in the foundation of the strategic map, and embraces objectives as personnel development and motivation, professional skills enhancement, and adoption of new organisational culture and philosophy.
- The business processes perspective reflects the operations managers' view on the practices, procedures and functions to be implemented in State Administration. Special significance is given to business processes whose implementation is of key importance to the success of planned initiatives. This perspective further provides for the development and implementation of standards, rules and procedures for inter-institutional co-operation, as well as means and technologies for their practical use. The relevant objectives here are information integration, identification and information security, and communication and collaboration between institutions.
- The services and users perspective reflects the viewpoint of citizens and businesses on the services offered by the State Administration. It is focused on user expectations and requirements about the quality and accessibility of administrative services. The objectives assigned to this perspective include consumer satisfaction, provision of public e-Services, and decrease of citizens' and businesses' expenses for public services.
- The perspective on transparency and dialogue among stakeholders covers citizens' and firms' desire to be involved in the

public dialogue, as well as the level of transparency and clarity in the activities and processes performed by the State Administration. Important here is the ability of citizens and firms to exercise structured involvement and control over the process of administrative services delivery, and the capability to use channels to access State Administration.

The order and direction of the cause–and–effect relationships between the objectives in the strategic map depends on the prioritisation of perspectives. The transparency and dialogue among stakeholders is assigned the highest priority, followed by the perspective of services and users. The clarity and transparency in State Administration, as well as the motivation of citizens and firms to participate in State Governance, can be achieved through the provision of high-quality accessible administrative services. Citizens and businesses will take advantage of the access channels to State Administration, if the channels are open, clearly indicated, low cost, and offer shorter service completion terms. Furthermore, the services and users perspective is followed by the business processes perspective. The higher quality and effectiveness of business processes, activities and functions, executed by public institutions, is a prerequisite for the higher quality of administrative services, as the end product, and for better customer satisfaction. Finally, the management and development perspective is placed in the foundation of the strategy map. The objectives assigned to this perspective influence directly the objectives included in the business processes perspective. The availability of qualified and motivated staff as well as leadership commitment to the process of modernisation and improvement is a precondition for administration's functional effectiveness and quality. The implementation of modern technologies and the adoption of best practices in the internal business processes, depends to a large extend on employees' qualifications, knowledge enhancement and skills improvement.

The main purpose of the strategic map model is to support the strategic decision making process and control. Another important purpose is to facilitate the consistent monitoring and analysis of key performance indicators used by the management system. A key performance indicator defines the degree of objective accomplishment quantitatively. As each objective is measured in a different way, a specific measurement model is developed for every objective. A measurement model includes specific and common elements. The specific elements are indicators and dimensions enabling multidimensional data analyses, while the common elements are functionalities such as calculations, benchmarks, forecasting and information sharing. In order to explain the essence and benefits of objective measurement, the model for the public e-Services provision objective is presented. According to the model, the Government gradually provides online all basic services for citizens and firms, as defined by the e-Europe initiative of the European Commission, and some additional services listed in the Bulgarian e-Government Action Plan.

The choice of measures is a challenging task in the design of the management information system. Effective measures are developed through identifying the factors that have direct correlation to desired results. The indicators have to observe the requirements to provide a complete, accurate, and true picture of performance, to be readily available and meaningful, and the related data should be gathered on a regular basis. Some of the data are gathered from internal sources in State Administration, and others are collected externally through end-user surveys, as a guarantee for a balanced selection of indicators. Dimensions are another important aspect in data monitoring and analysis. In the example, the dimensions are services, suppliers and sub-suppliers. Therefore, the percentage of basic public services available online may be examined across public services or across suppliers that provide the services. The predefined calculations, as percentage of plan, variation, etc., facilitate fast data processing. The benchmarks allow comparison between indicator values and accepted standards, and help with the current-status diagnosis of the e-Government implementation process. The forecasts provide trend analysis, and help in undertaking timely actions. Next, relating the management information system to the e-Government Action Plan, a second group of key performance indicators is added to the objectives' measurement models. The purpose of the additional indicators is to detect percentage of completion and costs for all projects undertaken to make achieving an objective possible. State officials and experts are given the option of projects' execution monitoring, which allows decision makers to report on the current status of e-Government implementation in Bulgaria and decide upon future development.

GUIDE Project

The third case study presents international collaboration at EU level. The Government User Identity for Europe (GUIDE) project is focused on creating a European standard for interoperable and secure identity management architecture for e-Government. Organised within the Sixth Framework Programme (FP6) of the European Commission, the GUIDE consortium involves 23 partners from 12 countries including Bulgaria, Denmark, Estonia, Finland, France, Greece, Hungary, Israel, Netherlands, Spain, Switzerland and United Kingdom (CORDIS, 2003). The main contractor is the Global Solutions division of British Telecommunications and the collaboration brings together the European industrial, financial and technical market leaders in e-Government solutions as well as leading academic institutes. It is the largest project of this type, with an overall cost of €12.47 million and EC funding of €6.9 million.

The overall goal is to create the critical requirements and principles for the development of Identity Management Open Architecture that will support the interrelations and interoperability between EU e-Government services. The interoperability is based on and achieved through transnational cooperation and consensus. The vision to develop a European service-oriented architecture will allow for dynamic services and applications throughout Europe. The Bulgarian partner on the project is Sofia University St Kliment Ohridski – the oldest, largest and most prestigious Bulgarian university. One of the directions in the work of its team is the identification, systematisation and representation of the circles of trust related to Bulgarian e-Government (Stefanova et al, 2006).

What is the impact of the project? GUIDE recognises the specific needs in Europe, based on the social, ethical and legislative differences regarding privacy and data protection. The research is tested, demonstrated and validated, through working closely with the State Administrations in a number of EU Member States and Candidate States. The effort is focused on the modernisation and innovation of the European Identity Management e-Government solutions. GUIDE contributes to the open mobility of European citizens and businesses, making European Citizenship and Common Market a reality.

Future Challenges and Conclusions

Implementing e-Governance is a strategic goal of the Bulgarian Government, in line with the strategic priority to develop the information society and knowledge economy in the country. The development of e-Governance solutions is considered as a tool to modernise the State Administration, as well as an important element in the process of change that extends the participation of citizens and businesses in a new knowledge-based economy. The Ministry of State Administration and Administrative Reform is committed to implementing good governance principles. In the Operational Programme developed by MSAAR for the period 2007–13, the strategic goal is 'to build a strong, effective and modern administration that is able to meet the high expectations of Bulgarian citizens, business and European Union for good service and highly professional ethics'. (MSAAR, 2007) One of the three main priorities in the Programme is to develop further and implement e-Governance through:

- re-engineering the State Administration in line with the methods and tools for electronic governance;
- improving the legal framework;
- developing a mechanism for the efficient management of the processes of e-Governance implementation;
- developing an adequate environment for systems integration and interoperability;
- building centralised technological resources for e-Governance; and
- developing unified standards for electronic services.

The information and communication technologies in use at separate state administration units will be harmonised and standardised. A dedicated effort will be made to improve the access to electronic services for all users, including people with disabilities and people from disadvantaged groups. Furthermore, the Coordination Center for Information, Communication and Management Technologies (CCICMT) is revived, and the State Agency for Information Technology and Communications (SAITC) is working to develop the infrastructure needed to implement e-Governance. The current Government has three years ahead – e-Governance funds are allocated in the 2007 budget and planned ahead. It is expected that further e-Governance principles will be implemented, and more electronic services become available to citizens.

Additional financing for e-Governance projects is expected from EU funds such as PHARE, e-Ten, e-Content. Bulgarian teams have already worked on projects within the Fifth and Sixth Framework Programs of the EC, and expect to take part in FP7. The US Agency for International Development (USAID) further funds e-Governance projects, particularly related to the judicial system. The international collaboration and funding allows Bulgarian Universities and NGOs to play an active role in building Bulgarian e-Governance.

Implementing e-Governance in Bulgaria is considered part of the economic and social transition. Transparency and anticorruption measures are essential for the improvement of services delivered to citizens and businesses, and the guiding principle of the e-Government strategy is to be citizen-centric. A lot of effort has been invested in developing the Bulgarian e-Government, though the considerable effort is in the area of the legal framework and strategic planning. The main problem is that the continuous political reform causes changes in strategies, and it is difficult to implement the changes in time, into the day-to-day operations in e-Governance. Therefore, more can be expected when considering practice, operations and coordination. The case studies discussed in this chapter, however, are evidence of the irreversibility, in a transition country like Bulgaria, of the process of acquiring experience and building excellence in e-Governance. This process should expand and allow stakeholders at different levels to find ways to work together.

Political will, availability of resources, and good coordination are the keys for successful implementation of e-Governance.

Bibliography

Administration Act (1998) State Gazette, Vol. 130 of 5/11/1998. Available online from http://www.mdaar.government.bg/docs/en_ZA_en.pdf [accessed 10 April 2007].

Balanced Scorecard Institute, *Basic Concepts, Examples, Performance Measures*, [Internet], BSI. Available from http://www.balancedscorecard.org [cited 10 April 2007].

Community Research and Development Information Service (2003) *GUIDE Fact Sheet*, [Internet], CORDIS. Available from http://cordis.europa.eu/fp6/projects.htm [cited 11 April 2007].

Coordination Centre for Information, Communication and Management Technologies, *Library of Documents*, [Internet], CCICMT. Available from http://www.ccit.government.bg [cited 11 April 2007]. (in Bulgarian)

Council of Ministers Decree No. 866 of 28/12/2002 on E-Government Strategy, (2002). Available online from http://www.mdaar.government.bg/docs/en_e-gov_str_en2002k.pdf [cited 9 April 2007].

Council of Ministers Decree No. 671 of 24/9/2003 on Strategy for Modernisation of State Administration: From Accession to Inte-Gration 2003–2006, (2003). Available online from http://www.mdaar.government.bg/docs/strate-Gia_modern.pdf [cited 10 April 2007]. (in Bulgarian)

Council of Ministers Decree of 26/1/2006 on National Strategy for Good Governance, Prevention and Counteraction of Corruption 2006–2008, (2006). Available online from http://www.government.bg/cgi-bin/e-cms/vis/vis.pl?s=001&p=0037&n=000019&g=target=_self [cited 10 April 2007]. (in Bulgarian)

Electronic Document and Electronic Signature Act (2001) State Gazette, Vol. 34 of 6/4/2001. Available online from http://www.mdaar.government.bg/laws.php [cited 10 April 2007]. (in Bulgarian)

Electronic Trade Act (2006) State Gazette, Vol. 51 of 23/6/2006, pp. 1–6. Available online from http://www.paragraf22.com/pravo/zakoni/zakoni-d/41669.html [cited 10 April 2007]. (in Bulgarian)

Gueorguiev, I., Dimitrova, S., Komitska, M., Traykov, H. and Spassov, K. (2005) 'Balanced Scorecard based Management Information System: A Potential for Public Monitoring and Good Governance Advancement' *Electronic Journal of e-Government*, [online], Vol. 3(1), pp. 29–38. Available from http://www.eje-G.com/volume-3/vol3-iss1/v3-i1-art3-gueorguiev.pdf [cited 9 April 2007].

International Telecommunication Union (2006) World Information Society Report 2006, [Internet], ITU. Available from http://www.itu.int/osg/

spu/publications/worldinformationsociety/2006/wisr-web.pdf [cited 9 April 2007].

Kaplan, R. and Norton, D. (2004). *Strategy Maps: Converting Intangible Assets into Tangible Outcomes*, Boston: Harvard Business School Press.

Ministry of State Administration and Administrative Reform (2006) Draft e-Government Law, Sofia: MSAAR. Available online from http://www.mdaar.government.bg/laws.php [cited 10 April 2007]. (in Bulgarian)

Ministry of State Administration and Administrative Reform (2007) Operational Programme Administration Capacity, Sofia: MSAAR. Available online from http://www.mdaar.government.bg/docs/en_OPAC_eng_09.03.2007.pdf [cited 9 April 2007].

National Statistical Institute (2006) *Statistical Reference Book of the Republic of Bulgaria 2006*, Sofia: NSI.

National Statistical Institute (2007) ICT Usage by Households and Individuals 2006, [Internet], NSI. Available from http://www.nsi.bg/IKT_e/IKT.htm [cited 10 April 2007].

Spassov, K. (2006) 'Application of the Digital Opportunity Index to Bulgaria' *Digital Opportunity Forum* 2006, Seoul, [Internet], International Telecommunication Union. Available from http://www.itu.int/osg/spu/digitalbridges/materials/spasov-paper.pdf [cited 9 April 2007].

State Agency for Information Technology and Communications, Library of Documents, [Internet], SAITC. Available from http://www.daits.government.bg/index_en.php [cited 11 April 2007].

Stefanova, K., Kabakchieva, D. and Spassov, K. (2006) 'Circle of Trust for Identity Management e-Government Infrastructure'. In Remenyi, D., (ed.) *Proceedings of the Sixth European Conference on e-Government*, Marburg, pp. 401–10, Academic Conferences Ltd.

Trifonov, R. (2006) 'ICT Cooperation Perspectives in Bulgaria' *Digital Opportunity Forum* 2006, Seoul, [Internet], International Telecommunication Union. Available from http://www.itu.int/osg/spu/digitalbridges/materials/trifonov-paper.pdf [cited 9 April 2007].

Vassilev, N. (2006) Priorities Statement 2006, [Internet], Ministry of State Administration and Administrative Reform. Available from http://www.mdaar.government.bg/priorities.php [cited 26 June 2006]. (in Bulgarian)

Vitosha Research, Library of Documents, [Internet], Vitosha Research. Available from http://www.vitosha-research.com/index_en.php [cited 11 April 2007].

Yalamov, T. and Mirski, K., (eds.) (2006) eBugaria 2006, Applied Research and Communications Fund Publications. (in Bulgarian) Available online from http://www.arcfund.net/fileSrc.php?id=1975 and http://www.arcfund.net/fileSrc.php?id=1975 [cited 10 April 2007].

Index